"Tecumseh" and Other Stories
of the Ohio River Valley by Julia L. Dumont

"Tecumseh"
and Other Stories
of the Ohio River Valley
by Julia L. Dumont

edited by

Sandra Parker

Bowling Green State University Popular Press
Bowling Green, OH 43403

Library of Congress Cataloging-in-Publication Data

Dumont, Julia L. (Julia Louisa), 1794-1857.
   "Tecumseh" and other stories of the Ohio River Valley by Julia L.
   Dumont / [with introduction by] Sandra Parker.
      p.   cm.
   ISBN 0-87972-823-X (cloth) -- ISBN 0-87972-824-8 (paper)
   1. Ohio River Valley--Social life and customs--Fiction. 2. Tecumseh,
   Shawnee Chief, 1768-1813--Fiction. 3. Frontier and pioneer life--
   Fiction. 4. Shawnee Indians--Fiction. I. Title.
   PS1555.D88 A6 2000
   813'.3dc21

                                                          00-058567

Cover design by Dumm Art

Dedicated

to my students, with whom I have studied

The people of the west should liberally encourage active and worthy efforts to contribute to the common stock of American literature that will justly represent the rich vallie in which our forefathers were pioneers. The mass of people of the west are not only careless in regard to home interest in literature, but they are ignorant of what that literature has been, is, or may be, and yet it is true that the great central valley has contributed 'a great and honorable share.'

—William T. Coggeshall,
"Lectures and Literature"

A novel is neither a plan of action nor a treatise on sociology. It is not to secure rational conviction. Addressed to human sensibility, it works on those strata of man's personality which are beyond the reach of intellectual argument. Its effectiveness derives from the realignment of sympathies which is caused by the experience of reading it. Its thematic content is not a matter of systematic and rational exposition of a problem, but is to be found rather in the pattern of aroused and redistributed sympathies which it creates. Thus though the novel achieves all its effects through a concretely presented situation, its moral or social truth does not depend on the exactness of its correspondence with present or historical facts.

—A. N. Kaul,
The American Vision

ACKNOWLEDGMENTS

I would like to express my appreciation to the faculty and staff of Hiram College who have helped encourage research and writing on this project. At our library I have been assisted by our Archivist, Joanne Sawyer, and interlibrary loan staff librarians Mary Ann Sielander and Jane Dye; special gratitude needs to be expressed to Reference Librarian Lisa Johnson, who has answered innumerable questions, led me toward tracking down a variety of details about the Ohio River Valley, and sought out holdings in other libraries.

Thanks also need to be expressed to a series of reference specialists at a variety of libraries where archival materials were located, in particular: Case Western Reserve, Kent State University, Ohio Historical Society, The State Library of Ohio, and the Ohioana Library.

Having worked with materials about Ohio's early writers for many years, I must also cite the place where these ideas first germinated, Hiram College's 1982 National Endowment of the Humanities grant for "Regionalism in the Humanities"; its campus coordinator, David Anderson, over the years has collegially supported my work on Ohio's early women writers. Our Writing Director, Joyce Dyer, has provided the invaluable asset of friendship and steadfast encouragement, criticism, and challenges as my writing on Dumont progressed. Additionally, I am grateful for Hiram College's 1999 Faculty Research Grant, which provided an incentive for speedy completion of this project before the century's conclusion.

CONTENTS

INTRODUCTION

Julia Louisa Corry Dumont is not a household name like Jane Austen or Emily Dickinson. She was born in the summer of 1794 on the Muskingum, and died on January 2, 1857, sixty-four years later, in a town on the Ohio River near Cincinnati. In her time, she was called a "fine specimen of female intellect," an example of "the great superiority of the educated female," and a teller of a good story "not surpassed by any similar productions of western genius." These words pronounced her gifts to Cincinnati's literary world in 1834 and were written by her mentor, William H. Gallagher, who became famous for his nurturance of the Ohio River Valley's tradition of rural press. His first literary newspaper, the *Cincinnati Mirror,* adapted the *New York Mirror* by adding regional editorials, letters, and a Poets' Corner. As he notes, Dumont's principal characters are drawn from the "mundane sphere," like her realistically conceived Ashton Grey, and unlike her early romantic characters, such as Elvira, who have little "claim on our regard." William Gallagher also called Julia L. Dumont the "first lady" of the Ohio River Valley, "in terms of literary talent, which our country has produced" (120). He concludes his early essay by mentioning that Dumont ought to be as well known as "the Hales, Sigourneys, and Sedgwicks of New England" (229).

William T. Coggeshall, a distinguished anthologist and editor, in 1856 described the decade of 1830-40 as a time when a number of western prose writers earned a "permanent name in American Literature," including Mrs. Dumont (99). He also admired her poetry and included her in the first collection of regional poets, his groundbreaking *Poets and Poetry of the West* (1860). Another prominent regionalist, Edward Eggleston, the author of *The Circuit Rider* (1874), along with his brother George Cary Eggleston, was taught by Julia L. Dumont during her thirty-five years in the profession. A dozen years after Dumont's death, Edward Eggleston praised her in *Scribner's Monthly*, saying she "occupied no mean place as a writer of poetry and prose tales. Eminent litterateurs of the time, from Philadelphia and Cincinnati, used to come to Vevay to see her" (750). A quarter of a century after her death, Dumont continued to be identified as a significant writer by W. H. Venable, who in his 1891 *Beginnings of Literary Culture in the Ohio Valley* called her the "Hannah More of the West" (91) and praised her for dealing with realities, creating picturesque vividness and representing "customs of pioneer days along the Ohio River" (101).

However, in the twentieth century Julia L. Dumont has been nearly forgotten, except for several writers in the first half of the century. Meredith Nicholson in 1916 commented that Dumont "was easily the woman of most varied accomplishment" in the region (89); she could not know the twentieth-century's ideas about realism because during her lifetime it was not yet "the fashion to transcribe with fidelity our American local life." He adds, "in the little school of storytellers and poets that flourished in the Ohio Valley in its early history, she was one of the chief figures" (92). Also there was a 1944 essay in the *Ohio State Archaeological and Historical Quarterly* by Lucille B. Emch, who described Dumont as "the first woman to achieve literary prominence in the Ohio Valley." She pointed out that the story-writers of the first half of the century usually published in literary periodicals and family newspapers, occasionally collecting their work in anthologies. No copyright existed at the time, so Dumont's stories were copied in magazines of both East and West. Emch went on to argue that Dumont's prose is historically significant because it reflects the era's popular story of sentiment (230). Then in *Indiana Authors and Their Books* Julia L. Dumont was described as "the first widely-known woman writer of the Middle West" (Banta 93), while William J. Coyle's entry in *Ohio Authors and Their Books* labels Dumont "the earliest native Ohioan whose writings have been preserved" (181).

As this brief accounting of her literary reputation suggests, Julia L. Dumont must be viewed within her own context as a person who created important images of her era, its people and mores, its culture. She was not a British writer like Hannah More (1789-1879), who was a famous Blue Stocking, or a replica of America's more famous eastern contemporaries, such as Sarah Josepha Hale (1788-1879), editor of our first women's publication, *American Ladies Magazine* and, for forty years until her death, of *Godey's Lady's Book.* Nor did Dumont much resemble Lydia Huntley Sigourney (1791-1865), a popular sentimental moralist. In one sense, Dumont most closely shares an affinity with Catharine Maria Sedgwick (1789-1867), a significant eastern novelist who cultivated New England's regional elements, using native setting, dialect, and characters who were local types, as in *Hope Leslie,* which includes the cultural conflicts of Indian captives.

This anthology is intended to begin the process of gaining recognition for Julia Louisa Dumont, a pioneer woman writer of the Ohio River Valley. It contains selected stories that are representative of each phase of her literary style and that continue to retain relevance for twenty-first-century readers who are interested in Ohio's early history. I have made an effort to represent a number of periodicals which published Dumont's work and to cover the spectrum of time—over three decades—during which Dumont's tales were among the significant staples of frontier Ohio fiction. If there is a bias to this collection, it is in the direction of illustrating representatives types, themes, and fictional trends in the writing of the era. I elected to order the stories chronologically so that a reader may observe how Dumont's narrative pattern developed over time and to demonstrate its growth and resilience.

The lesson to be learned from this moment in women's literary history is that Julia L. Dumont demonstrates the loss from our regional heritage of a marginalized woman who was once well known. Dumont's stories in the 1820s and 1830s are bravely critical toward such American institutions as racism toward Indians and masculine violence. In her later writing, Dumont attacks snobbishness, selfishness, and provincialism. The very existence of her sketches and stories which embody a woman's idealistic viewpoint also challenges common, "Daniel Boone"-type conceptions of the pioneer ethic. Her stories can still animate the reader, who will discover what contemporary issues concerned people in the Ohio River Valley nearly two hundred years ago. A final benefit from appreciating Julia L. Dumont's narratives about frontier culture in the first half of the nineteenth century is that they remind the reader of the continuing need to reassess women's contribution to American culture.

This anthology's ten sketches or stories by Julia Louisa Dumont represent her evolving style over thirty-two years of publishing fiction. The stories retain their original punctuation and spelling, except where there was indecipherable damage in the original copy. The literary newspapers that published her narratives were treasured items in the West, but during the Civil War, readers were asked to send their families' reading material to the boys at the eastern battlefront; consequently, few copies of these periodicals exist today.

Dumont's tales of western life in the nineteenth-century Ohio River Valley reveal two different phases in her themes and style. In her first phase, Dumont's writings reflect a preoccupation with themes connected to the era of her parents' settlement at Marietta between 1788 and 1794, during the Indian Wars, which, broadly speaking, ceased only after Tecumseh's defeat in 1813. One of her stories not included in this volume, "Scenes of the Wilderness," specifically refers to General St. Clair at Fort Washington in 1791 and his defeat on November 3 in which 630 soldiers were lost. Dumont was shocked by male violence, observing in 1830 that there is no "stormy joy in the battlefield," no healthy excitement, or guerdon. Indeed, her emphasis upon interracial conflict establishes a moral context for a series of stories beginning with the Indians Tecumseh and Okumanitas, victims of white men, and continues with white victims of the Indians—Theodore Harland, Ashton Grey, Hugh Mason. The victimization theme concludes in Dumont's 1833 romantic tale "Boonesborough."

After the 1840s Julia L. Dumont entered a second phase of her writing, which focuses upon her real-life experiences and knowledge. Several sketches concentrate upon her hometown of 43 years, Vevay, Indiana. Her other persistent themes include love of the Ohio River Valley, concern with prodigal sons, and sympathy for women's unacknowledged contributions. Her stylistic maturity culminates in Dumont's best-crafted story of her career, "Aunt Hetty" (1856), which realistically integrates a number of her concerns—victimization, domesticity, and unconquerable parent-child love.

The style of her early tales in the 1820s and 1830s reveals the influence of earlier literary practices, such as poetic quotations, metaphors, similies, allusions, rhetorical questions, and authorial intrusion. Her early punctuation, spelling, and grammar continue to challenge twenty-first-century readers. Two of the included stories from 1832 and 1833 are introduced by poetry, one anonymous, the second by "Hemans," Mrs. Felicia Dorothea Browne (1793-1835), an English poet. "Aunt Hetty" also includes several unattributed quotations and one by Thomas Moore (1779-1852), an Irish poet. Metaphors are often used to elevate Indian speakers, as when one says, "The tree of peace . . . spread its green branches over the waters of the Muskingum" (31), or the narrator comments on Tecumseh's mother, "a gleam of joy, like the red meteor of a stormy night, crossed the darkness of her widowed heart" (37). Dumont also uses a variety of allusions which expand the significance of the action—thus, the Ohio River Valley is variously connected to such things as Apollo, son of Zeus; Ruth, biblical daughter-in-law of Naomi; Tyre, the ancient Phoenician seaport on the Mediterranean, and Herman, a mountain in Syria. The author alludes to contemporary matters, too, explaining a historical source, for instance, as being Thomas Jefferson's *Notes on Virginia*; she also alludes to such things as Logan, friend of the white man, Sam Patch, Carroll, a musician, and the ditty "Dan Tucker."

After 1840, as with the changing nature of her themes, Dumont's style also grows away from derivative romanticism and toward simplified realism. Early American writers, like Dumont, who wrote self-conscious regional fiction, such as that of the Ohio River Valley between the Revolutionary and Civil Wars, usually include patriotic and moralistic narrators, as was a classical literary convention. Her narrators claim authority in their exercise of intruded judgments. In the more crudely styled early tales, this may take the form of a classical apostrophe which interrupts the plot—for example, Dumont defends love at first sight for Tecumseh's parents, writing: "The philosopher may laugh at the existence of love, and the moralist may talk of reducing it to system, but its vital influence still remains unimpaired" (30). Or, about a forest conflict, Dumont's narrator attempts to raise the readers' sympathy by exclaiming: "The boats! Merciful heaven . . . they had been unmoored" (116). Another device her narrators employ to increase the drama is rhetorical questions: "Where were the tents which rose on the path of the hunter?" (40) is asked just before the adolescent Tecumseh is dumbfounded at his arrival at Gnaden-hutten to find the Christianized Moravian-Indians have been slaughtered. Later, in the second half of her writing career, these devices disappear. The narrators even cease being conventionally male; Dumont's new female narrators are more realistic and stress "our" community while addressing female readers. Dialogue now conveys the plot, and the narrators in her later work comment on the story as involved personages.

To further explain the substance of Julia L. Dumont's fiction, it is helpful to review the Ohio River Valley's relevant history that so profoundly influenced her life and craft. The "Great River" or "Oh-he-yo," as labeled by the Indians, was later named by the French as "La Belle Riviere." Once it flowed up the Little Miami River out of Duck Creek, then came back down out of the Great Miami River bed. After the region's Mound Builders disappeared, the southwestern region above the Ohio River had no established Indian tribes, though many tribes used the fecund area for hunting, while other Indians migrated westward to escape eastern colonists. Later, tribes like the Seneca, Miami, Ottawa, Delaware, Wyandot, and Shawnee moved into the Ohio River Valley.

Once the French claimed much of North America, dueling with the British for control between 1689 and 1815 in the various French and Indian Wars. By 1760, the region came under British control. During the American colonies' War of Independence from Great Britain, Ohio country was entangled in a series of raids between Americans from Kentucky and Pennsylvania and the region's Indian population.

Congressional approval in 1787 of the Northwest Ordinance provided a way to pay war veterans, as well as create a new type of governance model in the territory. Less than a year before, March 3, 1786, General Rufus Putnam met with other Continental officers in Boston and agreed to accept western lands as payment for their military services. They organized the "Ohio Company" and Congress awarded them the opportunity to sell one and a half million acres along the Ohio River to the "Ohio Company of Associates." These pioneers were entranced by previous travelers' stories:

that watermelons as big as houses grew in the clearings of the West; that the flax plant in the Ohio Valley bore woven cloth on its branches; that honey trees were numerous along the Miami river; and that springs of brandy and rum gushed from the fortunate hills. (Venable 325)

Arriving on April 7, 1788, at the mouth of the Muskingum River, the Ohio Company of Associates became "the first legal white settlement in the present State of Ohio" (Ogg 81). Marietta, their settlement, contained a blockhouse and cabins, and eagerly greeted General Arthur St. Clair, the new governor of the territory. Indian skirmishes kept reoccurring. The worst incident was probably the white men's 1782 massacre of pacified, Christian Indians at Gnadenhutten, near New Philadelphia, which led to retaliations, making 1783 the "bloody year" in Ohio country. That year Congress claimed that, indeed, all Indians who lived in the West did so at the good will of the U.S. government. Six years later, in 1789, President George Washington authorized the use of military force, and despatched troops to Fort Washington in Cincinnati. The following year, 1790, the army was destroying Miami villages, which led the Indians to counterattack, and on October 21 they routed the American troops. A year later, Congress authorized the creation of a new army under General St. Clair, which again assembled at Fort Washington and from there sent out expeditions to attack nearby Indian villages. On November 3, a major confrontation led to St. Clair losing 630 soldiers, with another 283 men wounded. Indians demanded that whites respect the Ohio River boundary as promised in the 1785 treaty. The white men's response was President Washington's sending the experienced Indian fighter "Mad" Anthony Wayne to be commander in chief of the U.S. Army in the northwest.

General "Mad" Anthony Wayne, assisted by an aide-de-camp named William Henry Harrison, defeated Tecumseh's Indians in 1794 at the Battle of Fallen Timbers, a site near modern Toledo. This defeat led directly to the so-called end of the Indian Wars with the Treaty of Greenville, which proclaimed that Indians ceded the disputed Ohio region to white men. "Mad" Anthony Wayne died the next year, 1796.

Within the next eight years Ohio became a state, and the Indians' threatened annihilation was becoming increasingly likely. Perhaps only the idealistic Tecumseh continued to believe that it was still possible to prevent the Indians from being pushed out of their ancient lands. Today, 187 years after his death, Indians from diverse Canadian and American tribes are gathering a new Indian coalition under his name: "Uniting First Nations: Tecumseh's Vision" ("Tecumseh's" A18).

This is where Julia Louisa Dumont comes directly into the picture. In 1788 the Ohio Company arrived at Marietta, approximately eight hundred miles and ten weeks after leaving the Boston area. Almost immediately war whoops rang in the ears of the Ohio Company settlers. Several of the 47 original colonists, including Ebenezer Corry [or Cory], were killed during the first half dozen years of their settlement. His death, the summer of 1794, made Ebenezer Corry the posthumous father of an infant daughter born a few months after he was murdered by Indians. This daughter would later become the Ohio River Valley's first noteworthy woman writer—Julia Louisa Dumont.

Escaping the region's frontier maelstrom a few months later in early 1795, the widowed Martha Dyer Waterman Corry put her tiny daughter into saddlebags and returned to the East, settling near Saratoga, New York. Here she worked as a seamstress and eventually married a man named Manvill, a retired widower with six children, the youngest of whom is the subject of her epistolary story *Lucinda, or the Mountain Mourner* (1807). This book recounts the seduction, abandonment, birthing, and death of Lucinda, whose baby, Polly, stayed with her kindly step-grandmother, grandfather Manvill, and the young Julia Louisa, who, the story says, maintained a close relationship with Polly. Julia Louisa Corry was educated at nearby Milton Academy, became a teacher, and married into a family that traced its ancestry back to Sir Francis Drake. After her August 1812 marriage to John Dumont at Greenfield, New York, Julia L. Corry Dumont prepared for emigration back to the lands of her birth. They arrived in the spring of 1813, and John was immediately employed as a land agent for General William Henry Harrison, the politician and Indian fighter who was now in charge of all the troops in the northwest.

This fortuitous employment placed John Dumont's family within the orbit of Harrison, an advocate of western land speculation who was married to the daughter of a master speculator, John Cleves Symmes. William Henry Harrison, after the Fallen Timbers' Treaty of Greenville, was responsible for a variety of Ohio's Indian treaties that granted, between 1802 and 1805, over 33,000,000 acres of Indian land for white settlement.

William Henry Harrison is known in American history as the one-month, ninth president of the United States who was elected under the rubric "Tippecanoe and Tyler too." He resented the Indian leader Tecumseh's escape from his grasp at Fallen Timbers, and next attacked Tecumseh's people at Tippecanoe. Subsequently, the two leaders debated. When war broke out in the summer of 1812, William Henry Harrison pursued Tecumseh into Canada, where the chief was preparing to defend the British Fort Malden. Then the chief attacked Harrison at his stronghold,

Fort Meigs; Tecumseh was ultimately deserted by his redcoat British allies, abandoned by many of his Indian tribal coalition, and overpowered by military odds. Harrison's men wounded Tecumseh at McGregor's Creek and killed him at the Battle of Moraviantown on October 5, 1813.

The next day, when Harrison was taken to view the body, it was unrecognizable because of white men's desecration. The death of Harrison's "principal opponent" (Esarey 198) was omitted in his military report on the war. William Henry Harrison resigned his military commission and for many years held a variety of important political positions in the Ohio River region.

At this time, 1814, John Dumont and his wife Julia moved away from Harrison's direct orbit and out of Cincinnati, the Queen City of the West, a burgeoning riverfront city after 1811 where new steamboats were competing with traditional keelboats, flat vessels 75-100' long by 15-20' wide. Boomtown "Porkopolis" at that time had over 1,100 homes, three weekly newspapers, a theater, a library, and a university (Miller 33). In fact, until 1840 Cincinnati was "one of the great publishing centers of the continent" (Rusk 29). It was still the West, "ebullient but somewhat raw and unsophisticated" (Shortridge 14). The Dumonts desired a quieter domicile and moved nearby to a new down-river settlement at Vevay, Indiana. Two years later, in 1816, Indiana became a state.

In Vevay, John, a lawyer, became prominent in state politics, serving for years in the state's House and Senate and in 1837 unsuccessfully running for governor. It is Vevay's evolution from a "forest town" to an "embryo state" that Dumont in 1843 writes about in "Sketches from Life" and "Our Village."

Julia Dumont benefited from the fortuitous timing of her new life on the Ohio River. Unlike her husband's employer, William Henry Harrison, she was one of many whites who hero-worshiped the valiant Indian leader. Tecumseh's much-talked-about life became the subject of two of her earliest published essays, in Cincinnati's prestigious *Literary Gazette* in 1824 and 1825. Nearly a decade later, in 1834, the famous frontier editor William Gallagher commented in his essay "Brief Notices of Western Writers . . . Mrs. Julia L. Dumont" that she had a full manuscript *Life of Tecumseh* which he hoped western publishers would print. Seven years later, Benjamin Drake, the brother of one of Gallagher's associates, successfully published the first biography of this mythical Indian leader—*The Life of Tecumseh and of His Brother the Prophet* (1840). Dumont's manuscript about Tecumseh never appeared in its entirety and, according to her great-granddaughter, was consumed by fire in the late 1860s.

Modern readers may wonder why, indeed, anyone like Dumont would wish to immortalize Tecumseh, a man whose people harassed her family and murdered Ebenezer Corry, her father. Certainly, Dumont was not the only Ohio woman writer to sympathize with the Indians—others did the same, for instance, Pamilla Ball, Caroline Hentz, and Alice Cary—but none of them carried personal scars rendered by Indians' hands. Working with little historic perspective, and sorting out the chauvinistic justifications of Harrison and his cronies, Dumont composed stories that are designed to create sympathy for the great but victimized Indian chief. She shared the Indians' love of the Ohio River Valley and sympathized with their victimization by an engulfing government and frontier individualism. Perhaps it is not so surprising that Dumont identified with his persecution—both the Indian and the white woman were driven from the land of their birth, both had fathers murdered while defending their homes by the enemy, and, whereas Tecumseh responded by taking up arms against the enemy, Dumont's reaction was to take up the pen and valorize the Ohio River Valley as well as its advocate and famous local hero, Tecumseh.

In the first story included in this anthology, Julia L. Dumont describes a war between the Shawnees and Creeks which leads to Tecumseh's future father, Onewequa, being sent to the Creeks as a hostage or prisoner. While among them, he meets a sixteen-year-old Indian girl named Elohama, a Muscogule or Creek. They marry and return to the Muskingum, where Tecumseh is born. In 1774 a "party of adventurers," probably Kentuckians, murder Onewequa, whose wife commits her son to revenging his father's death. In Dumont's second installment of Tecumseh's biographical tale, she continues to present the Indian's maturation; this story is structured around a youthful Tecumseh who becomes attached to a young girl, "Yonca," a member of a Christian band living in southern Ohio. When Tecumseh returns to the Delaware village, it has been ravaged by whites, except for the resourceful Yonca, who recounts the devastation: "The white men came while darkness was on the earth; they came like lightnings from the stormy cloud!—their path became a rivulet of blood" (41). Tacitly the reader sees how Yonca's suffering, like his mother's, will intensify Tecumseh's commitment toward retribution against the whites. This episode is probably adopted from the infamous massacre at Gnadenhutten on the Tuscarawas that occurred in March 1792. Tecumseh was outraged by this blatantly cruel attack on noncombatants and in 1810 complained to William Henry Harrison about "the murder of the Christian Delawares," a slaughter that killed at least sixty-two men and women and thirty-four children (Hatcher 61). In fact, two boys escaped.

Modern historians, most notably the recent English biographer John Sugden, argue that Tecumseh's father was not Onewequa, but

Pukeshinway, a member of the Kispoko division of the Shawnees, and his mother was Methoataskee, a member of the Pekowi Shawnee living among the Creeks or Muskogees who provided haven to Shawnees. The couple returned north and are believed to have settled in the Indian town of Chillicothe on the side of the Scioto, where Tecumseh was the second born, probably arriving in 1768 and named "A Panther Crouching for His Prey" or "Blazing Comet." During his early youth between 1774 and 1782 there were at least five white incursions into his tribe's territory, and in one of these his father was murdered while defending his people.

In 1792, when Tecumseh was twenty-two, he returned from meeting with other tribes and was "determined to regain control of the north bank of the Ohio" (Sugden 79). The French and British were at war in 1793, and after General "Mad" Anthony Wayne defeated Tecumseh and his Indian allies at Fallen Timbers, the idealized hopes the chief had of an Indian Confederacy were threatened. His death concluded a life remarkable for its idealism and honor. After his death, both Indians and whites celebrated him as a noble martyr. Dayton's *Ohio Republican* called him the "greatest Indian general that ever lifted a tomahawk" ("More Glorious Still").

During the same time span when Dumont was writing her biographical essays about Tecumseh, she simultaneously published two more stories which sympathized with the broad issue of Indians' cultural disenfranchisement. In the first, the two-part "Okumanitas" (1825), she inverted the popular form known in the East as the "captivity narrative" by adopting an unusual perspective—an Indian youth is kidnapped by whites who massacre his people and is brought up in the East. Later he chooses to return to the Ohio River Valley, where he complains about being a misfit. He says, "I am floating on a pool which no breeze shall ever curl, no sun-beam shall ever illumine" (46). In the sequel to this tale, published a year later in 1825, the male narrator is replaced by an omniscient voice which presents a meeting between the lonely youth and the "compassionate" warrior, Tecumseh, who is depicted as he may have been before the War of 1812—tall, graceful, though fatigued and "attenuated with disease." Tecumseh takes Okumanitas to a village where the failing youth meets an old Indian woman who he learns is a priestess and physician. The youth is told to "build a wall round the remnant of our country" (51), but the sick young man is less troubled with the overall plight of his decimated tribesmen than with the loss of his immediate family. When the old woman recognizes a birthmark on his chest, she informs him that she is his only relative from the Montonga family, which two decades before was attacked by whites who killed his parents.

Upon his urging, she takes him to his mother's gravesite, where Okumanitas expires.

Another romanticized early tale is "Theodore Harland" (1825). Placed during Ohio's Indian Wars, it presents the reader with another Indian captive—this time a white. Its background is the East, where a Revolutionary War veteran named Captain Harland is disappointed in his son, Theodore, who has turned to dissipation. Though the young man is inspired to change when he falls in love with Elizabeth, his bad reputation interferes with the romance, and he flees. His disillusioned parents decide to start their lives over, too, and join others from their village who are emigrating "to the wilds of the West." They arrive in a beautiful region where utopia is threatened by the depredations of Indians. Captain Harland leads an expedition of men from the settlement who go out to fight the Indians. In the battle that ensues, he is out-maneuvered and then saved by a tawny savage who nurses, feeds, and returns him to the settlement. Calling himself "Hethlamico," the young man reveals that he really is Theodore Harland, the prodigal son, who learned of their departure, followed, and then—while descending the Ohio River—was captured by the Indians; saved by the pity of an aged squaw, he is mothered and after her death decides it is time to escape. In the Ohio River Valley, an egalitarian paradise, the transformation of Theodore Harland leads him to become a soldier and model of "filial piety." His reward is the renewed devotion of Elizabeth and the reconsecration of his family.

A few years later, in 1832, "Ashton Grey" was published, a more realistic story than Dumont's previous work, and one that became deservedly well known among literary editors. It won a $50 prize, and the narrative so pleased Dumont that twenty-three years later she included this "western story and romance" as the final selection in her collected anthology *Life Sketches from Common Paths* (1856). "Ashton Grey" is about the frontier world as remembered by survivors of pioneer days—the boatmen, soldiers, and villagers who fought so that the "cornerstones of our Queen City" (61) could be laid. The plot commences when a working mother returns home to her cabin to find it engulfed in flames. Panic ensues, but a nameless young man with a ladder appears and extricates her three children from the upstairs of the house. Described as having a "face which defied possibilities" (62), the youth leaves the scene with a wounded arm. One observer is a youthful orphan named Annabel Hampden, who is smitten by this youth. The omniscient author teases the reader by raising questions about the identity of the young man. The remainder of this long story unravels the mystery. The heroic fellow works in river commerce with the kind of men made famous by Morgan Neville's "The Last of the Boatmen," a story that celebrated keelboatmen as prodigious drinkers, jokers, and fighters. The youthful Ashton Grey has learned "self-reliant adventure" but is temperamentally very unlike his Ohio River cohorts. Dumont presents several boatmen discussing their awareness of this young man's unlikely, even noble character:

[N]atur is natur. . . . it ain't no use, no how, to try to force natur. I was jest minding that tree, growing out of the side of the bank there, below us, and thinking how it could a'growed up straight, that way . . . so one'll see it sometimes with a human. (71)

Before the romance between Ashton and Annabel can be made public, the weighty question of family background is raised. Two father figures intervene: her guardian is the upper-class Colonel Ainsworth; the youth's "father" is described as a dark and sinister "frontier adventurer" who raised the boy from a "cub." The noble lad was named after his "father's" dead younger brother, the original Ashton Grey. The story's Ashton was raised by the Indian trader, taught himself to read, took jobs as translator and surveyor for land-jobbers, and moved away from his "father's" "wild Ingen," Pottawatamie life.

Ainsworth repels Ashton Grey's address to Miss Hampden, saying the young man is an "improper aspirant" for her hand since his "class" is rude, though the aristocratic Kentucky emigrant admits that Ashton appear to be free of the "vices and habits of his caste." However, his suspicions seem to be validated when both Greys are imprisoned, accused of murdering a man on a riverboat. A series of revelations follow. Miss Hampden confesses to her guardians that she had already become Mrs. Grey. The elder Grey at the trial reveals that he is only a stepfather and in Kentucky saved the captive two-year-old boy from a bellicose Shawnee. Then that Indian, Walk-in-the-Water, strides into the courtroom to verify these events and provide details of the baby's abduction. The story they present amplifies the dying Grey's confession. He did murder the man on the riverboat, who long ago had unjustly caused Grey to be imprisoned; this initiated his escape to the frontier and a life of trade with the Indians. The story concludes happily with Colonel Ainsworth informing his wife that Ashton Grey is their abducted son and now they have two "children." Thus, his social conscience is clear, and class conflict on the frontier is avoided.

Julia L. Dumont over her decades living near the river observed diverse riverboatmen and sanitized them when she created her fictional boatman, Ashton Grey. Some surely were self-reliant, individualistic, confident, resourceful, and optimistic. In 1826 Timothy Flint described their western traits as rigorousness, rashness, and recklessness (21). He went on to label the Ohio River Valley's "yeomanry" as unique in dialect, enunciation, proverbs, and profanity. Flint wrote they are also frank, trusting, and, he adds, unusually courteous on steamboats. The post-Revolutionary Ohio River Valley was a place, he continued, where youths were given license to be extravagant, dissipated, and attached to the wandering life (15-16).

Indeed, in its early decades Ohio was a maritime state (Hatcher 107). It was attractive when men danced to fiddles on the decks of their craft, and during the era, many writers were fascinated by the free-wheeling boatmen. For example, Flint praised the boatmen's "charm for the imagination" (16); a decade later in 1838 an Englishwoman, Harriet Martineau, was similarly fascinated by the picturesque flatboats on the Ohio River. Even toward the end of the century William Cooper Howells, the father of Ohio regionalist William Dean Howells, wrote of the water craft as "enchanting" and added that he often watched them from the "bank of the river with longing and envy" (85). Later boatmen were memorialized for the twentieth century by Frederick Jackson Turner, whose *The Rise of the New West* (1906) romanticized riverboatmen as molded by the frontier lifestyle into "turbulent and restless" (102) figures.

Of course, ideas about the Ohio River's denizens were partially responses to regional myths, such as the one about Mike Fink, a man born near Fort Pitt around 1770 who for over 20 years was celebrated in the region as a scout, marksman, and keelboatman. Stories about this "ring-tailed roarer" were in print by the 1820s, the most famous being Neville's "The Last of the Boatmen," a story referred to by Dumont in "Ashton Grey" and published in James Hall's *Western Souvenir* in 1829. James M. Miller claims Neville "rescued an epic American character from oblivion" (161). However, modern commentators add that real boatmen were migratory, restless, and aggressive, and keelboatmen were especially rough frontier types. At the end of the twentieth century, historians describe the river's social and economic reality as growing increasingly complex. The rise of steamboats in the four decades between 1823 and the outbreak of the Civil War gradually diminished the flatboatmen's control of "total inland river commerce" (Allen 144) to no more than 20 percent. Perhaps, a few men were like Fink and wanted to be called "Alligator Horses" or "ring-tailed roarers," but far more were probably "poor, sick, womanless, alcoholic drifters" (Allen 215), colorful but ill adapted to represent "western life in poetic and literary form" (Hubbart 58).

Julia L. Dumont's riverboatmen are neither idealized from a distance nor transformed by bestial imagery. And, in one sense, Ashton

Grey is a recurrent type in Dumont's stories, a man who is victimized by events but survives. Despite kidnapping and a frontiersman's nurture, the boy's instincts are to distance himself and grow. The parable of Grey's transformation moves him away from the literal river scene, to the village courtroom, and into a home. It is thus that Dumont repudiates the Mike Fink story which had been popular for five years when she wrote "Ashton Grey." Her boatman represents a different frontier type—not a scalawag, but a youth whose inborn instincts democratically reveal him to be innately above his apparent "station" in life.

Setting the riverboatmen aside for a while, Dumont returned to the public's much-loved formula of the captivity narrative for the last time when she wrote "Hugh Mason" in 1833. This story focuses on the title character who, like Ashton Grey, operates at a disadvantage because of appearances. The romantic tale unfolds by a traveling narrator who visits the frontier cabin of the Browning family and meets Hugh Mason, a social outcast and apparent misanthrope who suffers from being an orphan with a humpback. Later, the child Edward is kidnapped by Indians. Marian, the distraught wife and mother, sympathizes with the blamed and forlorn Hugh Mason, despite knowledge of his inadvertent responsibility for Edward's abduction. The nameless narrator is also taken captive and, therefore, is able to testify about the next stage of the plot. He observes Hugh Mason—an unlikely hero who has let himself be taken captive by the Indians in order to care for young Edward Browning. This selflessness leads to Hugh Mason's redemption; he rekidnaps the boy from the Indians, and the consequence is that Mason wins self-respect, manhood, and community acceptance on the Ohio frontier.

Dumont's intentions for "Hugh Mason" are explained by its introduction, in which a traveler at a village inn hears complaints about the barrenness of America's native legends. The speaker complains, "If western literature is to have no broader field than that afforded by western history, it will need the aid of puffing." His tirade continues with a list of the absent features of the New World: it has no "grandeur in ruins, no classic associations, and no gorgeous pageants." Surely no one could wrest good fiction out of "half savage habits, and rugged and monotonous adventures," says the "Knight of the Classic school." But the western narrator responds that they do not need "pomp, pride and circumstance" since there is always in "*human* character a power, a mystery evincing itself in all conditions . . . to awaken interest" (93). The respondent then offers as proof of his democratic beliefs the observed story of Hugh Mason's heroism.

In the same year, 1833, Dumont's romantic story "Boonesborough" again exhibits her interest in frontier settlements under threat. Her subject this time leads her characters to a Kentucky fort begun in 1775 as a stockade to protect nearby cabins. Dumont's exciting frontier tale about Boonesborough, Kentucky, draws upon common knowledge of the fledgling community's significance fifty years earlier in the 1770s, when it played a key role in obstructing the plans of the British and their Indian allies, who worked to deprive whites from further western expansion. Indeed, modern historians say that if the fort at Boonesborough had fallen in 1779, "other forts would have been captured, and the whites would have been driven out of the West" (Clark 79).

It was the British plan to weaken George Washington's Revolutionary War army in the East by causing men to be drawn westward in order to protect pioneers. In response, General Washington sent George Rogers Clark and a small expeditionary force to attack the British in the northwest, and they won a key battle at Vincennes. Nonetheless, new settlements like Boonesborough remained under constant Indian harassment. In the words of one historian, "The Indians seemed to be everywhere. They were not able to take the stations, but they lurked about in the forests and made it dangerous for any man to hunt" (Lester 173).

In July 1776, Daniel Boone's daughter and several other girls were taken prisoner by Indians and soon were rescued by Boone and his men (Stewart 163). Boone went on to complete his fort by the spring of 1777; it was attacked by Indians on April 15 and May 23. It also underwent several sieges, one from French Canadians and Indians on September 7. Boone himself was captured on January 8, 1778, and, when he finally escaped and returned to the beleaguered Boonesborough, he learned that his wife had taken the children back to the relative safety of North Carolina until the borderlands were truly pacified. Indeed, twenty years later the region had become so civilized that the restless Boone forever left it, moving west of the Mississippi in 1797. Though Boonesborough was the first incorporated town in Kentucky, it never had "any commercial importance, and it soon disappeared" (Lester 79).

Dumont's story avoids retelling its military narrative while drawing upon the nostalgic flavor of the era in which Boone's daughter was abducted and saved, while the whites within the palisaded fort lived under constant Indian threat. "Boonesborough" commences in Washington, D.C., in the period at the end of the Revolutionary War. Its plot introduces a prodigal son who flees civilization in order to move into western borderland forests and draws to a close in a microcosm of white civilization, the new fort at Boonesborough. Its storyline is simple: the widowed, childless Major Worthington offers to help his friend Howard Everill by giving a job in his office to his ineffectual son Verni; the young man proves to be untrainable, is accused of theft, and disappears. The major soon adopts a niece and nephew and employs a recently injured war veteran called Herbert Allen. When disease devastates Major Worthington, Allen proves invaluable, though his courtship of Worthington's niece, Avoline, is rejected. Allen then decides to go to the West, where he has heard there is a "stirring call to a rich field of stormy but ennobling adventure" (111).

By water they all journey westward, but while mending a boat Allen and a border man named Bryan are taken prisoners. The wounded Major Worthington escapes by boat, and Avoline comes out of hiding, a desolate figure until her two traveling companions return after getting their Indian captors drunk and killing them. The party of three proceeds to find Major Worthington and locate Boonesborough, where they are surprised to learn that Howard Everill is the officer of the garrison. Conversation about Verni Everill, his "missing and wretched" son, is interrupted by the ironic appearance of a dying soldier who confesses that he was responsible for the theft blamed on young Everill. As the plot winds down from this revelation, father and son are reunited. Avoline is asked if she still loves Verni Everill, the childhood friend who once saved her from drowning, and she responds that her mature love has now been earned by the sterling character of Herbert Allen. Learning finally that the two names refer to the same person—Verni is Herbert—allows Avoline to marry and completes the redemptive story of an American prodigal son who "was lost but is found."

What is, perhaps, most interesting about this romantic frontier tale is that it, like "Ashton Grey," was a $50 prizewinner which brought Dumont considerable contemporary fame. Nineteenth-century American readers were curious about the past and patriotically hungry for stories with happy endings about reconstituted family alliances; they wanted to see Daniel Boone-type frontiersmen in action, and were always gratified by the triumph of romantic love. All of these romantic formulas are utilized by a young Dumont in her rustic tale "Boonesborough."

By the 1840s, as Ralph Leslie Rusk points out, Ohio's pioneer period had essentially ended (23), and the mature Julia L. Dumont's style becomes transformed; she now foregrounds her interest in the post-frontier nature of village life. The writer turns her attention away from rustic tales of the Ohio River Valley's frontiersmen and toward its settlers, which leads to a different sort of story—one that examines the modern consequences of the Ohio River Valley's thirty years of domestication. Her 1843 stories "Sketches from Life" and two-part "Our Village" realistically illustrate this poignant reassessment of the changing lifestyles generated by the Ohio River.

"Sketches from Life" is essentially an "allegory" directed to those who have not been stirred by "the world of thought" (127). Her allegory presents a valley that is turned into a pleasure garden, which deceives its dwellers with "slow and insidious poison" (125). When a second garden is laid out as a place of health, few visit it. Dumont's poetic moral explains this rendering of Ohio River Valley life: people should learn what is real and earnest. She comments that the Methodist-sponsored *Ladies' Repository* is an appropriate vehicle to provide open-minded readers with prose that helps them to honestly see the "garden" for what it is; after all, this periodical was the "most extensive and most expensive literary periodical ever published West of the Allegheny Mountains" (Venable 97). Dumont's forty-nine-year-old voice adds that an author's skill is needed to reveal the breadth of human experience—tenderness, trust, love, joy, hope, and their opposites like sorrow and suffering. The storyteller rejects the city's loneliness, the countryside's barrenness, and then turns to village life, "where we shall feel ourselves a part and parcel of those about us" (129). This is Julia L. Dumont's "true arena," a place to discover "manifestations of character and feeling" (129).

The village to be examined is located on "our own Ohio—la belle riviere—associated with a thousand romantic legends and thrilling recollections." Flatboats carry freight to New Orleans, "our southern emporium," and are loaded with "ungentle slang" (129). She realistically describes two boatmen, one with a family is starting on his first commercial adventure; another is experienced and has an innocent wife joining him who must face "rugged accommodation, the incidental exigencies, and rough encounter" of a river trading voyage. The ferryman speaks:

to see that little skeery woman a-starting to Orleans! Why I tuk her wunst across the river here when a bit of a gale come up; and she'd no more blood in her face than the white caps popping about us. (131)

Then the drama proceeds: the two boats push off, reach the current, and go out of sight. Four months pass and the wife of the neophyte boatmen reappears, impoverished by the "incubus of debts" (133) caused by a debilitating illness, country fever, an unremitting ague. It is then learned from the returning boat that her young husband has died upon the passage and been buried in "a grave upon the shores of the Mississippi." Dumont observes the wife's shrieks and comments: "This is reality . . . a scene of common, real life" (135).

The next month she published in *The Repository* the first installment of "Our Village," a history that fundamentally continues the themes of "Sketches from Life." She begins with a description of the village's history—forested land thirty years before was turned into a rustic village, which thrived because of its proximity to the "natural thorough-fare" of the Ohio River. New emigrants continually arrive, including a vast contingent from Switzerland. New families in the frontier village are briefly described, like the young wife who is taught by cruel experience how wrong it was for her to see "the *West*" as merely "a land of romance" (236).

The second segment of "Our Village" begins with a long narrative about reentering the village years after it has grown and lost its simplicity. Class distinctions have now "poisoned" life; disease has taken "nearly a fourth of the population" (146). At one point the autobiographical narrator physically enters the story and futilely attempts to help a pestilence-stricken family. Nearby, a debtor's family is dying because he cannot legally go to their cabin for nursing duties. Both "inebriate carousal" and church meetings are described. At the sketch's conclusion, Dumont addresses her readers about how these swirling memories must ultimately be abandoned, as it is indulgent to stay too long in a "retrospect of the past" (155).

The next story included in this anthology, "A Family History," appeared the following year, November 1844, in the *Western Literary Journal and Monthly Review*. It illustrates the maturity of the fifty-year-old Julia L. Dumont. She herself serves as the narrator, though she is preceded in the earliest part of the story by an initial narrator, an older woman in Cincinnati who was many years a confidante of the Ellesly family. The sophisticated double narration allows far more development of psychological characterization than is found in Dumont's early frontier stories. Her framing device is an arrogant family which is rude to a first-born but eventually is humbled and forgiven by the grown youth. Between the circular presence of George Ellesly at the beginning and end of the story, the two women narrators reveal many aspects of the region's psychology and sociology when Ohio was still the West.

The unique perspective of a person who was fifteen when first attached to the Ellesly household in the East allows the now old lady to comment as an involved first-person participant and observer. She describes the family's formidable patriarch, his second wife, their two conventional children. Also there is the sad boy named George, first-born son of Mr. Ellesly. George's dying mother had demanded of her husband that this son be allowed to spend his first decade in the care of Mary, her sister in the country. The narrator observes how the country-bred boy was later treated coldly by the aristocratic Ellesly family. She even confesses her own failure to support and protect George when he was unfairly abused by his half-brother, Edward, who killed George's pet bird; the old woman adds that her heart "smote" her for not defending him. George is subsequently ill and returns to his beloved Aunt Mary. Glad to be rid of a son he perceives as being stupid and without pride or character, Mr. Ellesly moves his family to Cincinnati, to the house that initiates Dumont's storytelling, and lives there for ten years with the addition of a four-year-old daughter and a older orphan cousin named Alice.

Then, on their way to Cincinnati from Pittsburgh by flatboat, the family meets a "denizen of the West" (169) named Brown, who injures his arm while intercepting a runaway horse, thus saving the patriarch Ellesly and his daughters. This is "not story-telling" (169), the old woman notes, but a real event. Brown briefly recuperates at the Ellesly home.

Later Mr. Ellesly moves his family yet further west, and Dumont's voice as narrator continues the Cincinnati crone's story. The town described seems to be Vevay, Indiana. It is new, has fewer than two hundred homes, a single street, and a population that includes many indigenous backwoodsmen, "lineal descendant[s] of Boone or Leatherstocking." The narrator comments that at the village grocery they talk about:

commerce, politics, legislation . . . magnificent metaphors and figurative brevity, so properly in keeping with the ample features and nerve of the country. Thanks to Western legends and Crocket Memoirs which enable us to imagine these, for truly we have not time "to tak' notes." (173)

Edward Ellesly's high-flown manners and snobbery leave his law office empty until one of the locals is told by Brown that "yes"—a "fellow in a linsey coat . . . [can] get to speak to him nigher than a set-pole's length" (174). The emergence of Ellesly's and Brown's friendship leads to the lawyer's real "education." He wins a law case and soon runs for the state legislature. The neophyte lawyer learns that not all backwoodsmen are illiterate, nor coarse-minded, though some phrases of "concentrated Westernism" need to be translated for him by his campaign manager, Brown. Young Ellesly wins and becomes euphoric about the beautiful countryside and its disparate western population; he even brags about being nearly "half horse–half alligator" himself (177).

In the story's epilogue, the two young men go to visit the Ellesly home, only to discover it engulfed in fire; they save its occupants and build them a log house. The humbling of Mr. Ellesly is nearly complete; he finally admits to pitying his lost elder son, George, and is amazed to be told that Brown, who had taken his aunt's name after she died, indeed, is George Ellesly! The narrator, Dumont, comments upon how the reader has certainly known this and adds that—after the transformed patriarch dies—the banished cousin Alice is invited to return and soon marries the loyal George.

Thus this long story provides Dumont with a chance again to adapt the parable of the prodigal son—inverting it and developing a tale of multiple dwellings that transforms arrogance into humility. Along the way her two complementary female narrators offer refreshing counterpoints; the old woman expiates childish sins, and the mature Dumont intrudes an account of frontier life and politics in a place that apparently is based on Dumont's hometown, Vevay, Indiana, where rough-and-ready politicking, including "stump" activities shown in the story, were inevitably a part of her husband's electioneering activities. The story's vital portrait of the era grows from "common affection and minor currents that are flowing on always and everywhere" (157). Dumont's subject also mocks the pretensions of green New England emigrants from "the land of classic shades and ultra observances" (158) and praises "Western . . . home material" (157).

A year before she died in 1857, and in accord with the literary conventions of her era, Julia L. Dumont published *Life Sketches from Common Paths*, an anthology of her short fiction which balances early frontier stories like "Ashton Grey" (1832) against stories conceived in a more domestic vein, like "Aunt Hetty" (1856). The anthology's framing device is provided by a matriarch named Aunt Quiet, who describes how a series of young people need to learn, through sketches and stories, the consequences of vice and virtue.

The "American Tales" in this volume are dedicated to J. L. Dumont's remaining children, two sons, survivors of a "mirthful band." The preface warns that a "small portion of the stories have strayed singly into the journals of a past day," which notably includes "The Pauper," a revision of her award-winning 1825 story "Theodore Harland," "The Soldier's Son" (1828), "Ashton Grey" (1832), and "The Family History" (1844). The remaining contents of *Life Sketches* include two introductory tales about boyhood friends who have an "anniversary dinner" reunion where they share stories. This produces seven stories, each of which represents a clear moral theme and is in accord with her preface, which warns the stories are designed to offer youths a "guiding hand." As stories written to inculcate lessons about adult life, Dumont intentionally supplements her frontier stories of the Ohio River Valley. Nonetheless, many of these stories exert their "moral influence" within the framework of pioneering and farming in early Ohio—her characters struggle with sibling rivalry, youthful folly, career disillusionment, estrangement, poverty, debt, and alcoholism. One, told to please a childish family auditor, is a love story.

For a modern reader, perhaps the most interesting and original story in *Life Sketches from Common Paths* is "Aunt Hetty," a story about a rampaging cholera epidemic on the "western waters" of the Ohio, perhaps modeled after a terrible one in 1833 (Knepper 154). The male narrator has a sprained ankle and helplessly watches a corpse being laid out by a German emigrant woman, Aunt Hetty, who serves the riverfront village. After Aunt Hetty discovers a German Bible with "Henrique Van Ernstein" written in it, the mystery of the corpse's identity is solved, for her dissipated but penitent son has returned to her for "safe housing."

Dumont adds a closing endnote to *Life Sketches from Common Paths*, explaining that she sees frontier stories as being about "the sober details drawn from *common paths.*" She then in the tradition of Ohio's frontier writing offers the reader her last intruded comment before being stilled when she introduces the concluding narrative, her 1832 "Ashton Grey." This story, Dumont continues to believe, best embodies the "warp and woof" of Ohio River Valley culture.

*   *   *

When William H. Gallagher's essay "Brief Notices of Western Writers" appeared in the *Cincinnati Mirror and Western Gazette of Literature and Science* in 1834, he qualified his praise of Julia L. Dumont's skill as a writer by sadly implying that her potential was limited by her mothering a large family and thus lacking adequate time for literary pursuits. Three decades later in 1860, Thomas Eddy similarly qualifies his admiration of Julia L. Dumont's literary work by lamenting that she was overburdened by household cares, feeble health, and consequent "distrust of her own abilities" that "prevented her from attempting more" (45). He adds an interesting proviso about her generous motives:

While her productions were sought after with avidity by publishers able to pay for them, she felt so much desire to build up and sustain the local press and home literature, that she more usually would send her best songs [poems]to some new village paper, struggling for existence. (45)

Before returning to the question of whether Dumont's domestic responsibilities adversely affected her literary work and prevented her from joining the ranks of single, childless women writers like Jane Austen, the Brontë sisters, or Emily Dickinson, one must note that the facts are true—Dumont's life was very full. When she and John Dumont moved to Vevay in 1814, his parents, Peter Dumont and Mary Lowe Dumont, also came and lived with them there. Two of John Dumont's brothers, Peter and Abraham, came to live in Vevay as well. Additionally, Julia L. Dumont's widowed mother also emigrated from the East to Vevay and moved in with her daughter and the rapidly expanding family. Eleven children were born to Julia and John over the years, and during her lifetime five of her beloved boys died. The male survivors were: the eldest, Peter, and Ebenezer, who followed his parents' footsteps by becoming a lawyer, teacher, and legislator. He died after being named as the territorial governor of Idaho. Four female children also survived, including the eldest, Mary; Martha who as a widow in 1856 returned from Lawrenceburg to help her declining mother and after her death kept house for her father, who died in 1870; Marietta; and the youngest, Julia, who assisted her mother as a teacher and posthumously collected her manuscripts, including poetry and some narratives, like her unpublished Tecumseh biography.

Over the years Julia L. Dumont's teaching career paralleled her role as mother and eventually fed into her writing career. She first taught in a Vevay log house, then in rooms in several homes and was surprised, after a trip to New York City to work with her publisher on her 1856 volume *Life Sketches from Common Paths*, to discover that John Dumont had built a new schoolroom for her alongside their Vevay residence. She is lovingly described by her great-granddaughter, Lucille Skelcher, as combining in one room infant care and teaching, while assisted first by her mother and later by her daughter. Dumont writes about her children being her inspiration, "around her feet as she wrote."

Her teaching was inspired, and in her own time made her regionally renowned. Indiana's Brookville College, as a case in point, named its Debating Society after her and proudly printed her photograph on their publications. Dumont's pedagogy was based on nurturance and affirmation, a revolutionary approach during this era in American history. One of her students, George Cary Eggleston, was taught to write by her when others had declared him to be hopelessly illiterate; he warmly wrote in "The First of the Hoosiers" that she was a "Dr. Arnold in petticoats" (350). His more famous brother, Edward Eggleston, was also deeply influenced by their benevolent Indiana mentor. He composed a novel, *Roxy* (1908), about the era of Harrison's presidential campaign in Vevay, and the main characters inherit "the House of the Lombardy Poplars," which was the home and school of Julia L. Dumont. In this novel her son Aurelius, who died at age 26, is represented by an unpleasant character named Mark Bonamy, and the title character, "Roxy," is based on Aurelius's real-life wife, an idealized Vevay native named Harriet Dufour.

While the shadowy figure of Julia Louisa Corry Dumont ran a complex household, operated a series of schools, including Vevay's high school after she was 60, and occasionally wrote, her husband, John, pursued an independently vigorous career as: lawyer, legislator, real estate salesman, nurseryman, Justice of the Peace, Coroner, Inspector of Elections, and even President of the Vevay Literary Society. Julia L. Dumont remained within women's private sphere, although she had ambitions when she was young; in 1831, she issued a prospectus for a new Cincinnati journal to be called *Literary Parterre and Ladies Magazine.* Dumont did not edit this publication, since funding was not forthcoming (Coggeshall, "Literary" 98). In the preface to *Life Sketches from Common Paths,* Dumont claims she "had no ambitious aims" and has learned not to care about criticism—in the author's third-person voice, "The time has been when she might have been flattered by its notice, even while she shrunk from its scrutiny."

Dumont's view of herself as a writer is indirectly suggested by the changes that took place in how she presented herself to the public. Over the several decades of her writing career, Dumont's literary signatures evolved—growing from the nearly anonymous "D," to "Mrs. Dumont of Vevay," to plain "Mrs. Julia Dumont," to an even simpler "Mrs. Dumont," to being without a name, just identified as the author of some of her most famous stories, for instance, "the author of the 'Soldier's Son,' 'Ashton Grey,' Etc." In her concluding anthology, *Life Sketches from Common Paths,* she retains her first name and middle initial, plus the title Mrs. and her husband's last name: Mrs. Julia L. Dumont, while her dedication is simply signed J. L. Dumont.

There are also significant changes evident in her use of narrators' voices. Early stories adopt the period's convention of direct or indirect male narration, as in "Tecumseh" or "Theodore Harland." Later Dumont's narrator evolved into a female, as in her two mature 1843 "Sketches from Life," and "Our Village," as well as in the double female narration of "A Family History" in 1844. More than a decade later in 1856 when she undertook her anthology, Dumont finally and uniquely spoke directly to the reader in her dedication and preface. The female narrator and character within the framing device for the story sequence is introduced as Aunt Quiet, a domestic matriarch, who says in a postscript to "Aunt Hetty" that she is writing western realism with "sober details," not romance. This collection demonstrates a feature Dumont in 1833 called "the softer traits of mind and feeling which a woman can only appreciate." The character Aunt Hetty, for instance, reestablishes the genuine merit of westernness while the enfeebled male narrator observes the cholera epidemic raging on the east bank of the Ohio River Valley. These changes in signature and narrator reveal Dumont's growing confidence and sense of voice.

Over the years several of Julia Dumont's male critics, like Gallagher, Eggleston, and Eddy, sympathetically blamed her lack of productivity upon the pressures wrought by her health and household cares, yet one could as well claim that it was the experiences of being a teacher, wife, and mother that generated the most original content in her career as a story writer. Certainly Julia Dumont's wisdom and ideas for themes and plots grew from her knowledge of life as experienced in her Vevay home and schoolroom. These arenas enriched Dumont and led her toward realistic subject matter and style. Dumont's writing conveyed her domestic sympathies, a supportive corollary to her experiences as a mother and career as a teacher. It is within the traditional womanly guise of Aunt Quiet in *Life Sketches from Common Paths* that Dumont fades from Ohio's literary scene, and perhaps this is the ultimate illustration of how domesticity complemented her literary career.

Indeed, Julia L. Dumont's hectic life was atypical in comparison to other women of her culture, who for the most part were restricted to the domestic sphere. The medical doctor Daniel Drake in his 1834 "Discourse on the History, Character, and Prospects of the West" described women's roles. They faced toil, danger, deprivation, and depression or "sickness of the heart" but discovered joy in being a pioneer man's companion, a role which elicited her courage, bravery, and self-possession (34). But Julia L. Dumont's double career and growing assertiveness as writer and teacher never concentrates on women's frontier joy.

She admits in *Life Sketches from Common Paths* that children's demands have made her "slow to complete the purposed offering" (7), and the autobiographical voice of its third-person narrator, Aunt Quiet, confesses to the experience of a "sick heart," or temporary loss of inspiration after the deaths of many children. Judging in terms of literary productivity, it appears that after the mid-1840s Julia L. Dumont's mental and physical health declined, including illness so severe that she went to Florida to recuperate. After going through a fallow period, in the early 1850s she somehow roused herself and was "induced once more to resume her task" (8). Dumont was galvanized and set out to complete the retrospective anthology, *Life Sketches from Common Paths*, which was to be based on the theme, the "reality of goodness in a bad world" (9).

Although not a prolific author, Julia L. Dumont, nonetheless, contributed to the tradition of popular literature in the Ohio River Valley. Rather than imitate British or American authors of the East, Dumont responded to western calls for vigorous "indigenous talent," such as was expressed in the *Western Monthly Magazine* in 1833, in which an article on "American Literature" protested "intellectual vassalage" to Great Britain and urged cultivation of "native intellect" and an "American feeling" (189).

Julia L. Dumont's prose fiction was written in response to such patriotic injunctions, and they continued beyond the opening decades of the century. For instance, an 1855 editorial in a literary newspaper called *The Genius of the West* sought "a literature partaking of the spiritual energy of our people, inspired by our past and full of legend, and story of peril and romance" (342). After the Civil War, this characteristic regional patriotism was abandoned as America decried sectionalism, forcing literary taste to change and forever altering American culture. Nonetheless, it is important to remember that during the first half of the nineteenth century, the Ohio River Valley's intellectual leaders were passionate about creating pride in its sectional uniqueness. Probably the most influential of all the commentators who promoted the need to celebrate regional culture was Dr. Daniel Drake, intellectual gadfly and professor at Transylvania College. He sang the praises of the Ohio River as "one of the most interesting boundaries among the republics of the West" (24), and gave a famous 1833 speech, published under the title "The Importance of Promoting Literary and Social Concert in the Valley of the Mississippi." In retrospect, Julia L. Dumont's literary career as a writer of fiction may be viewed as a response to Drake's prophetic words: "We should foster western genius, encourage western writers, patronize western publishers, and create a western heart" (26).

Chronological Bibliography of Selected Dumont Stories

"Okumanitas." *Cincinnati Literary Gazette* II.1 (3 July 1824): 1-2.

"Tecumseh." *Cincinnati Literary Gazette* II.15 (9 Oct. 1824): 113-15.

"The Life of Tecumseh." *Cincinnati Literary Gazette* III.20 (14 May 1825): 153-54.

"The Sequel of Okumanitas." *Cincinnati Literary Gazette* IV.9 (16 July 1825): 225-27.

"Theodore Harland." *Saturday Evening Chronicle* I.7 (21 April 1827): np.

"Ashton Grey." *Cincinnati Mirror, and Ladies Parterre* I.17 (12 May 1832): 132-36; reprinted in *Life Sketches from Common Paths*. New York: D. Appleton & Co., 1856. 245-86.

"Boonesborough." *Cincinnati Mirror and Ladies Parterre*. II.16 (16 March 1833): 97-103.

"Hugh Mason." *Cincinnati Mirror, and Western Gazette of Literature and Science* III.4 (9 Nov. 1833): 23-24.

"Sketches from Life." *Ladies Repository* 3 (July 1843): 206-10.

"Our Village." *Ladies Repository* 3 (Aug. 1843): 233-36; 3 (Sept. 1843): 297-302.

"A Family History." *Western Literary Journal and Monthly Review* 1 (Nov. 1844): 34-46.

"Aunt Hetty." *Life Sketches from Common Paths.* New York: D. Appleton and Company, 1856. 227-42.

Works Cited

Allen, Michael. *Western Rivermen, 1763-1861: Ohio and Mississippi Boatmen and the Myth of the Alligator Horse.* Baton Rouge: Louisiana State UP, 1990.

"American Literature." *Western Monthly Magazine.* Ed. James Hall (April 1833): 184-89.

Banta, Richard Elwell. *Indiana Authors and Their Books.* Crawfordsville, IN: Wabash College, 1949.

Briscoe, Orah Cole. *The Hoosier School of Fiction.* Thesis Indiana U, 1934.

Clark, Thomas O. *A History of Kentucky.* New York: Prentice Hall, 1961.

Coggeshall, William T. "Lectures and Literature." *The Genius of the West* 4.11 (Nov. 1855): 342.

___. "Literary Enterprises in Cincinnati." *Genius of the West* 5.5 (April 1856): 97-100.

Coyle, William, ed. "Julia Louise Corry Dumont." *Ohio Authors and Their Books.* Cleveland: World, 1962. 181.

Drake, Daniel. *Remarks of Daniel Drake on the Importance of Promoting Literary and Social Concert in the Valley of the Mississippi.* Louisville, 1833.

Eddy, Thomas M. "Julia Dumont." *Poets and Poetry of the West.* Ed. William Turner Coggeshall. Columbus: Follett, Foster, & Co., 1860. 43-45.

Eggleston, Edward. *Roxy.* New York: Scribner's, 1908.

——. "Some Western School Masters." *Scribner's Monthly* 17 (March 1879): 370-73.

Eggleston, George Cary. *First of the Hoosiers.* Philadelphia: Drexel Biddle, 1903.

Emch, Lucille B. "Ohio in Short Stories, 1824-1839." *Ohio State Archaeological and Historical Society Quarterly* 53 (July-Sept. 1944): 230-33.

Esarey, Logan, ed. *Messages and Letters of William Henry Harrison.* 2 vols. Indianapolis: Indiana Historical Commission, 1922.

Flint, Timothy. *Recollections of the Last Ten Years in the Valley of the Mississippi.* Boston, 1826. New York: Johnson Reprint, 1968.

Fry, Mildred Covey. "Women on the Ohio Frontier: The Marietta Area." *Ohio History* 90 (Winter 1989): 55-73.

Gallagher, William D. "Brief Notices of Western Writers . . . No. IV. Mrs. Julia L. Dumont." *Cincinnati Mirror and Western Gazette of Literature and Science* 3.29 (3 May 1834): 129.

Hatcher, Harlan. *The Buckeye Country.* New York: H. C. Kinsey, 1940.

Howells, William Cooper. *Recollections of Life in Ohio from 1813 to 1840.* Gainesville, 1895. Gainesville, FL: Scholars' Facsimilies and Reprints, 1963.

Hubbart, Henry Clyde. *The Older Middle West 1840-1880.* New York: Russell & Russell, 1963.

Hurt, R. Douglas. *The Ohio Frontier: Crucible of the Old Northwest, 1720-1830.* Bloomington: Indiana UP, 1996.

Kaul, A. N. *The American Vision: Actual and Ideal Society in Nineteenth-Century Fiction.* New Haven: Yale UP, 1963.

Knepper, George. *Ohio and Its People.* Kent: Kent State UP, 1989.

Lester, William Stewart. *The Transylvania Colony.* Spencer, IN: Samuel R. Guard, 1935.

Lewis, Thomas W. *History of Southeastern Ohio and the Muskingum Valley, 1788-1928.* 3 vols. Chicago: S. J. Clarke, 1928.

Manvill, P. D. *Lucinda: or the Mountain Mourner.* 3rd ed. Albany: J. Munsell, 1852.

Martineau, Harriet. *Retrospect of Western Travels.* New York, 1838. New York: Johnson Reprint, 1969.

Miller, James M. *The Genesis of Western Culture: The Upper Ohio Valley 1800-1825.* Columbus: Ohio State Archaeological and Historical Society, 1938.

"More Glorious Still from General Harrison." *Ohio Republican* 1.22 (25 Oct. 1813): np.

Nicholson, Meredith. *The Hoosiers.* New York: Macmillan, 1916. 88-95.

Ogg, Frederick Austin. *The Old Northwest.* New Haven: Yale UP, 1920.

Parker, Sandra. *Home Material: Ohio's Nineteenth-Century Regional Women's Fiction.* Bowling Green: Bowling Green State U Popular P, 1998.

Rusk, Ralph Leslie. *Literature of the Middle Western Frontier.* New York: Columbia UP, 1925.

Skelcher, Lucille. "Julia L. Dumont and Her Descendants." Paper read at the Switzerland County Historical Meeting of 13 Jan. 1938 and printed in *Vevay Reveille-Enterprise* (10, 17 Feb. 1938): np.

Sugden, John. *Tecumseh: A Life.* New York: Holt, 1997.

"Tecumseh's Vision: Indians in Canada, U.S. Seek Closer Ties." *San Diego Union-Tribune* 22 July 1999: A18.

Turner, Frederick Jackson. *The Rise of the New West, 1819-1829.* New York: Harper & Row, 1906.

Venable, William Henry. "Pioneer Poets and Story-Writers." *Beginnings of Literary Culture in the Ohio Valley.* Cincinnati: Robert Clarke & Co., 1891.

TECUMSEH, PART I

In the year 1767, the Shawanese Indians then scattered along the waters of the Scioto and Muskingum committed some depredations on the Creeks, who inhabited the interior of Georgia. This warlike and numerous nation threatened their immediate extermination, and would probably have accomplished their vengeful purpose, but for the timely interposition of the Delawares; who were warmly attached to the Shawanese, having, at a former period lived with them as neighbors and allies, on the borders of the Susquehanna. A party of the Delawares, who inhabited New Jersey, had recently crossed the Allegheny mountains, and were seeking, on the waters of the West, a suitable place for a settlement. They were immediately applied to, by their old friends, the unhappy Shawanese, who trembled beneath the expected vengeance of the Creeks, had no other hope but the influence of their former neighbors, whose character as peace-makers had been long established: and this hope was eventually realized. The Delawares immediately stepped forward between them and their exasperated enemy, and a treaty was at length concluded on condition, that the Shawanese should yield up a certain number of their principal young men, as hostages for the future good conduct of their nation. Among these hostages was Onewequa the father of Tecumseh: Tecumseh, the celebrated warrior, who moved a few years since like a stormy cloud, dark, terrible and mysterious on the horizon of American prosperity. Onewequa was the son of Shekellimus, an old and respectable chief, whose voice was heard with deference by the councils of his tribe. The young savage would gladly have exchanged the fate that now awaited him for the hatchet or the death fires of the enemy, but there was no alternative. To rush unbidden thro' the gates of eternity, is deemed the death of the coward by the philosophic savage; and he walks proudly on thro' the rocking billows of existence with a spirit, cold, silent and settled, moving the wave it encounters and scorning the demon of the tempest. The aged Shekellimus saw the flourishing scion, which had been the prop of his declining years, torn rudely from his side and transplanted to a distant soil; yet neither the father nor the son betrayed the least emotion. Calm and sullen as the fearful pause which precedes the shock of jarring elements, so Onewequa departed, and Shekellimus was left joyless and bare like a tree, which the whirlwind has stripped of its branches. Arrived among the Creeks, his superior skill and daring prowess as a hunter, soon obtained for Onewequa the respect of the nation; for the children of the forest, independent of every adventitious circumstance, invariably pay the most flattering homage to the spirit of the brave. But the smile of hospitality and the glance of respect were alike indifferent to the haughty soul of Onewequa. Elevated by the consciousness of native freedom, and indignant that his nation had stooped to superior power, he disdained even the shadows of servitude. However, as time rolled on, a softer passion rose like a beam of light on the darkness of his path, and Onewequa forgot that he was in effect a prisoner.

Roaming through the forest in pursuit of game, he startled a wolf from the thicket; it fled from him with the swiftness of the wind, but lo, an arrow from the summit of a hill suddenly arrests its flight; he looked up and beheld the archer advancing to her victim. It was an Indian girl, apparently about sixteen. Her bright jetty tresses flowed to the ground, and measurably veiled a form of the most exquisite symmetry. Onewequa approached her with admiration and astonishment. She had burst upon his soul like the full moon emerging from a cloud. Health and animation flashed from her eyes as she smiled bewitchingly on the handsome Indian who stood before her. Language was here unnecessary. The union of congenial hearts is every where the same, whether they throb beneath the tawny bosom of the savage, or heave the snowy breast of nature's fairer race. The philosopher may laugh at the existence of love, and the moralist may talk of reducing it to system, but its vital influence still remains unimpaired; and its electric flame is less amenable to control than the flames of heaven. Onewequa and Elohama were perfect strangers; yet a moment passed away and their spirits mingled for ever. "You are weary," said Elohama, "but I will lead you to my wigwam and you shall forget the fatigues of the chase." She then led him to Kewaytinam, a venerable chief of the Muscogule tribe. The old man received him with benignity, while his daughter brought him some food and ran to bring some cool water from the fountain that bubbled thro' the broken rocks. From this moment Onewequa ceased to regret his native wilds, for Elohama met him in the forest and clambered the hills at his side. Her father, who loved her to idolatry, had taught her the use of the bow and arrow, and the deer fled from her in vain. She marked Onewequa with attention. She saw him, regardless of fatigue and fearless of danger. She heard her tribe applaud the intrepidity of the stranger, and her artless bosom swelled with triumph. She soon listened to his impassioned tales with undisguised delight and reciprocal professions of attachment. "Thou art dearer to me," said she, "than the cool breeze at noonday; I see thee darting thro' the thicket, and I forget my weariness. Ask Kewaytinam for Elohama; he has noticed thy deeds in the chase, and thou art dear to the soul of the warrior." Onewequa flew to obey the mandate. Kewaytinam heard his proposals with complacency, and the marriage was soon consummated. Tecumseh, whose origin has given rise to such various conjectures, was the fruit of this union. Previous to his birth the father of Elohama died, and Onewequa, who had gained the perfect confidence of the Creek nation, was permitted, by the desire of the dying chief, to return with his countrymen to the shores of the Muskingum. Here Tecumseh first saw the light. At this time the most extensive harmony existed between the white people and the different tribes, who were settled on the western waters. The former frequently came to the Indian villages for the purpose of trade; and the savages reposed the most unlimited confidence in their friendship. Onewequa soon acquired a knowledge of our language, and like Logan, "was the friend of white men." He admired their arts, and earnestly endeavored to inspire his tribe with a desire of attaining them. Alas! He had yet to learn, that the blackest vices still prowled amid all the refinements of civilized life. Who has not read the story of the interesting Logan? Who has not execrated the name of the detestable Cresap? Yet a thousand Cresaps have disgraced the sacred title of Christian, and many Logans have been sacrificed on the red altar of that exterminating hatred, which thousands of our people yet bear his scathed and unfortunate race.

In the year 1774, while the most perfect tranquility reigned through all the interior of the Indian country, a party of adventurers, who were engaged in looking out for settlements on the Ohio river, were unhappily robbed by some wandering savages; and so exasperated were these wretches, that equally regardless of the claims of humanity, or the safety of their exposed countrymen, they determined on the indiscriminate massacre of the Indian villages. The lovely temples of peace from this moment were abolished, and repeated murders were committed by the whites, under the mask of friendship. Jefferson, in the appendix to his incomparable "Notes on Virginia" gives a detailed account of these massacres. For a time, the voice of Onewequa was exerted in the councils of his tribe to suppress the resentment which this carnage had awakened; but continued outrages eventually destroyed his confidence, and he dared no longer attempt the defense of a government which permitted slaughter where they had promised protection. His much injured people called loudly on him for vengeance, and pointed out the numerous encampments where murder had rioted in the blood of the unsuspecting savage. "The tree of peace," said they, "spread its green branches over the waters of the Muskingum; but the white man approached it, and it withered. He laid the sword at its root and dug up the hatchet that was buried beneath it. Let us dye it deep with his blood; let us avenge the death of our countrymen." Onewequa felt the justice of their claims; but death unnerved his arm at the very moment when vengeance called for its utmost tension.

Deeply engaged in the pursuit of a buffalo, he one day met a party of men, who had recently assisted in the massacre of an Indian settlement. They knew Onewequa and presuming on his long and well known friendship for the whites, requested him to accompany them as a guide through the forest. The soul of the Indian darkened as they spoke. "Are not your hands," he exclaimed, "yet red with the blood of my countrymen. Even now, I hear the spirits of my slaughtered people, calling for revenge. Beware, sons of treachery"———. The unfinished sentence was lost in the convulsive struggles of death, for the leader of the party had discharged a musket at his bared bosom. He fell without a groan. The white men passed on, and the dying Indian was left in the solitude of the forest! The day declined, and Elohama clambered the rocky steep, to watch the return of her husband. Daughter of nature, repress the throbbings of thy bosom; the heart of Onewequa no longer beats with responsive feeling. Deep shall his sleep be in the silence of the desert, and often wilt thou call on his name, but he shall not awaken! Elohama threw her anxious gaze through the deep shades of the wilderness, but in vain; she listened in breathless stillness for the light footsteps of the hunter; but no sound was heard, save the hollow murmurs of a gathering storm, and wolf howling loud and discordant from his hills. Clasping her infant to her bosom, she sought the narrow path that wound through the forest, determined never to return till she had joined the side of her husband. The night gathered dark round the wandering savage, and the thunders now rolled deep and heavy through the sky. In the pauses of the wind, a dying groan struck her ear. She followed the sound; it led her to the body of Onewequa! A flash of lightning streamed across the stormy bosom of nature, and shed a livid glare on his convulsed features. Elohama sunk at his side! Successive flashes now discovered the blood which lay congealed on his bosom. Her shriek recalled him for an instant to life. He opened his eyes, and fixing them on his wife, distinctly said "behold the faith of white men."

Oh, Onewequa, has thou fallen thus, and is there none left to avenge thee? The arm of the warrior is broken, since thou art laid low; but behold the young plant at my breast, who shall yet gather strength to crush thy destroyers! When thou has past yon sky of storms, thou shalt see and converse with the Great Spirit, mid his clouds! Then let thy petitions all rest on the name of Tecumseh: For him shalt thou ask the soul of the warrior, and the strength of the mighty. Then shall he be as a whirlwind and a storm, scattering desolation and death; as a fire, raging through the forest when its leaves are seared on the winds of Autumn. The race of dark souls shall wither before him; and thou shalt behold his deeds as thou lookest from the skies, and thy very ghost shall rejoice in the fullness of revenge.

Elohama paused. The winds died away, and the storm was suddenly still. The full moon rent her thick mantle of darkness, and her clear light streamed here and there through the trees of the forest. The heart of Onewequa had ceased to beat, but a smile of approbation rested on the features, now fixed in death; for the words of Elohama had been heard, and the passing spirit assented as it fled.

The night passed away, and the mourner transferred her gaze, from the mangled body of her husband, to the placid features of her sleeping child. A lock of her own long hair, yet wet with the storm, lay across the face of the infant warrior. Softly she put it back, while she contemplated his countenance with a kind of holy reverence. "The Great Spirit," she said,

has smiled on the ghost of Onewequa, and granted his petition for our son. He hushed the howling tempest, and bade the moon and stars come forth in their beauty, as tokens of his assent. Tecumseh, thou shalt avenge the death of thy father, and appease the spirit of thy slaughtered brethren. Already art thou elected the chief of many tribes, for the promise of the Great Spirit is everlasting. Thy feet shall be swift as the forked lightning, thy arm shall be as the thunderbolt, and thy soul fearless as the cataract, that dashes from the mountain precipice.

Such were the consolations of Elohama, and she looked anxiously forward to the time when Tecumseh might realize her prophecy. Four years had marked his birth, when she led him to the grave of his father. It was at the close of day, and the most perfect silence reigned around the hillock of death. "Seest thou that little mound of earth?" said the savage. The boy fixed his steady gaze on the spot, and was silent. Elohama threw herself on the wild grass, that grew rank around the grave and drew her child towards her.

My son, thou art dearer to me than the cords of existence; thou art the sweetest flower that greets my eye as I wander through the forest. Thy voice is the music of my ear, and thy affection is the fountain which cools my scorched brain, when it burns in phrenzy. My son, who, like thy mother, would have cherished thy helpless infancy? Who like her rejoices in thy growing beauties?

The boy rolled his dark eye on Elohama; it shone in all the radiance of gratitude and filial affection. "My son," she resumed,

mark me, and remember what I say. Thou hadst once a father, for whose tender cares the fondness of thy mother is but a shadowy substitute. Tecumseh, had he lived thou wouldst have been the light of his soul, and the reward of exertions that would have never tired. For thee, he would have climbed the mountain steep, and braved the angry storm, when the Great Spirit frowned in darkness. He would have taught thy infant feet to explore the secret paths of the forest, and pointed out to thy inexperienced eye the faint traces of thy enemy on the fallen leaf. He would have guided thy young arm when it first aimed the arrow at the bounding buffalo. He would have taught thee to build the light canoe, and ride the deep waters in safety. But he is no more. In the summer of his days he has fallen, and he sleeps in the earth before us.

Elohama paused. Tecumseh for a moment seemed lost in thought—then suddenly exclaimed, "Mother, why does he not awaken?" "My son, his is the sleep of death." "Death?" said the boy, in an accent of inquiry, and evidently ignorant of her meaning. "Today," resumed Elohama,

you saw a deer bounding through the forest. He was lovely in strength and beauty, and fleeter than the winds which parted before him. Suddenly the hunter crossed his path, and an arrow cleft his heart. I led you to the spot, and bade you look at the struggling animal. A short time passed away, and the warm blood, which flowed from his wound, grew dark and chill. He was stiff and cold, and his beauty was departed.—Such is death, and such is the sleep of thy father.

An awful pause ensued. The features of Tecumseh assumed a ghastly ferocity. "Mother, whose arrow cleft the heart of my father."

My son, thou hast been told of a people beyond these wilds, who are the enemies of thy race. Their souls are dark with treachery, and their hands are red in blood. They came with the pipe of friendship to our forests, and smoked the calumet with our nation: but they met thy father alone among his hills; they pierced his bosom and fled! He was a warrior, and his arm was the arm of strength. Great might have been his deeds, but his heart is now moldered to dust, his eye is shut in darkness, and the wolf and buffalo bound over his grave unheeded.

Tecumseh burst from the encircling arms of his mother, and the fearful glance of his eye changed suddenly to flashes of lightning. "Mother, give me my hatchet, and lead me to their villages! I will drink their blood! I will consume their race!" Elohama smiled at the enthusiasm she had so anxiously endeavored to awaken. "My son," she replied,

thy arm is yet too feeble, and thy arrow is still unsure. Thy hatchet must lie in its rust, till the blossoms of many a spring shed their leaves round the grave of thy father. But time still rolls on without ceasing; the winter passes quickly away, and the summer is again here. Thou shalt soon rejoice in the strength of manhood, and thy enemies afar off shall hear thy name and tremble.

THE LIFE OF TECUMSEH, PART II

Tecumseh listened with a gloomy kind of submission; the playful animation of childhood no longer gladdened his countenance; the joyous light of his eye was quenched, and a settled shade rested on those features, that were wont to beam with pleasure. From that moment a deep and inextinguishable hatred was planted in his heart,—corrupting the fountains of gaiety and destroying the elasticity of his infant mind.

Elohama saw the strong impression she had made; and a gleam of joy, like the red meteor of a stormy night, crossed the darkness of her widowed heart. She now suffered no opportunity to escape nursing the deadly passion. Traditions of injuries long since past;—of blood long since spilt;—of territories lost, and nations exterminated: these were the themes which now daily amused him. The destruction of his enemies, was the prayer he was taught to utter; and songs of death were chanted in his ears, as he mingled at evening in the frenzied dance of these warriors, or sunk, overpowered by fatigue, into a fitful and disturbed slumber. The gay and airy visions of boyhood fled for ever. One absorbing sentiment took possession of his soul, influencing all his views, and strengthening with revolving years.

Elohama found it necessary to smother the rising flame, though she fanned its concentrated heat. "Behold those stars," she said to the musing boy, as she pointed to the clear blue sky of a summer evening:

such, Tecumseh, are the enemies of thy race. No eye can number them, and they roll on, year after year, still undiminished in their brightness.—Look again at the pale fire-flies, that glimmer through the trees: such, few and feeble, are the native children of the forest. Our warriors have lost their strength: the spirit of the Red man is broken, like a tree which the lightning has riven. Yet think not, my son, that the vengeance of the Great Spirit shall slumber for ever: it will yet waken, like the strong tempest that sleepeth in the clouds. He shall then clothe his warriors in new strength, as the spring covers the naked branches with green leaves. He shall send them forth, mighty as a herd of enraged buffalos. Then, Tecumseh! Shalt thou, also, rise in the summer of thy manhood, and wash the dark rust of his blood away from the hatchet of thy father. Till then, my son, thou must be calm and still, as the chained floods that are hushed by the breath of winter, or the smothered fire, ere it catches the added fuel!

Such were the frequent counsels of Elohama, and Tecumseh heard them with deference, even while his ardent spirit panted with unutterable fury.

Let the white man's favored offspring, who turn careless and unimproved from the voice of paternal instruction,—let them go and observe the tawny boy of the forest. With him coercion is unnecessary: he listens fondly to the accents of experience, and implicitly follows the counsel of maturer years.

Tecumseh became immoderately fond of hunting, in his earliest childhood. Disdaining every kind of hardship, he soon inured himself to hunger and thirst; to the damps of midnight, and the fervors of meridian day. His body seemed to acquire a kind of supernatural invulnerability. Fatigue had no power over him, and he laughed scornfully in the face of danger. Nothing could elude his vigilance, exhaust his perseverance, or thwart his determination. The deer could not out speed him, and he swam the proud waters with the skill of their native tenants. Ere he was ten years of age, his mother's lodge was decorated with the richest spoils of the chase; and the tribe to which he belonged, already looked upon him as their future chief. The old men admitted him to their councils, and the youth emulated his example. A kind of mock fight was frequent among the boys of the village; and prizes, composed of fantastic trophies, were awarded to the victors. Tecumseh was invariably the leader of his band; and he soon became the terror of his youthful antagonists.

The education of the savage is peculiarly calculated to call forth the native energies of his character. Taught from his earliest infancy to depend on himself for support, he discovers at once his own resources. The infant's lullaby is the wild song of the bird that perches on the bough, from which he is suspended; his moss-covered cradle is rocked by the winds of the forest; his caudle is the blood of the buffalo; his play things, the claws of the panther. His earliest exercises are the use of the bow and arrow—the hatchet, and the tottering canoe. No trembling mother deprives him of the fearful instrument, or warns him of the danger that lurks beneath the wave. Elevated by the consciousness of manly daring, he soon rises above that instinctive fear which operates on all human creations; and relying wholly on his own strength and skill, both are continually exerted. Thus the Indian boy, who is ignorant of all the arts of civilization, would hold, and perhaps justly, our effeminate striplings in the most sovereign contempt.—Among the bravest of the Indian boys, however, Tecumseh was still pre-eminent; and the Shawanese youth shrunk into conscious insignificance before the intolerable lightning of his eyes.

He was fond of solitude, and spent day after day, alone, in the extensive wilds that stretched their shades along the waters of the west. His spirit was dark and gloomy, and reveled with delight in the wildest visions of anticipated revenge.—The deepest recesses of the wilderness, the wildest scenery of nature, were most congenial with his feelings. In one of his daily excursions he followed the windings of the *White-Woman* till the lovely stream of *Muskingum*, burst suddenly on his view. Still impelled by the restlessness of an unquiet spirit, he wandered along its margin; and an Indian village at length rose before him. The red rays of the sinking sun trembled on the wild landscape; and the inhabitants were assembled together before the door of their principal tent. Struck with the appearance of the boy, who stood leaning on his gun, one of the oldest chiefs with an aspect of benignity, pointed to a mat and bade him to rest from the fatigues of the day. Tecumseh obeyed, and silently observed the interesting group. The men sat smoking with serious and composed countenances; the children rested quietly on the ground, and the women joined in chanting a hymn in the Shawanese language. Tecumseh listened with astonishment. The music was soft and mellifluous, and the words fell like dew on the summer blossom. Its theme was Love,—and praises of a Being whose attribute was *mercy*, it ceased, and the old man who first addressed him, now spoke to a little girl, whose long hair fell in thick masses on the ground as she sat at his feet. "Yonca," said the aged chief, "go fetch water from the fountain, and bring food for the youthful stranger." She rose, and throwing back her clustering tresses, discovered a face of the most exquisite beauty: Descending the hill like a shooting star, she returned in a moment, and presenting Tecumseh with the pure and cooling beverage, ran to procure him more substantial refreshments. The youthful hunter received the proffered repast, with silent thankfulness; and then stretched himself on the mat which was spread for his repose beneath the wide shade of the sycamore.

As the day began to dawn, the sounds of music awoke him. Was it the songsters of the wood, caroling their morning lay?—No, it was the unwonted strain of devotion—it was the deep and holy melody of the preceding evening. The poor Savage of the wilderness lifted the voice of praise to the Author of his being. Tecumseh rose immediately: an undefinable sensation rushed through his heart. He saw the crimson glories of the eastern sky, and the beauty of the rippling waters, which reflected the rising sun. He felt the dewy freshness of vegetation, and inhaled the pure and healthful breath of the morning. Creation dawned on his soul in a new and soothing light. The spirit of devotion hovered like an angel's wing over the sacred spot; and the haughty youth bent before its power.

The insufferable brightness of his eye grew dim; a tear, the first—the last—rolled over his tawny cheek! He advanced instinctively towards the pious band and his softened features expressed the language of Ruth when she exclaimed—*"Thy people shall be my people, and thy God my God."* Alas! Tecumseh, the yielding tenderness of thy heart shall soon give place to a hatred yet deeper than midnight, and yet more stubborn than the grave. The holy light, which now breaking on heathen darkness shall set in gloom: the white man shall quench it in blood, and the footsteps of him who bears the name of a Christian, shall dry up the fountain of love and tenderness for ever.

The thoughtful boy now returned to his tribe, in a state of mind which seemed like the soft influence of a pleasant dream. The voice of devotion yet sounded in his ears. That Being whom he had hitherto worshiped, assumed a new form. He no longer beheld him clothed in storms, and delighting in human blood—but a God of light, dispensing the dews of mercy, and pouring out his bounties with a lavish hand. An irresistible impulse impelled him, soon after this, to revisit the hallowed spot where these impressions were first received; and his heart throbbed with unwonted pleasure, as he trod the flowery wilds of Muskingum. He at length reached the site of the Moravian village; but where was now the busy hum of living habitation: Where were the tents which rose on the path of the hunter? Alas, they were a heap of ashes! Their inhabitants were already mingled with the dust. Tecumseh rushed forward with a thrill of unutterable horror. Ninety skeletons lay bleaching among the melancholy ruins. All was frightfully still and desolate. The green earth was scorched and blackened with the flames: the corn-fields were consumed; and the neighboring trees were blasted and burning. Tecumseh loitered long and mournfully on the gloomy spot. A kind of stupefaction seized his senses, and he remained incapable of moving till the chills of midnight fell around him. A torpid slumber then stole gradually over him; but it was frequently broken, and visions of horror rose on his dreaming fancy. Suddenly, a form, wild, emaciated, and unearthly, flitted before him. Was he sleeping or awake, he knew not, but he started on his feet, and the specter fled. "Yonca, Yonca!" he exclaimed, for the moon was at her full, and he well knew the shrieking phantom, whose long hair streamed on the midnight blast. "Yonca!" he repeated in a soothing voice, and the unhappy girl sunk exhausted on the ground. Tecumseh raised and addressed her with the soft accents of compassion. Alas! Where was now the brightness of her jetty eye? Terror had fearfully glazed it, and the beauty of her polished cheek was despoiled by the withered fingers of famine. Tecumseh carried her to the well remembered fountain, and brought to her the remains of his last repast. She devoured it with avidity, for she had been some days without food. She then pointed to the ruins of her village—"Look," she said,

they are all gone! My tribe—my parents—my kindred—where are they now? The white men came while darkness was on the earth: they came like lightnings from the stormy cloud!—their path became a rivulet of blood. They came to slaughter friends, and not enemies,—friends who had watched over their safety, and warned them of approaching danger; friends who acknowledged their God, and received with kindness their Ministers of peace. The people of Otulaska made no resistance; they implored no mercy. The hatchet of defense rested at their feet—no one lifted it up. Hatred was extinct in their hearts, and the hand of the murderer could not kindle its flame. The warriors bowed their heads to the stroke of death, and the mother yielded up her babe to the red knife of slaughter, ere her dim eye had closed on its struggles. Why did Yonca fly? Why did the daughter of Otulaska live? Too well I understood the words of him who turned the sword another had pointed at my heart. Yes, Yonca was to be a prisoner, and carried away the slave of him who headed the murderous band. I heard no more, but my strength was renewed; I burst from them and fled. The deer would have fallen behind me; and darkness covered me like a host of friends. The shout of the wretches grew faint on my ear. I hid myself in a thicket, and lifted my voice to the God of the red man alone. The Great Spirit heard and answered me: a strong wind arose from the woods, and drove back the clouds from the glittering stars. I heard the sound of water murmuring at my feet; and I bathed my burning brain in the cold stream. I ascended the hill, and looked through the trees on the scene of slaughter. A thick smoke now rose from the lodges; a bright flame streamed on the air, and the night fled before it; the trees were red with its glare, and the river shone as if a hundred suns had risen on its waves. The white man shouted with triumph, and shook his sword in the air, while it yet dripped with blood. I fled from the horrid scene, and wandered in the forest till the second sun had risen on the ashes of my kindred. I then returned, but all was dark and silent. The murderer had departed, but his track was the footsteps of the whirlwind. Sometimes I have clambered the neighboring hills in quest of fruit, and again I have sat here on the withered ground, gazing on the ruins of my people. Here among the white bones of my kindred, I have mourned along, on the very spot where they lifted the song of praise to the God of the white men.—But I now listen in vain for the morning or evening hymn;—Death only is here; and the soothing voice of music has ceased for ever!

OKUMANITAS, PART I

I was ascending the Mississippi on my return to Philadelphia, when the illness of our principal steersman, obliged us to land. Tired of the dull monotony of our voyage. I could scarcely regret the accident, and sprung on shore with the glad impatience of a school boy. I had been some time at the prow, watching the receding shores, and felt an irrepressible regret at gliding thus rapidly past scenes whose unspeakable grandeur invited the spirit to pause, and the imagination to riot. The sun was sinking amid brilliant clouds of gold and purple, and his dying glories gleamed, in reflected light, from the smooth surface of the river, winding through forests of impervious depth. The Arkansas here poured his tributary wave into the burnished bosom of the Mississippi, which seemed like a vast sheet of molten gold, mocking the narrow limits of description.

The Cypress tree lifting its dark green head to the clouds, threw its deep shadows far over the margin of the river and shaded the gorgeous colouring of the scene with lines of the gloomiest magnificence. Ravished with the beauties of so wild a landscape, I seated myself on a little eminence, and taking from my pocket a case of drawing materials, attempted, but in vain, to sketch the surrounding scenery. How futile was the effort; a plant—a flower—any abstracted object may be successfully drawn, but the combined features of nature, in the fulness of her majesty and beauty, are as indescribable as the visions of immortal bliss. Vexed at being foiled, I made repeated trials to no purpose. The red glow of departing day faded slowly into darkness, and the scene I would have drawn, was lost in images yet more lovely. Every unpleasant idea now subsided into a holy calm. I rose from my seat, and strolling along the wild margin of the Arkansas, indulged in all the luxury of a fervid imagination. The sound of the boatmen was no longer heard in the distance, my companions were forgotten, and I followed the windings of the stream through the deepest shades of the forest. The full moon had risen in the softness of her chastened light, and streaming here and there through the trees, partially discovered a scene of the most exquisite wilderness. The owl hooted over my head, and I heard the wolf howling from the hills, yet I listened without fear, insensible to danger, and unconscious of materiality. Through the splendours of creation, I beheld the Creature and, my soul sublimated by the contemplation of his works, seemed to burst the fetters of mortality. My course had been impeded by fallen trees, and now I stood in motionless rapture, gazing at the clear blue sky, while visions of unutterable import floated before me. Suddenly a strain of music, rich, wild, unearthly, rose on the stillness that surrounded me. It seemed like the harps of heaven, hymning the soul to realms of bliss. I listened in breathless amazement: was it the effect of heated fancy? No, the sounds approached me, and I distinguished notes, that were once familiar to my ear. An Indian canoe came floating slowly down the stream and its solitary passenger was breathing from his flute a deep strain of unspeakable melody. He passed on without appearing to see me—I hailed him, but received no answer. In a burst of uncontrollable emotion, I plunged into the river, and in a few moments reached the canoe. He ceased playing and turned towards me as I approached him, while the full moon now clearly revealed the long hair, wild dress, and dark features of a savage. "What do you want?" he said, in perfect English and a voice that struck deeply on my recollection.

A crowd of distinct images now rushed on my mind at once. The music—the voice,—I no longer doubted to whom they belonged. Okumanitas, a young Indian, who had been educated at college by some gentlemen of Philadelphia, had been one of my favorite associates. The wildness of his character, the graces of his person and manners, the brilliancy and versatility of his genius, alternately flashing in the clouds or shedding its lambent light on "airy trifles" rendered him an object of interest abstracted from the idea of his race; but associated with, and heightened by the recollection of his origin, they created an intensity of admiration. Courted and caressed by the first circles of Philadelphia he seemed formed to animate and embellish society. Gay, ardent, enthusiastic, possessing nothing of the frigid temperament ascribed to our northern Indians, his conversation was like a mountain stream, sometimes rushing with the impetuosity of a cataract; then flowing in smooth and gentle murmurings. Yet to those, who best knew him, the darkening of his smile frequently evinced strong but suppressed emotions; and his flute which he played with matchless skill was often heard in the stillness of his chamber, breathing forth a strain of melancholy music, that told a tale of sadness.

At length Okumanitas disappeared—curiosity traced him to the verge of the western wilds—then lost him forever. Soon after this I also left Philadelphia, and altho' three years had now elapsed, yet I still recognized the voice of my Indian friend. "What do you want?" said he, in a grave but gentle accent; while I replied, "Okumanitas, have you forgotten me?" He extended his hand and drew me into the canoe without speaking; several moments elapsed in silence, for I could find no utterance for my feelings. The voice of Okumanitas was the same, but his features had changed their character. They were settled in gloom, their playfulness was gone, and the light of his smile was fled. At length I said, "Okumanitas, what means these savage habiliments? For what are they assumed?"

"They are best suited to my feelings," said the Indian, and again he was silent.

"Is it possible," I now asked, "that you, who have realized all the elegancies and refined pleasures of civilized life, have voluntarily abjured the haunts of enlightened men?"

"Yes," said he, "for ever."

"And can you," I continued, "whose mind is irradiated with the genial rays of science, again mingle with the savage children of the forest?"

He answered me with vehemence: "I associate with no one. I have no intercourse with civilized or uncivilized man. I stand alone, like the last being of a race that is extinct."

"And why," said I, "have you left the wide circle of your friends? I am now returning to my native place, and you must accompany me. You cannot hesitate again to seek the social pleasures of life." "This language," said the Indian,

to me is mockery, fostered by a people who have almost exterminated my race; education has unfitted me for an intercourse with the miserable remnant, that remains. But does it afford an equivalent advantage? I have now no country, no kindred, no people. Where then for me are the vaunted sweets of society? My soul is a desert, where the fountain of bliss is dried up. The calm pleasures that flow from an intercourse of equality—the soft emotions of brother, parent, child—the proud glow of the patriot and the triumph of the mighty shall never gladden the wintry gloom of my heart.

"You thought not always thus," I resumed. "A few years since, and I saw you with all the elasticity of youth, sporting in the bowers of pleasure, or treading with equal ardor the rugged paths of science." "Yes," he replied with an indignant smile,

I once fancied myself a link in the chain of creation, and visions of imaginary bliss floated around me. But the mists of enchantment are fled; like the traveler of the wilderness who dreams of love and joy and festive mirth, I have wakened to the reality of desolation. I form no part of the human family. I look vainly round me for a being whose spirit might mingle with mine. My soul communes neither with the living nor the dead.

"Okumanitas," I said, "you are guilty of injustice. How many of your former companions have felt for you, the warmest glow of friendship?" "There is a complacency of feeling," said the Indian,

growing out of circumstances, which sweetens the intercourse of man, and this I have experienced from most of my young associates: but call it not friendship; that can only exist between beings whom birth, nature and education have rendered equal. In the gay scenes of conviviality, every face wore the smiles of welcome; but they vanished like the fitful glow-worm that glitters from the tomb. In the silence of solitude who thought of Okumanitas? Was there one heart in the universe that throbbed for my happiness? Not one—existence for me is the darkness and the shadow of death!

A pause ensued; for the vehemence of his manner inspired me with something like awe. At length he exclaimed, "I saw her married; I played her epithalamium!"

"Who?" I enquired. "Ah true," he replied with an indescribable convulsion of feature,

of whom was I speaking; but 'tis no matter, the tawny lips of Okumanitas would profane the name they might utter. She knew not the guilty passion she inspired. I smothered the sacrilegious flame and fled from the world she inhabits. The tempest which raged in my soul is still. I am floating on a pool which no breeze shall ever curl, no sun-beam shall ever illumine.

We had now reached the Mississippi and Okumanitas rowed me rapidly to shore. I struggled to speak; at length pointing to the glowing heavens, I said, "there are worlds beyond those stars." A gleam of pleasure crossed the darkness of his countenance. "True," said he, "and the journey is short." He then set me on shore, and a moment after his little canoe seemed a speck on the distant wave.

OKUMANITAS, PART II

Okumanitas stood on a rocky summit, which overlooked the waters of the West. The silence of solitude was broken by no sounds save the howlings of the wolf, or the shrill cry of the panther. In the gloom of the wilderness, Okumanitas wandered alone. The storm of passion had subsided; but his soul was dark and still as the desert, where the *Samiel* has left its track of desolation. He had now broken the fetters of society, and stood like the last wreck of a sunken world. Hope was extinct for ever; and his spirit, like the worm of the grave, loved to riot on its blasted and decayed images. Alas, unhappy Okumanitas! Thou wert formed to revel in the fond endearments of social life. Education had called forth all the energies of thy nature, and thy olive bosom throbbed with the softest touches of feeling; but despondence has blighted the opening blossoms of the mind, and touched the fountains of thy existence with corruption. "Even here," exclaimed the despairing Indian,

even here the rude tenant of the forest finds its mate, rejoicing in the ties of kindred and the bonds of society. The wolf rears a numerous family in her den of rocks, and the eagle calls to its mate on the mountain summit. For me alone, the earth is a joyless waste—not a beam of gladness crosses the gloom that surrounds me.

The day passed away, and Okumanitas at length sunk exhausted on the ground. A peaceful slumber stole over him, and visions of ecstacy rose on the dreams of the night. The image of her he loved hung over him, and her light brown hair fell on his tawny cheek. She smiled like an angel of mercy, and music soft and holy floated around him. He stretched forth his arms, and the dream departed. It was day—the birds were caroling their matin song—the yellow rays of morning streamed through the tall trees of the forest. A rustling near him drew his attention. On looking up, he saw a panther springing from a neighboring tree, to a limb immediately above him. He started on his feet, and a new sensation of terror rushed through his frame. His gun was uncharged, and stood at some distance from him. The glassy eye of the prowler had already marked his prey.—Another leap, Okumanitas, and he revels in thy blood! What sound is that? Who is it that arrests the fearful spring? The animal has fallen—his green eye ball rolls in death—his talons are fixed in the earth—his struggles are past. Okumanitas, behold thy deliverer! Far, on an almost inaccessible cliff, stood an Indian, cold, silent and collected, reloading the unerring rifle, which at an incalculable distance had thus secured its victim. Advancing towards him with the liveliest emotions of gratitude, Okumanitas suddenly paused. Who is the warrior that stands thus high and proudly before him? His party-colored belt is richly decorated with hieroglyphical emblems; his silver breastplate glitters in the rising sun—the plumes of the eagle wave over his expansive forehead, and the deep stains of war measurably obscure the bright olive of his cheek. The fires of youth are no longer gleaming from his eye;—its expression is dark, fearful, and determined. Yet he lifts his searching gaze to the wasted form of the youth before him, and a ray of benevolence brightens his gloomy features—he speaks to him in the accents of compassion—the haughty bearing of the warrior is changed. "And why, young man," he said,

is thy cheek so hollow, and thy lip so bloodless? Hast thou just risen from the withered spell of sickness, and seekest thou in exercise the renewal of thy strength? Thou dost well in this, but thy feeble arm yet trembles beneath the weight of thy musket, and thou hadst best return to thy village.

"Warrior," said Okumanitas, "the grave shall soon afford me a home, but I am now a wanderer without a resting place—a stranger on the earth, without kindred or country. I am hastening to the tomb alone, and no one shall ask for Okumanitas."

"I understand you not," said the warrior. "The race of the red men is not yet extinct, and the tents of every tribe are open to receive the stranger. Comest thou not from the dwellings of white men? Thy accent is theirs, and thy feeble form, unlike the children of the forest, betrays the withering breath of luxury." "Yes," said Okumanitas, with a ghastly smile,—

I was reared on the very lap of luxury, and in the dwellings of white men I learned to shrink from the mildest dews of heaven. My tongue there forgot its native language, and the remembrance of my people flitted before me like the dim and fitful recollection of a dream.—From the chiefs, who sometimes visited the white rulers beyond those mountains, I first regained a partial knowledge of the Indian tongue; and long, though vainly, have I sought among these western wilds some trace of my origin. Among the numerous tribes who inhabit them, the name of Okumanitas was never heard. I shall pass away unregretted, and the feet of the hunter shall press careless and rudely on my ashes.

"And why carest thou?" said the warrior,

for the narrow distinctions of kindred? The red man is thy brother, and the wilderness thou treadest is thy country. Young man, thy spirit sleeps. The nation that fostered thee are the enemies of thy race, and are now trampling on the bones of thy people. Rouse, Oh youth from this torpor—thy strength may yet be renewed, and thou mayst then go forth to the rescue of thy injured brethren. Behold, the tribes of the forest are rising—the foot of the invader approaches our last possessions, and the hour of vengeance has come. Go young man, and join our warriors: they will teach thee the arts of war, and recount to thee the numerous oppressions of our nation. If worthy of thy race, thou wilt soon grasp the hatchet and bathe it in the blood of our enemies. Every tribe shall then hail thee as a brother, and thy fathers shall behold thy deeds from the residence of the Great Spirit.

The warrior paused—his strong muscular arm was raised with a fearful expression, and a dark smile crossed his feature, like a lurid glare of lightning on the sable skirts of a stormy sky. But his words fell on the soul of Okumanitas unheeded as the voice that calls the mouldering dead. The spring of feeling was broken forever; and he looked, with a dim and languid perception, on the billows of existence. Still the warrior beheld him with an aspect of compassion. His tall, graceful figure, though deeply attenuated with disease—his lofty, though pale forehead—his eye, sunken indeed and bloodshot, yet darkening with a bright and unutterable expression as he lifted it silently to heaven, still rendered him an object of interest, even to the haughty savage who strove thus vainly to animate him to exertion.

"I will accompany you," he said, "to the nearest village. We shall reach it ere the sun completes half his journey. You will there find rest and food, and no one shall behold you as a stranger."

Okumanitas assented, for the voice of kindness even yet awakened the feeble vibrations of decayed feeling. They commenced their little journey, and the warrior carefully measured his pace by the languid step of his companion. It was a sultry day, and Okumanitas felt himself sinking beneath its heat; but the warrior was unconscious of its enervating power. The sound of murmuring water was at length heard, and Okumanitas sprung eagerly forward. Cold and transparent a fountain gushed through the rocks of the dell that intercepted their path, and breathing with new life as his parched lips touched the stream, he bathed his fainting limbs in the pure element. But why does the warrior pass the spot unheeded?—there is no breeze stirring on the hills—the deer lies panting in the shade, and the dark green trees of the forest droop in the searching vapour. Yet the fountain of the valley rises vainly before him, and he strides across its limpid current, with a step that seems to mock its inviting murmurs. "Warrior," said Okumanitas, "can you pass this stream untasted? Behold how clear it gushes from the solid rock." "I see it," said the chief, carelessly, "but the Great Spirit often commands his warriors to spurn the idle wants of the body.—Their souls are thus purified, and the dreams of the night carry them to the dwellings of their fathers.—They are then instructed how to conquer on the field of battle, and the soul of Tecumseh thirsts only for the blood of his enemies."

"Art thou, then, Tecumseh," said Okumanitas, gazing almost fearfully on the stern countenance of the lofty chief. "I have heard the name, and know thee terrible as the tempest; yet I find thee also compassionate as the summer dews, and surely thy arm is strengthened by *Him* who builds up and destroys at pleasure." While he yet spoke, the distant village broke on his view, and ere they reached it, Tecumseh was recognized by its inhabitants. The youth thronged forth to meet him, and the old men gathered round the door of their principal tent to receive and welcome him. Presented as an invalid, Okumanitas was also received with kindness. Refreshments were brought him, and the females of the village employed all their little art to amuse the sick stranger. Tecumseh was immediately conducted to the council house, where he spent the remainder of the day with chiefs of the tribe; and at evening, the commencement of their war dance, wild, frantic, and peculiar, revealed the result of their deliberations. At some little distance from the fearful troop, Okumanitas rested on a mat, and gazed at the scene with the mingled sensations of delight and horror. Their light and spectral figures, at one moment drawn up to their utmost height, then bending like a reed in a strong wind;—their fantastic dress streaming on the evening breeze;— their arms flashing in the yellow moon-beams, as they brandished them in the air;—the clashing of the weapons;—the tinkling of their ornaments;—the deep hollow music of the drum;—their cries, and the chilling tones of their war song, all struck with an overpowering force on the decayed soul of Okumanitas. Exhausted with fatigue, the warriors at length seemed to pause. An aged squaw now approached the scene, and as she passed the spot where Okumanitas was reclined, he instinctively shrunk from her appalling aspect. As she joined the warriors, her hollow eye gleamed with unhallowed fire, and her skinny hands were clinched with unutterable fury.—They struck their arms at her approach, and she immediately commenced singing in a voice that seemed to issue from the tombs.

Young men, arise, go forth to the field of battle. The night has passed away. The mist rolls back from our hills—the morning breaks on the darkness of our country. A warrior comes in the strength of the avenger. He comes to save the expiring race of the red man. He calls them to rise from the furthest bounds of the wilderness, and build a wall round the remnant of our country.

Young men, ye have slumbered beneath the feet of your enemies. They have danced on the graves of your kindred, and you have not awakened. Rise, now, and bathe your languid limbs in their blood. A Chief cometh to guide you in the field of battle, and your enemies shall pass away before you.

While yet the Sun was young, the Red Man was planted on the earth. His race was like the leaves of the forest, and his hunting grounds spread before him like the blue sky, whose bounds no one has ever found. But the white man came over the great waters, and scattered desolation around him. He drove us from our hunting grounds; he burnt our villages; he deceived our warriors; he slaughtered whole tribes, and washed their names from the earth with their blood.

Warriors, arise! The fire of vengeance is kindling. The white man faints at its approach. Go forth, and give him to the flames. Already I hear his groans on the air, and our slaughtered countrymen are laughing at his agonies.

The song and the dance at length ceased, and Okumanitas fell into a kind of death like slumber. His system was nearly exhausted, and the morning found him extremely ill. The aged Songstress of the preceding evening came immediately to his assistance. She was considered a kind of priestess in the village, and possessing some medicinal skill, was also their physician. The old woman, notwithstanding her fearful aspect, evinced some interest in the situation of Okumanitas, and had him removed carefully to her lodge. In the course of the day, as she bent over him to administer some salutary preparation, her eye caught a deep stain on his breast, and she suddenly exclaimed, "whence are you, and to what tribe do you belong?" Roused from his state of torpor by this exclamation, and the frantic look that accompanied it, he exerted himself to reply, and gave his history in a few words. The old woman interrupted him with a deep cry of untranslatable import. "Yes," she at length said,

thou art indeed the last descendent of the family of MONTONGA, and in me, young man, behold the mouldering wreck of all thy kindred. Thy mother's family, with all my growing branches, were lopped away by the white man's sword. Our enemies approached us, and thy father, the last hope of Montonga, went out with our young men to meet them. He was slain, and the white men pressed forward to our village. We fled in canoes at their approach; but their guns were pointed across the stream, and thy mother's blood reddened the wave. I knew not *thy* fate. Thou hadst escaped the eye of watchfulness, and we had traced thy little footprints along the path thy father had taken, when the shouts of the enemy approached us. We thought thee sacrificed, and fled. But I alone of all thy kindred escaped in safety. Since that hour my soul has withered up, and I have panted vainly for vengeance. In thee, I see a long lost scion, sprung indeed from my blasted root: but the canker of death is already at thy heart, and thou shalt soon mingle with the ashes of my slaughtered offspring.

Okumanitas struggled to reply, but in vain. His inmost heart yearned for the maternal embrace. But alas! He shrunk with a kind of horror from the wild and withered form that bent over him. "See," she exclaimed, as she removed his clasped hands from his heaving bosom,

behold the united emblems of the bear and the panther, the symbols of mine and thy mother's family. These hands impressed the unfading stain on thy infant breast, ere the second sun had risen on thy birth. But thou must be calm, Okumanitas; that tear—it suits not the tawny cheek of the Indian. Thou shalt not live, indeed, to avenge thy kindred; but shalt meet them in the clouds. Rest thee, then, Okumanitas, and wait calmly for the summons of the Great Spirit.

Montonga was now silent for some moments; at length she resumed, "Hadst thou strength, I would lead thee to the grave of thy mother. At this very spot the waves bore her to the shore, and I laid her in the rocks, which raise their white cliffs above the stream. But 'tis no matter, I will lay thee beside her, and her spirit shall meet thine, in thy journey to the skies."

A kind of supernatural animation now rushed through the system of Okumanitas, and his soul resolved to take its flight from the tomb of his departed parent. He rose without an effort, and adjured Montonga to lead him to the sacred spot. She acquiesced in silence, and Okumanitas followed her with a firm and decided step. In the deep recess of a rude and rocky precipice, Montonga had formed a kind of coffin, on which she had piled a mass of rock that had defied the hand of time to loosen. It yielded easily, however, to the touch of filial piety, and on lifting his cover, a skeleton, with long black hair, met the eager eye of Okumanitas. A bracelet composed of shells still compassed its fleshless arm, and here and there a silver ornament glittered in the glossy tresses which lay in thick masses round the hollow temples. Okumanitas knelt beside the coffin, and gazed wistfully for some moments on the fearful image of decayed mortality. The sun was sinking in a flood of glory, and reflected a strong glare of light on the features of the dying Indian. Their expression at length changed—he stretched forth is emaciated hands to heaven; his bloodless lip moved—a smile of unearthly brightness passed over his face—his uplifted eye became fixed, and the next moment was closed for ever.

THEODORE HARLAND

Theodore loved! and the vapid temperament of his mind, produced by long habits of dissipation, suddenly gave way to the deepest intensity of excitement.—Satiated with the gilded cup of pleasure, he was chained to her unhallowed haunts, and unable to break the spell which bound his morbid faculties. From this moral incubus—this disturbed lethargy of the soul, he was raised by a vision, bright and lovely as the rainbow of promise on a stormy sky. Elizabeth,—but who shall describe her? The ethereal lightness of her form baffled the gaze of scrutiny, and the beauty of her features was of a cast beyond even the magic of the pencil. It was the undefinable expression of Intellect,—the radiance of youth,—the impress of innocence, the seal of virtue. A halo of light dwelt around her; folly checked his unholy sallies, and vice receded at her approach. Such was the being who crossed the path of Theodore at a time when his bosom was scorched and withered with the heat of uncontrolled and corrupted passions. She passed over his soul like a clear and healthful breeze, amidst pestilential vapors. Her voice, breathing in mellifluous tones the sentiments of a pure and exalted mind, came like seraphic music on an ear sickened with the siren strains of dissipation.

Man is a being of inconsistency! Theodore loved Elizabeth for the purity of her character, but heeded not the stains that marked his own. He approached her with hope; he addressed her without embarrassment. The graces of his person met the dark eye of the maiden, and she listened to his conversation with complacency. The language of Theodore assumed a new tone. Chaste and elevated, it was fit even for the ear of Elizabeth. Yet the soul of Theodore was above deception, and hypocrisy had never deepened the shades of his character.—Who has not felt the sublimating influence of that hour, when the curtains of night are drawn on the silent world, and the moon flings her silver light o'er the quiet scene? Such was the presence of Elizabeth; such was the mystic spell, so pure, so holy, that hushed every passion to rest in the bosom of Theodore, and called forth sentiments, exalted as the Being that inspired them. Elizabeth heard him with delight and believed his soul congenial with her own. Succeeding interviews confirmed the fatal illusion: Visions of bliss float around them, and the pure heart of Elizabeth, beats high at the approach of the profligate! 'Tis past, the vale of deception is rent for ever! The hand of a friend has torn it rudely away, and the character of Theodore, wild, dissolute, and irreligious, is delineated to her astonished view. Theodore again beholds her—but the glow of her cheek is fled, and her eye is lifted coldly at his approach.—What means this fearful calm, this chilling composure? Theodore is not formed to endure suspense, he demands his destiny, and the answer of Elizabeth, gentle, but decisive, blights at once the blossoms of promised happiness. Astounded at the stroke, as if a thunderbolt had fallen at his feet, he scarcely believed it real, and even yet hope is not extinct in his heart. Accustomed from infancy to all the elegancies of affluent life, Elizabeth was the child of penury. The casualties of trade had stript her father of wealth, and she now shared with her family the homely bread of indus-try. "I will restore her to that sphere in which she was wont to move" said the impetuous Theodore, and he mentally determined never to resign her. Day after day found him at the cottage of her father, but Eliz-abeth invariably retired from his presence, or met him with a cold, politeness which congealed the warm current of his heart. Stung at length to madness, and scorning himself for thus brooking the contumely of others, Theodore again plunged into the vortex of dissipation and strove to lose, in the haunts of folly, the pure image of Elizabeth. But Theodore had long been descending the steps of ruin and an arrest for debt suddenly checked his mad and reckless career. He heard its amount with a start of convulsive horror:—"No," he exclaimed. "I cannot again apply to my father," and refusing to give bail, he followed the officers of justice immediately to prison.

A week had passed away and among the idle circle of gay charac-ters whom Theodore called friends, no one was found to visit him. All around was desolate—not a gleam of light crossed his darkened, tempes-tuous spirit! His liberation is at last announced, and a note in the well-known hand of his father, placed in his eager hands—his blood-shot eye glanced over it with an expression of despair.—"Where is he," he exclaimed, and rushing from the house, he beheld his father at a distance walking with hasty and irregular strides. "My father!" exclaimed Theodore, springing wildly forward, "you give me liberty, but forbid me your presence? Pardon me that I cannot obey you.—Will you not hear me? Once more, oh my father, say that you will hear me!"

"And what would you say?" said Captain Harland, coldly, while he yet evidently struggled with emotions. "I would say that my future life"—"Stay rash young man, add not another promise to the many already broken:—the season of confidence is past—you have exhausted every plea of youth—you have mocked every hope of amendment—my forgiveness shall no longer sanction your vices, and you have at length drained the fountain that ministered to your extravagance. Go wretched boy—I can no longer shield thee from want, and thy presence, lost and degraded as thou art, will render yet more bitter the bread of poverty." "Stay oh my father! for the sake of her who bore me, stay and tell me your dreadful meaning."

"Claim you yet an interest in the heart you have broken? Presumptuous Theodore! The mother who cherished you is now without a home—the scenes of your childhood are already trodden by the foot of strangers. But for this, you had still been a prisoner."

Captain Harland now tore himself from the grasp of his son, and disappeared.—Theodore stood appalled as if the earth had yielded up her skeleton dead. His vices rose before him in terrible array—fearful as the corruption of the tomb—his whole frame was wrought as with a tempest. Suddenly his features assumed a settled though dark expression, and a lurid gleam of troubled joy passed over them. He walked to the lodgings he had formerly occupied, and locked himself in his apartment. After spending half an hour in writing, he arose and looked cautiously round as if fearful of being observed. He then took a pistol from his desk, and loaded it with desperate calmness.—At this terrible moment, a book which he accidentally threw from his table, fell heavily on the floor; he stooped mechanically to raise it, and a small but highly finished drawing dropt from its leaves.—Had the portals of Heaven opened on his view, the countenance of Theodore could not have changed more suddenly. The pistol fell from his trembling hands; a universal tremor passed over his frame; a sweat as of death broke out on his forehead, and the blood which had curdled around his heart, rushed back to his ash cheek: a tear suffused his fixed eye, and falling on his knees, he lifted his clasped hands in deep and convulsive prayer

Impetuous as the mountain cataract, Theodore had been precipitated from folly to folly, and vice to vice, by the ardent temperament of his nature, rather than the perversion of his principles: he had once been the child of promise, but an early introduction to dissolute companions blighted the opening blossoms of his mind, and planted in their stead the gloomy weeds of corruption.

At a time when his irregularities first withered the hopes of paternal love, Theodore returned unexpectedly and late at night to the house of his father. Passing his mother's apartment with a noiseless step, he heard the low deep tones of prayer, and through her half open door, beheld his mother, kneeling at the throne of Grace. He listened in breathless silence: she was supplicating pardon for her erring son—she implored the protection of the Most High for the weakness of youth. The prayer ceased; the sobs of the mother only were heard. Theodore retired, but not to sleep. "I will perpetuate this scene," exclaimed he, "it shall strengthen me in the hour of trial."—Theodore drew with a master hand, and he now sketched a strong and touching representation of the recent scene. The kneeling attitude of his mother—her interesting form, now scarcely past the zenith of her beauty—her pale countenance deeply touched with sorrow but marked with the fervor of devotion—her clasped hands and upturned eye, all were drawn with a correctness and strength of expression, which gave to the lifeless paper an interest as deep and affecting as the original.

This drawing had been carefully preserved but time had effaced the impression, and it was now forgotten.

Such was the picture that met the darkened eye of Theodore, at the moment when his impious hand had raised the instrument of self-destruction; and the words of his mother which he had written on its margin again sounded on his ear.

"Subdue, Oh Heavenly Father! the stormy passions of his soul, and guide his wayward feet in the paths of piety and virtue." "Hear, oh God of Mercy!" exclaimed the kneeling Theodore, "hear her prayer, and for her sake pardon the guilt of this dreadful hour." And that prayer was indeed heard, for a peace such as he had never before known now dawned on his throbbing bosom; he rose with confidence and meditated what course he should pursue. "I will not again intrude myself on my father, till I am worthy of his forgiveness. I will direct all the energies of my mind to the profession I have so long virtually abandoned, and look forward to the time when I can restore that wealth which my vices have so wantonly scattered."

Such was the determination of Theodore, but in his professional career he at once foresaw obstacles of the most fearful weight; he had forfeited the confidence of the public and must necessarily remove beyond the reach of distrust. Having written to his mother and obtained her pardon and her blessing, without daring again to address his father, he left the scenes of his misguided youth and buried himself in a distant metropolis.

Unable to contend with poverty where he had long known better days, Capt. Harland formed the determination of removing to the wilds of the West, whither a small party of adventurous families from his native State, was now preparing to emigrate. On a lovely stream, which rolled its clear waters through limitless forests of luxuriant fertility, the weary travelers at length formed a permanent residence.

All around them was gay as the garden of Eden. The blossoming earth teemed with plenty, but it was the wild prodigality of nature, and the pampered child of affluence looked vainly for the luxuries of a culti-vated soil. But Capt. Harland had been a soldier of the Revolution, and scorned the gratifications of the sensualist, while Mrs. Harland, with a constitution delicate, even to sickliness, possessed an elevation of soul that lifted her above the common wants of mortality. Concentrating every wish within the domestic circle, she felt not the loss of general society, and the friendship of one lovely being, whose character resembled her own, threw its gentle charm over the shades of solitude. Elizabeth had been the companion of her toilsome journey, for among the emigrants that accompanied Capt. Harland, the family of Elizabeth had formed a part. Struck at once with the mild virtues of her character, Mrs. Harland soon regarded her with maternal affection, and received in return all the nameless but sacred offices of filial love.

Regarding the surrounding scenery with an eye of enthusiasm, and beholding in perspective days of returning prosperity, Mrs. Harland, but for one absorbing sentiment, might have been happy. Theodore, to whom she had repeatedly written since their arrival, still continued silent; Capt. Harland at length addressed his Eastern friends, soliciting information of his son: none could be obtained. Theodore could be no where traced and the wretched parents foreboded some fearful catastrophe. Meanwhile their new abode had already become one of terror. The Red Man beheld with dismay the rapid encroachments upon his native soil, and the tomahawk was raised to repel the invaders. Death was every where around them, and the white blossom of the forest was daily crimsoned with blood. Immured within a rude and crowded fortress, yet still exposed to the wide bosom of desolation which the proud savage wielded over the scattered settlements of the white man, the parents of Theodore passed two years ignorant of his fate, and losing, under the absorbing influence of parental anxiety, the sense of individual suffering. Increasing numbers at length gave them strength to contend with the savage foe; and Capt. Harland, at the head of a few volunteers, joined a detachment sent out by the Executive to destroy the Indian villages. The wary savage still fled before them, and as yet nothing intercepted their march. Near one of the deserted villages, Capt. Harland saw a grave freshly made; a wild rose was planted over it, and an Indian name was cut on a rude stone that marked the spot. The soldiers passed on, and the red glare of battle suddenly gleamed around them. From the long grass of the Prairie, the painted savage, desperate in revenge, and laughing wildly with demonic fury, rose on the unsuspecting party in the terrible array of countless numbers.

The conflict was short and decisive: many of the soldiers were as yet unused to the arts of savage warfare, and the troops gave way in every direction. Maddened at beholding his flying soldiery, Capt. Harland, with some others remained on the field of slaughter a few daring moments, but resistance had become desperation, and even *they* were at length driven to the alternative of flight,—a flight marked with blood and intercepted by the mangled and convulsed forms of the dying. Wounded and faint, Capt. Harland soon fell behind his companions. A party of savages rushed past him a little distance. Two of them stopped and the one uttering a loud war whoop sprang towards him with an upraised tomahawk. Harland was exhausted and silently commending his spirit to the author of his being, bowed his head to receive the expected stroke. At this moment the younger of the savages darted forward like an infuriated panther, and buried his tomahawk in the head of his tawny companion. The fallen warrior rolled in the dust and expired. The surviving savage now turned to the astonished Harland and beckoning him to follow, plunged into the thicket. Harland, instinctively obeyed, and the Indian led the way thro' the thickest part of the forest. At length suddenly pausing, he plucked a green plant, and approaching Harland with respect, applied it to his wounds. He then pointed to a fallen tree with a look not to be misunderstood. Its hollow trunk afforded the exhausted soldier a place of concealment, and the Indian disappeared. Nature was spent, and Harland slept long and quietly. He woke to a perception of renewed strength. Through a cleft in the tree, he saw the stars glittering above him, and leaving its narrow environs, the first object he saw was the Indian, standing pensively before him. He approached Capt. Harland, and presenting him with some wild meat which he had just dressed, inquired in broken English at what distance were the white settlements. Capt. Harland informed him, and, pointing out their course, added, "you will accompany me to my people."

"Yes" said the Indian. "Hethlamico will live with the white man." They travelled with the utmost caution, hiding themselves by day, and shunning even the wild paths of the hunter. Hethlamico seemed insensible to fatigue, and anxious only for the preservation of his companion. He still dressed his wounds with the medicinal plants of the forest, procured him food while he slept, and supported his fainting steps when exhausted with suffering.

They emerged from the wilderness;—the forts of the white man rise before them, and Capt. Harland points out to his preserver the place of his abode. A scene of unutterable emotion succeeds. Hethlamico is presented as his deliverer. Mrs. Harland struggled in vain to speak; language was lost in the excess of powerful feeling, while the Indian, dropping for a moment on his knee, rose and precipitately retired. "'Tis mysterious!" said Capt. Harland, and he almost believed himself in a dream. Mrs. Harland was not alone, during the absence of her husband; the presence of Elizabeth had been her support, and Elizabeth now participated in her joys. An hour of calmness arrived, and again the Indian youth stood before them, dressed in the wild habiliments of the savage: an air of elegance still marked his form; and his fine features, though disfigured by the deep stains of war, yet beamed with a strong expression of unaltered meaning.

To the various questions of Captain Harland, he replied only in monosyllables, and even then with hesitation. His eye at length rested on a flute lying near him and he raised it mechanically to his lips: no one spoke, for his first breath had called forth a strain of seraphic melody: he played the Soldier, and the deep rich tones seemed to bear on their mellow wing, the words to which they had been appropriated:

> His faded features, have lost their light,
> And suffering had marked his form,
> His brow is marked with the scars of the fight,
> And his spirit is weary, and dark as the night,
> That follows the wreck of the storm.

He at length paused, and began a sacred air of which Mrs. Harland was particularly fond. It was the return of the Prodigal, and a slight tremor in his tones was now distinguishable. The pallid cheek of Mrs. Harland grew yet paler while Hethlamico proceeded, and dwelt with a lengthened and unearthly pathos on the notes accompanying the words:

> Behold the lost!—receive the wanderer home.

An audible cry escaped the convulsed bosom of Mrs. Harland; the instrument fell from the hands of the tawny musician, and the lost Theodore, now clearly revealed, knelt at the feet of his deeply injured parents. Who shall describe the scene that followed:—as well might the painter attempt the holy but dissolving colours of the Rainbow.

Apprized of the dangers that hung over the infant settlements of the West, Theodore learned the removal of his family with horror. "I will follow them" said he unhesitatingly; "I will exert every energy of my soul in their defense." But it was otherwise ordained. Descending the Ohio, Theodore became a prisoner; designed for sacrifice, he was conducted to the scene of intended slaughter, but female pity interposed, and he was consigned to the cure of an aged squaw whom war had been rendered childless. The name of *mother* was sacred to his soul and the tenderness of her who adopted it excited his gratitude. Regarding his sufferings as the just reward of his vices, he bowed submissively to his fate and though he looked forward to the season of escape, evinced not the lightest symptom of regret. He studied the character of the savage and acquired his confidence. He learned their rude arts and strove to supply to his Indian mother, the offices of her departed children. His efforts were successful; she regarded him with maternal approbation, and smiled benignly on the son of her adoption, at the moment when her weary spirit fled through the valley of death.

The one tie was now broken, that bound him to his captors, and the moment of desperate resolve had arrived.

He visited, for the last time, the spot where his Indian mother slept, and plucked the weeds from the rose bush, planted on her grave.

He then went forth to the battle field, prepared to join his countrymen or perish in the attempt.

Such was the simple tale of Theodore, and in his speaking countenance, the dignity of settled virtue, now mingled with the humility of conscious error. But there is still a restlessness in his searching eye, a look of deep and anxious inquiry.

Where is the bright being that met his astonished gaze on his first arrival? Has his presence banished it, or was it only a vision of his morbid fancy? Elizabeth had indeed fled, for the high throbbings of her heart, alarmed the purity of her principles. Time passed on, and the acknowledged virtues of Theodore sanctified the emotions he had long since exiled. Peace again reared her lovely temple on the Western waters—the war whoop no longer echoed through the wilderness, the green earth was gladdened with plenty, and round the habitations of the Harlands the hand of cultivation called forth the fruits of luxury and the flowers of paradise. The pride of Capt. Harland gloried in the deeds of his son, for Theodore had enrolled himself among the defenders of the soil, and became a pillar of strength in the fabric of their national prosperity. The lacerated bosom of Mrs. Harland, now healed by the hand of filial piety, beamed with that peace, which passeth show. Theodore, shuddering at the past, continued rejoicing in the course of virtue, and Elizabeth, like the stars of evening, shed a mild and sacred radiance on his path of existence.

ASHTON GREY

There are doubtless yet a few survivors of the pioneers who laid the corner-stones of our Queen City, to whom its aspect at the opening of our story is still a "picture of memory." The long conflict with a terrible foe was then finally, though recently terminated; the fires of the Indian were at last extinct, and a peace like the dews of Hermon had settled on the fair land that had been for years the arena of deadly strife. The soldier's huts that had covered the site of our modern Tyre had disappeared; the fortress that had protected our armies was dismantled, and a population, composed of almost every nation and every class, hurrying on like many waters and meeting with resistless impetus, was about to carry up a proud city from the very bosom of a hitherto almost unbroken and interminable wilderness, with a rapidity that made it seem like an isle sprung in the "night-time" from the everlasting solitudes of the deep.

But the place as yet retained much of its character of primeval wildness. The heavy shadows of the old forests, that still stretched from it on either hand in "boundless contiguity," lay darkly over it; and within their embosoming glooms little more than rude evidences of the mighty influences already at work met the eye. Charred and blackened trees, with all their glories in the dust, yet lay across its remoter paths. Pools and spots of marsh, yet undrained, sent up their dank miasmas, and glancing myriads of fireflies, and the hoarse music of the dwellers of the pool, were the accompaniments of the evening. But already the mingled hum of a people elate with hope, and pressing gaily forward to the goal of promised affluence,—the bustle of incipient commerce, the sound of various rafts, the quick tread of men impelled by cheerful and stirring impulses, the rich broad laugh of conscious and independent freemen, and the harsher voices of rough and untamed spirits, whom the call of peace had bidden from the war-path to employments perhaps less suited to their stormy natures,—were all heard in this city of the wilderness.

Here and there a dwelling had already risen, distinguished by palpable indications of wealth and pretension; and from one of these a woman, whose appearance denoted poverty and servile occupation, issued one cold November evening, and bent her steps towards, in western phrase, a *cabin*, in the outskirts of the place. There was weariness upon her countenance; but as she drew near the humble domicile, to which her eye had been directed as she hastened forward, it required no effort of a fine imagination to read in her still quickened step, and the brightening expression of features, till then wholly commonplace, the history of a mother returning from a day of toil to the family of helpless ones, whom she had left but to procure them bread. We almost fancy that we hear her murmuring some fond expressions of maternal yearning, as her eye exclusively rests upon the rude dwelling, and we feel how to her that dwelling is consecrated by the tender ones it shelters. Her step has seemed weary—it is now quick and almost joyous; she is in thought already clasping her little ones—she is within a few paces of her threshold. They are probably locked in slumber, but she will lay the little dainties she brings them upon their eyelids.

At that moment a flame, broad and vivid, shot up from the roof. Its glare upon her face revealed the wild and sudden agony that went out the next moment in a scream of curdling horror. Thrillingly it went out upon the calm evening—thrillingly it must have met the ear of all within the sound; and they came running—laborers, craftsmen returning to their own homes—neighbors, strangers, all gathered to the spot. The mother lay on the ground. She had broken open the door of the dwelling and fallen suffocated and senseless. It was thoroughly on fire, and a volume of smoke and flame was pouring forth upon the air. The crowd, too paralyzed to act, stood round in deep but unavailing sympathy. Was it certain that her children were in the house? The inquiry ran through the circle. The cry of infant voices gave an appalling answer. The mother, for that cry had restored her to a frenzied consciousness, was held back from the flames only by force. Strong men were there, and stern ones—men upon whose rough lineaments the red glare revealed the scars of ferocious conflict; but even these were subdued as those childish screams reached the ear of the delirious and struggling mother.

At this terrible moment a young man, who had been seen only for an instant amid the crowd, reappeared with a ladder. The throng gave place in silence—hope sprung in every heart as they looked at him; there was that in his face which defied impossibilities. The ladder was placed against a corner of the house that the flames had not yet reached, and rapidly ascending it, he tore away the materials of the roof with a strength which the exigence of the moment only could have given him, and disappeared amid a shower of cinders that streamed up through the aperture. In the opposite part of the building the lower logs seemed already about to give way, and every moment threatened to precipitate the whole into one indiscriminate and burning mass. There were a few moments of agonizing suspense—of a silence more breathless, more terrible, than that with which men await the last gasp of the dying—and then a shout, such a shout as the throng sends forth under the most powerful excitement of the soul's better sympathies, which rung far and wide over the now rushing sound of the combustion. The young man stood above them, almost surrounded by flames, a witness of the superhuman *might* there is in high purpose. Two children enveloped in a blanket, which he had torn from the cot from which they had been awakened by the flames, were in his arms; and tossing them into the far brawnier arms below, he turned to assist yet a third boy of some eight years old, who was struggling of himself to get up to the roof, and was the next moment in safety on the ladder, now upheld by strong hands, rather than the tottering building.

Who shall meddle with the feelings of the mother now? Her children are in her arms—her soul is pouring itself out to her God. We leave her with them and Him. But the crowd are asking for the young man who had imperiled his life to save them; they would applaud the heroism that effected the rescue. But the *hero* is not among them. When there was no more to be done, he had sprung to the ground with the bound of the mountain cat, and disappeared, as all eyes were drawn to the crash of the falling ruin.

The hour of calmness comes to the strongest scene of human emotion as it does to the wildest tempest. The sobs of the mother and the gratulations of the crowd grew silent. The many dispersed, and the few that remained were immediate and kind neighbors, who gathered around her with contending offers of a temporary home. Among the last of the lingerers of the less familiar crowd was a young girl, who had manifested throughout the scene an intensity of feeling that her delicate frame seemed unable to support. While the issue remained doubtful, she had stood silent, but with clasped hands, and a face as still and as colorless as marble; but when the rescue was at last certain, her tears fell fast, and she shrunk back as if to hide her emotions. Yet once or twice she had approached the mother, as if wishing in some way to tranquilize the agony of joy that seemed as far too mighty for the maternal heart as had been the moment of despair; but if such were her purpose, timidity had checked the effort. Now, as she at last glided away with the matron by whom she had been accompanied, she murmured, in the sweetest and saddest of tones, though scarcely audible, "I have no home to offer her."

The exceeding beauty of the young face had attracted notice. Curiosity is a distinctive trait in the social habits of all new settlements. "Who is she?" was an inquiry that was scarce suppressed till it would no longer meet her own ear, and now taking no small share of interest with the benevolent arrangements being made for the houseless neighbor. Nor did the little details thus elicited fail to deepen the truly kind feelings her look and manner had awakened. She was, it would seem, the daughter of a stranger who had been buried a day or two previous in the village—was still at the boarding-house where her father had died—"and as far as I can gather," said one who seemed to have learned something of her history, "is left without a friend to care for her, or any means of support, except perhaps a few fine notions that'll pay her way for a while, maybe."

"Poor thing!" said another, who from her look of deep pity was probably undergoing her own novitiate in wild-wood life; "poor thing! She does not look like one accustomed to the smoke of a western cabin."

Ah! little used enough to aught but summer airs and sunshine was the unconscious subject of these remarks; but there was deep sorrow on the fair, pale face now, and no eye could have followed the drooping figure, as she walked slowly back to her lodgings, without interest. The first object that met her melancholy eye, as its dark silken lashes were timidly lifted at her entrance, was the young man whom she had just seen in a character of such exceeding heroism. The bandages with which one arm and hand were bound, and the many suggestions of relief with which friends were crowding around him, at once told that he had been no inconsiderable sufferer in the recent scene. But the glance of pitying interest that Annabel Hampden (that was her name) lifted unconsciously to his face, and met by a look of animation—a glow of satisfied and happy feeling, that disclaimed all title to compassion. Whatever he endured, it had failed to cast a shadow upon that glow. The young mourner shrunk back from the deep gaze he flung over her own form; and bidding the matron, upon whose arm she had still leaned, a low and silvery good night, she stole quietly from the apartment. But she bore to her own an excited and haunted fancy. Sorrowful memories, and recent deep regrets, were strangely blended, as she sought her pillow, with new and strongly intruding images. That of the youthful stranger was not indeed calculated to be thrown aside at will; and when they met the following morning at breakfast, the unwonted glow on the maiden's delicate cheek might, to one who had known her, have half revealed the troubled and vivid fancies that had hovered round her pillow.

Who could this young man be? We deem not that Annabel even *thought* the question. But a slow fever, the consequence of his injuries, confined him to his lodgings, and his increased sufferings, receiving as they did, from the inadequate facilities and the claims of a crowded house, a very irregular and inefficient attention, were not wholly in his power to disguise. And gradually she was led on, with the timid approaches of a partly tamed bird, to proffer some little service of herself to the sufferer; making at time the prescribed teas—smoothing the buffalo robe on which he tossed so restlessly; and at last venturing, with her own white and trembling fingers, to dress the terrible wounds. A most perilous position this for the young nature that looked out, while she was thus busied, from those ardent eyes! they were neither blue, nor black, nor brown, nor hazel, nor any one of the approved colors of romance, save as the expression of feeling that perpetually clouded or irradiated their depths varied their hue; and had the fair nurse been a physiologist, which in those days young ladies were not, she would have soon discovered how with every day the young pulses throbbed more and more wildly at the touch of these, her own delicate fingers.

While these very natural results to the young knight-errant were rendering him with unwonted meekness less and less anxious to disavow his *invalid* claims, the peculiar tone and bearing of a character entirely new to her, was acquiring a strong power over the pure but perhaps somewhat dreamy imagination of the gentle Annabel. Something there was about him that fully accorded with her beau-ideal of the distinctive characteristics of the fearless and self-sustained backwoodsman. The untamed horse that tosses his mane in the green savannahs, could scarcely have moved with more freedom; and the perfect development of limb and muscle evidently arose from the conscious vigor and habitual action of one accustomed to tread, not the gay saloon, and prescribed walks of fashion, but the rough paths of danger, and the limitless range of voiceless solitudes. But then his manner! How could it be so utterly exempt from the imposing conventionalities of civilized life, and yet without a touch of the rude, the coarse, the commonplace, or of aught that could lessen one's sense of his well-tested chivalry? If he was indeed a son of the west, the wild unreclaimed west,—and various allusions to early forest adventure and associations, drawn out by chance remarks from those around him, and to which she had been a listener, was confirmation of this,—to what did he owe that strange tone of refinement? a refinement not of fashion, nor poetic culture, nor classic taste; but yet coloring every word and action. These questionings certainly found no definite shape, much less a language, in Annabel's girlish and innocent mind. But without such attempt to trace its developments, she was unconsciously yielding day by day to the power of a high nature, whose innate delicacy was refinement, and whose generous impulses, chivalry. Her thought did not even rest on the extreme beauty that, from fair lips, rarely failed to find mention with the name of Ashton Grey.

We would by no means aver, however, that it was *unfelt* by the young susceptible heart. Alack for those who are thrown within the bewildering spell of youthful beauty!—but it is not our cue to moralize. That of our hero was perhaps the more impressive from its fine keeping with his backwoods character. The crisped and glossy curls, flung so carelessly back from his brow owed all "their propriety" to inveterate tendency; the smooth white brow was contrasted strongly by the dark hue of a cheek that had been touched not lightly by embrowning suns. Yet an artist, sketching an Apollo, might have been well satisfied with such a model; and Annabel, the dreamy, the impressible, the *desolate* Annabel—was it possible she should drink in the language of the eyes so tenderly, so passionately lifted to hers—of the smile so rich, so dazzling, so lighting up the whole face like a positive glory, and not at last lose the very sense of her own being in his?

Ere Ashton Grey could no longer avail himself of the immunities derived from his disabled arm, when he was again called out of the life of action and emprise to which he was accustomed,—he had become to the young trembling heart the sole rest on which it now leaned; while to him, the strong, the impassioned, the full of soul, she was at once an object of such protective tenderness as the outstretched hands of infancy inspire, and the adoration of a nature whose deep inborn sense of the pure and the beautiful has found its *first*, yet full realization.

Annabel Hampden was yet scarcely sixteen. She had been educated in retirement by a widowed father, who had no other object upon which to lavish the wealth of garnered-up affections; and although adversity had finally compelled him to seek a home amid western wilds, she had been still carefully shielded from its pressure. Her form and face were like her character, calculated to awaken an immediate sentiment of protective tenderness—the former slight and fragile, the latter resembling the lily in its exceeding purity. The complexion was of marble delicacy, relieved only by the dark penciling of her arched brow, and the still darker braids of luxuriant hair that were parted over it. Emotion not unfrequently imparted to her colorless cheek a slight rose-tine; but when in repose, she resembled some waxen impersonation of purity or innocence. It was only in motion—and the bend of the willow was not more graceful—or when, in the excitement of feeling, she lifted her eye of the softest hazel to yours, that you fully realized she was a thing of life. In character, she was strikingly like the forest fawn, which our hunters tell us, while it starts wildly away from human footsteps, yet attaches itself at once to him who succeeds in arresting its flight. What wonder that, between these young hearts, their communion had grown into sudden sacredness? Pity it is that the tame realities of life should cast their dust and shadow upon the brightness of an existence thus hallowed! should call the soul from the sweet fountains of feeling, to the trodden ways of baseness—to the labors of need; binding it down with its throbbing pulses to the cold calculations of profit, and fettering it with a weight that, in its strugglings against it, becomes a sickening weariness.

That species of wild and hardy adventure belonging to the commerce of our infant west, had originated its own appropriate *Order*. To those familiar with our current literature a few years since, "The Last of the Boatmen," a sketch touched by the hand of genius, afforded a most life-like representative of the class. Yet little as the habits and feelings of Ashton Grey could assimilate with those of men, whose general recklessness of moral obligation was only relieved by the scrupulous honor with which they fulfilled their trust, circumstances had made him, not unfrequently, a sharer in the kind of emprise that formed their distinctive character. His early habitudes had familiarized him with uncertain and self-reliant adventure, fitting him for all difficult enterprise; and the constitutional ardor to which *position* permitted no other channel, found something of allurement in the *trade* that had been already introduced upon our then gloomy and even dangerous waters. Young as he was, he was still known, not only as the most efficient of agents, but among the most skillful of western *boatmen*; and the trader, whose whole fortune was often invested in the richly-laden keel committed to a perilous navigation, was glad to secure his service at the most unstinted of terms. His engagement in an undertaking of this kind had been, much to the chagrin of his employers, delayed by the accident of his injuries; and that delay, however to him "it had sped on golden wings," might be drawn out no longer.

And did he leave the fair girl, who sat, as he spoke to her of these cold business arrangements, as pale and silent as if hope had just parted from her heart,—did he leave her without avowing the hopes, the passion, the purposes of his own? Such course did not belong to the character of Ashton Grey—all was avowed, and with a manly tenderness, a truthful eloquence, that inspired confidence, and won the vestal heart to unveil its own timid depths. They must part for a season, but beyond it, bright and green paths were opening away into the far future. When the farewell was at last spoken, and the lover had turned back once more to the life of vigorous action and strong endeavor that was again before him, the fairest and gentlest of human beings was "his own betrothed bride."

II.

> And why should I the past recall,
> To wither blooms of present bliss?
> Thou'rt now my own—I clasp thee all—
> And Heaven can grant no more than this.
> Moore.

And with the remembrance of their pledged faith, Annabel's desolate heart grew tranquilized; and whether alone or surrounded by intrusive voices, she sat day after day with the image of her lover pressed as it were to her soul, and shutting out every other. But from these soft dreams she was at last aroused. Her hostess came to bring her tidings that, upon her first arrival, had been the subject of her almost hourly inquiry, and to which she had looked forward with absorbing interest.

"Colonel Ainsworth has arrived, Miss Hampden."

"Colonel Ainsworth! oh, yes—he has?" and a gleam of troubled feeling went over her face, instead of the expression of pleasure her informant had so reasonably anticipated.

"Shall I send to let him know you wish to see him?"

"If you please—yet no," said the young girl, striving to fling off the startled feelings that, she knew not why, had come over her. "Colonel Ainsworth knows nothing of me, but my father left a letter that I promised to deliver in person. Will you please direct some one to attend me to his house?"

Annabel sat down to try to collect her strangely scattered thoughts. Colonel Ainsworth—a native of the Old Dominion, and many years since one of the adventurous and noble spirits that, in seeking to win them homes from Kentucky forests, were involved in a long conflict with the most terrible of foes,—was her father's friend in the season of youthful ardor. Years of subsequent separation had failed to weaken the bond of reciprocal regard, and Mr. Hampden's purpose of migrating to our infant city was not a little strengthened by the knowledge that his early friend had become one of its denizens. Business had called Colonel Ainsworth to the east, a short time previous to the arrival of Mr. Hampden, and his family had accompanied him. The dying father, whom a fatal disease had met at the anticipated haven from a toilsome voyage, had little other solicitude but for his gentle child; and a brief letter, consigning her to his friend's future care, and left her with a charge to deliver it in person at his return, soothed his parting moments. But the sudden light which her meeting with Ashton Grey had flung upon the sorrowful path of the bereaved girl, had banished, till now, the very remembrance of hopes and expectations so much colder and dimmer. Now the recollection came with something to which her guileless heart was wholly unused—a something of its own rebuke. The image of a beloved and lamented parent, the many soft memories of years of indulgent fondness, again swept mournfully over it, and it grew faint and chill as the warm visions so recently cherished faded before them.

Pale and drooping as "the bent lily overcharged with dew," she stood, a half hour after, before her appointed guardian; and placing in his hands the deed of her father's dying trust, awaited its perusal in silent and trembling emotion. Colonel Ainsworth was a man in whom a dash of aristocratic hauteur, fostered by that species of isolation which high tone of character, united to superior wealth, draws around one amid the common walks of life, was redeemed from all ungraciousness by rich feelings and benevolent principles. It needed not the exceeding beauty of the delicate and sinking being who awaited his reception, to create an immediate interest in the orphan daughter of his friend. Yet as he at last kissed her pallid cheek, and, bidding her a fervid welcome to his home and heart, presented her to Mrs. Ainsworth as a sacred bequest by one whom he had held in fond and early regard, he felt, with a glow of most animated pleasure, that Annabel Hampden might be loved for herself alone.

And Annabel *was* taken joyfully, and at once, into the closest folds of paternal care. The sudden interest with which circumstances had invested her, was soon and forever confirmed by the enduring charm that a spirit of perfect innocence, and a mind deeply as well as delicately toned, diffused through her every word, look, and movement.

Mrs. Ainsworth was a lovely woman, around whom the impalpable lingerings of some early sorrow, melted by time into indistinctness, but not to be effaced, hung like the perpetual shadow of the cypress upon the rose of the cemetery, and giving a deepened interest to a character that seemed to have been made up of the kindest elements. To her the young and seemingly desolate orphan soon became inexpressibly dear; and had Annabel's heart in reality acknowledged no other ties than those that death had severed, the new sense of affectionate adoption would have soothed her by degrees to perfect happiness.

But the fever of an unacknowledged passion was preying upon her young spirit, and the pure instincts of her nature recoiled from its concealment. Yet for one like Annabel Hampden, so timid, so resembling the plant that shrinks from the slightest touch,—to throw open unencouraged, unsolicited, the veiled sanctuary of her young affections,—it was an effort to which her strength was all unequal. In vain she strove to utter the name so engraven on her heart; it died away as it reached her crimsoned lips, and she would flee to her chamber to hide the overpowering emotion.

But the time her lover had named, when he should again be with her, was speedily at hand, for the *southern* voyage had not been yet undertaken; preparatory to that, Ashton Grey had gone to bring a boat from some of the upper waters. Becoming with every hour more and more anxious and disturbed, Annabel had stolen one day from the house alone, scarcely conscious where her feet tended, and stood at last on the margin of the Ohio, whose swollen and turbid wave, now lashed by a strong gale, was little illustrative of its early name of La Belle Riviere. But it was the stream that her lover was descending, and Annabel stood gazing upon it with a crowd of half uneasy, half delicious fancies.

"A rough morning for so delicate a rambler," exclaimed a familiar voice. "Have a care, my dear girl," continued Colonel Ainsworth, who was now at her side; "the breeze that hardly lifts the gossamer might all but bear you off; much more the winds that have lashed the bosom of our usually quiet river into so rough a mood. A little occasional season- ing after all," he added, drawing her shawl more closely around her, "may not be amiss for so tender a plant; and by remaining a few min- utes, you may chance to see on its way one of our western broad-horns."

He drew her arm affectionately through his, and they remained together gazing upon the bleak distance and the agitated waves that were now dashing against the shore with almost terrific violence. But though Annabel's eye was thus directed, her ear was intently turned to a group of some three or four persons who had just approached the bank, and now remained stationary, scarcely three paces from her. They were earnestly engaged in a species of conversation peculiar to the class of men who, with half-civilized habits, were now found floating on the wide current of the better order of population. To the untrained ear of our fair emigrant it would have seemed somewhat strangely colored; but the name of *Ashton Grey*, familiarly repeated, chained all her faculties. Their rudeness of aspect was in full accordance with their language; and but for that magnetic name, the glance she at first turned towards them would have been at once and wholly averted. But her interest was becoming too intense for the recollection of aught else. There was one of the group whose appearance, or rather countenance, was singularly dis- tinct from that of his companions. The harsh mold of his deeply-bronzed visage, and the strong proportions of his muscular and heavy-set frame, together with the strange garb in which it was arrayed, and the wild slang that marked his low muttered remarks, were in different degrees shared by all. But in place of that cast of open and ready defiance pecu- liar to the frontier adventurer, whose character was formed by habitual encounter with dangers and difficulties, in which physical prowess was the most exigible of all virtues, the countenance of this man bore a dark, and set, and sinister expression—an expression that seemed to speak, not of the mere adventitious ferocity, acquired in the rough play of hardy adventure, but of evil habitudes—of a familiarity with ferocious thought and gloomy passions.

"You seem to have liked Pottawatamie life so well," said one of the group, addressing the remark to this man particularly, "I wonder you didn't stay with 'em altogether. You left them, it seems while Ashton Grey was a mere cub yet."

"May-be," said another of the party, passing his hand round his own unkempt head somewhat significantly, "may-be they'd take a fancy to your hair in order to square up some old dealings. The red skins have a *pertikeler* slight o'hand that way in straitening accounts. Men living with the Indians, I've heerd say, were apt to forget their arithmetic, and more than one trader has closed up old balances at last with his scalp."

"The Indians are not slow at such handicraft," replied the person addressed, grimly; "but as to the cause of my leaving 'em, that is my business. The red skins have a fashion of not meddling with more than they need."

"I 'low you'd good reason enough," said a third one, evidently desirous of leading the way on to smoother ground; "the young one, I've heerd *yourself* say, never tuk to an Indian wigwam; and I should no s'pose you'd a'liked to have jest naturalized him among them, any how."

"Better shots might have hit wider of the truth," responded the other; "if the boy would a' staid willingly, I'd a'been content with 'em all my life. But natur is natur, and one must larn what cursed villians there are among *white* men, before he can make up his mind to be satisfied with Indian life. And it ain't no use, no how, to try to force natur. I was jest minding that tree, growing out of the side of the bank there, below us, and thinking how it could a'growed up straight, that way. But it has growed up, and up, with nothing on airth to help it; and so one'll see it sometimes with a human."

"It's a fair shake, any way, to bring such a tree up along side of Ashton Grey," responded the other, "for they've both got up as straight as them as had broad ground to start from. One of the old prisoners told me once that Ashton larned to *read* and *write* among the Pottawatimies, but that I 'low was running the tin over. Pottawatimie schools, I take it, is raither scarce."

"'Tis truer than you may think, man," was the reply, the speaker's look of inaccessible in duration having taken, in the course of these remarks, a perceptibly softened expression; "the boy did larn himself to read somehow. Once in a while a prisoner got among us that had a bit of larning, and he got one of these to mark the shape of the letters for him, and then he cut 'em out of bark and worked with 'em till he knew 'em. And now and then he got hold of a book, or some leaf of a book, that some one would leave in the towns; and so he got on. A French missionary was sent to convart the tribe. They posted him off, not long after, to his own upper hunting grounds; but he took a liking to Ashton, and larned him to write upon a birchbark copybook. All the more trouble I had with him, for these things made him all the more restless to get with those of his own feather. Not a party of land-jobbers but would draw him off, sometimes as guide, sometimes as runner or chain-bearer, or something of that sort; and I thought at last I might as well come in with him to the settlements for good. I did not like to contrary him much, no how; for, boy as he was, he had stood by me in some darkish frays."

"I heerd something of that, too, from the old prisoner I spoke of. He said they were a lettle inclined, now and then, to suspicion you of selling 'em bad powder and the like, and the boy got you off more than once by pushing himself between you and their tomahawks. You might well keep on his track if he was bound to leave them."

"Well, I *could not* bring myself, you see, to do without him. When I tried it for a while, I got as hungry for him as a famished wolf. To be sure, I don't see him often now,—Ashton always strikes out his own track,— but when I do get a glimpse of him, he has always a kind word for me; and if it was not for him, there's not a soul on airth to mind whether I was dead of alive."

There was a touch of feeling in the harsh speaker's tones that was not to be mistaken. "It is time now," he said, after some moments' silence, "that Ashton should get down with his boat. Hard rowing he's got," he added, looking earnestly at the river, "if he's bringing her on to-day. Why, the waves heave like a dying buffalo,—there's a boat *now*, if my eyes don't deceive me!"

Colonel Ainsworth at the same moment was pointing it out to the impassive Annabel.

"And that is Ashton Grey at the oar; no one else could manage it alone as he does. He would doubtless bring her safe to shore, but a little help will make it surer in a swell like this."

He quietly unmoored a canoe, and stepping into it, was soon alongside of the young oarsman. The boat, with the strength of a new arm, came speedily to shore; and while the silent girl's cheek was yet colored with the rush of startled and painful, though indefinite feeling, to which the name of her lover, so revoltingly associated, have given rise, Ashton Grey sprung lightly from its bow, and dashing the perspiration from his fine brow, and shaking off somewhat impatiently the greetings of our own last acquaintances, as they advanced to meet him, stood before her with a countenance for one moment absolutely flashing with pleasure.

"Miss Hampden!"—the tone was full of passion,—"is it possible—" But the words he would have uttered faltered on his lips. He had an immediate sense that the position of his betrothed had undergone something of change. Yet the look with which he met that of Colonel Ainsworth, as the gentleman returned his bow with a glance of the coldest recognition, lost nothing of its singularly open and manly character;—it was but the hesitation of delicacy that silenced the impassioned accents.

"Shall we return, Miss Hampden?" asked the Colonel, drawing her away with a movement not exceeding deliberate, as he spoke; "or would you wish to walk further?" Pale and trembling in every nerve, Annabel bowed slightly to her lover, and obeyed the impulse of her guardian in silence.

"That young man seems to be known to you, Miss Hampden," said Colonel Ainsworth; "may I ask where and when the acquaintance was formed?"

Annabel rallied herself. Her truthfulness of character came to her assistance. Simply and at once she detailed the circumstances under which they had met, and been subsequently consorted under the same roof. Colonel Ainsworth looked more than grave. But that the look and bearing of the youthful figure from which he had just turned were still before him, he might have thought little, perhaps, of any danger in all this to his gentle ward; but the handsome and glowing face—the air of high spirit—the tones of thrilling power,—all were in his thought as he listened. He was deeply pained.

"And was there no one," he at length inquired, in an accent of mingled chagrin and tenderness, "to tell you that this young man was an improper aspirant to the notice of Annabel Hampden?"

"Improper!" she repeated, almost inaudibly, but the suppressed voice did not disguise its unconscious emphasis.

"Yes, my dear child, *improper*—unquestionably so; and not the less that there is something in his person and manner so at variance with his class."

"His class!"

"Yes, Annabel—his class; for it is a fact that Ashton Grey,—though, to do him justice, I ought perhaps to say, I believe he keeps himself mostly apart from it,—is of that class which, to say the least, is a very uncertain and rude order of society. Have you been told nothing of his parentage? Do you know nothing of the elder Grey?"

"Till now I never heard such a person mentioned."

"Well, my dear, you have just seen him. That man with the grizzled hair is Ashton Grey's father. You might have learned as much had you been listening to the conversation he was carrying on so grimly with his companions, when his son made his appearance,—an Indian trader for many years, and engaged now only in those precarious occupations congenial to his former habits of pursuit. Such is Ashton Grey's origin; and though he may be, I believe in truth he is, quite free from the vices and habits of his caste, yet I need not add that a delicate young girl, moving in the sphere that Annabel Hampden can alone fill, cannot with propriety acknowledge hardly a personal recognition of one so hedged in with vile and low associations. Nor need I say, my dear," he added, after a moment's hesitancy, "that, informed as you now are, I shall expect you at once and for ever to renounce an acquaintance so unfitting."

Happily for Annabel, no reply was requisite—they were entering the house. The Colonel looked a little anxiously at the fair face, as his gentle wife, with affectionate solicitude, though with tender chidings, took off her shawl and bonnet; but it was too calm and still for his scrutiny. Men cannot often read emotion, that from its very weight settles down into the deep heart. The smile with which she met the maternal attention was as soft as ever. He did not mark the deep, deep sadness it played over, nor the troubled light of the eye whose heavy lashes, he was thinking at the moment, drooped so beautifully over it.

But Annabel had letters to write, and retired to her room. Letters to write! A vague purpose of writing to her lover had indeed furnished her with the pretext, but long hours wore away ere Annabel assumed the pen. How to her anguished thought had all of life faded out within the last half hour! How was the spell which Love had thrown over her young imagination,—how suddenly and rudely had it been broken! The bright visions of happiness—the charm, the freshness, the beauty, with which it had invested existence, was stricken from it forever. The future, so lately a dream of brightness, lay before her a cold, lengthened waste—dim, darkened, colorless. She was to renounce him whose companionship struck out from the dullest hour a glow and warmth the whole world else might not bestow. The founts of rich feeling he had awakened were to be again scaled, and vows, holy and *unforfeited* vows, to be blotted out. And had Annabel made up her mind already to do all this?

We may not pretend to individualize the surging thought that, in the first hour of conflict, swept over her heart. The young maiden was not altogether a thing of tender impulses. Duties within the grasp of her innocent mind had no light power over it, and that which she owed her guardian, as the representative of her beloved father, was distinctly before her. True, it sometimes dwindled to a mere spectre, as the vow she was bidden to break rose also; but like other spectres, it still beckoned in its retreat, and its indicating finger was not to be silenced. She prepared to obey it. She revolved and re-revolved the manner in which the sacrifice should be fulfilled. Her purity of nature would have suggested entire openness with Colonel Ainsworth; but even to her inexperienced thought, it could not be matter of doubt that it would call out, towards her lover, a high displeasure, not unlikely to lead to indignant reproaches and humiliating contumely, that she trembled to think of. No! only from herself should he learn her faithlessness; only in her own words be told the revocation of her plighted faith!

Nor could she again meet him. Poor Annabel! she knew her own weakness. She hid her face as she thought of his passionate remonstrances, his seductive tenderness. Her own heart was sick with the agony of crushed hopes and bleeding affections. To write, and at once, was the only course before her; it was the *kindest* way in which this most cruel renunciation was to be made. With a faintness, almost as of death, upon her whole frame, she took up her pen. She did write! That her letter was a little incoherent—that it had some tell-tale blots—that it breathed throughout a tenderness of which the writer was unconscious,—for she meant it to be very calm, and cold, and decided,—we have not a doubt; but, *n'importe*—the letter was not fated to give hindrance or advancement to the progress of events. The fates, as they were quietly weaving the web of our lovers' history, might have had a sly laugh to themselves at the interference that was being attempted by other hands.

Annabel Hampden, when her letter was finished, went out once more alone—now with a conscious and hurried step. She went forth to commit it to the conveyance of the poor widow, whose gratitude to the young preserver of her children had formed a ready link between her and his affianced. Her cabin had been rebuilt by kind and efficient hands need we say at the instance of Ashton Grey? From the windows of her chamber the beaming eye of Annabel had followed his lithe and agile figure, as, with his right arm still in a sling, he managed to render not unfrequent aid, apart from the rich tones and the whispered bonus with which he cheered on the work. As she paused upon the humble threshold, in the effort to overcome the crowding regrets and bitter self-reproach that filled her heart at the moment, a well-known step was beside her—and Ashton Grey withdrew the hand she had pressed upon her aching brow. Why was it so passive—so cold! He was pouring out the full floodtide of his earnest soul, with an ardor that the presence of the simple and devoted matron, who opened the door at the sound of his voice, did not at all restrain. But Annabel is only silent—shrinking—pale. He has led her into the rustic dwelling. Trembling from head to foot, she has sunk on a seat. The letter is crushed in her hand; but she has lifted her eye to him in solemn purpose, and a few words have told him the parental claims of her guardian, and that their betrothal was a matter of nought. It was no idle trial of a half-formed renunciation. She believed the sentence irrevocable. She thought she had become firm. Alas for such illusions! The lover was now before her, his entreating eyes beaming down on her face—his deep tones of sorrowful and eloquent passion poured on her ear; and all with which she had striven to nerve her heart—the suggestions of prudence, the scruples imposed by circumstance,—all were fading from her sense. Duty! She still grasped it to her heart, but it had taken a new form. It was no longer a pale, stern presence; but it whispered only of the vow that nought could cancel but the unworthiness of her lover. And had aught she had heard cast on him such a shadow? The acknowledgment of her prejudiced guardian, the allusions to his boyhood's history, to which she had so breathless listened, had but flung a new brightness over his young name.

"Dear Miss," said the humble matron, as the young man paced her floor, "if ye promised him, God heard the promise, sure," and the simple advocacy told. The faint rose-tine came back to Annabel's cheek; her heart filled once more with happiness; she was again her lover's, his only. What was the world to her now!

At an earlier stage of their intercourse, the true manliness of Ashton Grey's character would have withheld him from seeking to lure her from the guardianship that was now hers. But now, the maiden loved him; and love!—had it not been to him a light that paled every other? The hindrances of position were to him but a sound. Strong in himself, the young backwoodsman felt able to trample them all under his feet, and to bear up his beloved above all the ills of life.

But something of the *real* was already pressing upon him. The moments to be permitted him were fast lapsing. A long separation, at best, was at hand. A few days, and he was bound to that mart, which, though long since considered by it as a *neighboring* emporium, at that time presented a distance as imposing as the voyage was wild and perilous; and the lover's heart grew faint as the thought of this separation bore upon its high pulses. How could he tear himself away from her, and leave her, so gentle, so young, so dependent still, hourly subject to the strong influences that had already so nearly estranged her from him? One manner of vow only could tranquilize his fears; but could he wish the public consummation that would at once deprive her of the fostering guardianship, for which he could give her no answering protection? A private marriage would alone secure her his; and leave him with the assurance of a watchful kindness still over her,—without which, the thought of his voyage was madness,—till his return. Then he might himself assert those claims that no human authority could countervail. What wonder that to our young backwoodsman these reasons were strong as his own sweeping streams? or that during those brief, agitated, hurrying moments, they prevailed? Another promise had been given, when Annabel's trembling form at last escaped from her lover. A yet more sacred vow was to seal that she had so lately essayed to revoke.

Within a week after, upon a morning when the earth seemed, from a sudden caprice, to have put off all ungenial influences, and arrayed herself, as for a gala, in all the glittering sheen of frost and sunlight, Annabel, to whom, despite her more than usually pale cheek, the exhilarating tone of the sparkling atmosphere afforded pretext for the early stroll, bent her steps towards one of those mysterious mounds, that yet afford so peculiar a feature of romance to our western river landscapes. She had more than once stood beside it with Ashton Grey, wondering at its origin; and now she knows her lover is there, awaiting her. Once more they meet—he has supported her steps to the humble dwelling where they last met; and there, under that cabin roof, and with no other attesting witness but its faithful occupant, her fate was irrevocably united to his, whatever it might be.

III.

Though the world should all witness against thee, my heart
to itself is a witness they cannot outweigh;
I am now all thine own—and I know my own part,
In life or in death, by thy side 'tis to stay.

Strong indeed was the sentiment that carried our shrinking heroine through the precipitous step we have detailed; but while her purpose was sustained by its ascendancy, her delicate nature also sank beneath the effort. Her finely toned mind had an instinctive revolt to aught that was clandestine, and she had not courage to lift her eyes to those now beaming upon her with hourly increasing kindness. Colonel Ainsworth's house overlooked the river, that was hurrying on, again dark and turbid, to the yet gloomier stream to which it was tribute; and, cold and pale as "monumental marble," she stood, on the morning of the following day, at her window, gazing fixedly at a laden boat that was being just loosened from its moorings. About it the flitting form of Ashton Grey might be seen, moving with the quick step and hurried air of one preparing to leave the shore. Annabel scarcely breathed; she pressed her hands upon her pallid brow, and directed her thought to Him who could alone calm the tempest of feeling, or shield the young voyager from the dangers of his way. When she again lifted her eye, her husband was standing in the bow of the boat; but he was at that moment closely surrounded by a group of men, in whose manner there seemed something of strange and hurried import. They turned to leave, after what seemed a brief parley, but it was with Ashton Grey in their midst. Thus they ascended the bank, and walked slowly on, till, in the turnings of their way, they were at last hidden from Annabel's strained view. What could it mean! Surprised, startled, anxious, she still remained motionless, momently expecting her husband's return to the boat; but minute after minute lapsed silently away, and he came not. The boat had been again moored, and there were two or three persons that came and busied themselves about it, but they were unknown to her. There was something like commotion among the citizens. Men were hurrying through the streets as by some common impulse, and craftsmen and laborers, dropping their respective implements, were hurrying with loungers and idlers to some common point of interest. Gradually the stir subsided, and all again was still, save in the heart of the young bride to whom this strange suspense had now become agony.

It was surely no little thing that thus detained him whose purpose it had been to depart with the early morning. The day—the weary, the endless day, wore on, and still the boat swung idly from its moorings, and the wind came with a mournful tone from the deserted and solitary river. Her half-frenzied eye grew dim with watching, as she still sat at her window, counting the long moments with feverish anguish. Again and again had Mrs. Ainsworth entered the apartment, and striven to draw her from it, but she plead illness, and begged entire quiet with so beseeching a tone, it repressed even the expression of the anxiety her manner awakened. Twilight at last gathered over the spot where her gaze had been so long and vainly fixed, and Annabel sunk on her bed in utter exhaustion. Still her ear remained quick to every sound. Not a leaf rustled, that her pulse did not seem to pause; and now at last hears, what had been her own name, repeated below in a tone that was little calculated to silence apprehension. It was the voice of the poor woman that had witnessed her bridal. ·

"May I speak with Miss Hampden, that was, ma'am?" The inquiry chanced to be addressed only to a servant, and the speaker was at once ushered into Annabel's chamber. The excited listener started wildly to her feet.

"My God! Mrs. Wilson! You have come to tell me—"

"Why, pray, now, dear Miss—that is to say, *ma'am*, you're so overcome. What is it ye've heard about it?

"About what Merciful heavens! What is there to hear?"

"Why, ma'am if ye was not so flurried—"

"Well, well, I am not—I am calm, you see—perfectly calm;" and Annabel seated herself with a stifling and haggard composure.

"Why, after all, it mayn't be as bad as one thinks. Murder somehow will get back to them as has done it."

"Murder! For God's sake, Mrs. Wilson, say, what *has* happened? Speak, or I shall go mad."

The kind woman made a great effort to get through the terrible detail,—we give it to the reader as briefly as possible. It appeared that for some days past a small trading craft had lain at the river; that on the morning of the present day it was found to be gone; and the owner having mostly disposed of his wares, it was thought he had left in the night. An hour or two after, however, his body had been found floating below, and with a deep gash in the breast that but too clearly revealed a work of violence. Some singular circumstances, that Mrs. Wilson said she "disremembered the particulars of, though of course it would be all cleared up," had, despite a general belief of his innocence, fastened suspicion upon Ashton Grey. His father, too, was implicated; "though I heard 'em say," said the narrator, "it was more from something sort o'unsartain in his character that any thing in the evidence. But I'm loth and sorry to say they are both now in jail."

Annabel listened as if she heard not. Mrs. Wilson was alarmed at her stony aspect.

"Dear me! how pale you are, *Miss*! and cold—cold as death! Dear, dear! I *must* call her friends; she is dying, sure."

The stricken Annabel roused. "No! no!" she exclaimed convulsively, "I am better—better," she repeated, struggling for calmness as for life; "and proceed! I am able, quite able to hear all."

"I've told all, dear *Miss*, except the message Mr. Ashton sent you."

"The message! Gracious heaven! have you yourself seen him?"

"Seen him! How can you ask, *ma'am*? Wan't my three children playing round me, and should it need any one to tell me he was innocent? But if I'd knowed him the *very murderer*, 'twas my place to go to him, and see if I could do any thing for him in his need."

"God bless you for ever! But the message—the message!" said the young wife, still gasping for breath.

"Why, he said, Miss, or—or my dear young lady—I can't mind somehow how to call you, but I'll try and tell you his very words, for that's what he over and agin charged me. He said he was clear of what they laid on him; he'd never harmed a human being in a way that men take hold of; but he had done a great sin for all, and it was to you whom he loved better than life. He'd no right, he said, to almost force you into such an out o' the way marriage,—I can't get his exact words,—but any way, he give you up; the law would nullify the marriage, for it wan't a fair one, that God could bless; and that—well, that's the amount of it; 'tis his own wish to set you free, sure. He said it was all that could clear his own soul, and then, come what would, he'd be content."

A ghastly smile touched the features of Annabel. Does he rate my love then so low? Does he think that for such a love I became his wife?

"Mrs. Wilson, you know not what feelings I trod on in uttering that final promise. But there is no separate path for us now; and now, yes, now Heaven be praised! that vow has been spoken. It is such that no power can separate us—for death even will but unite us for ever."

Annabel's face and manner grew calm as she spoke. She was girt up at once by strong purpose, and the sustaining power of that passion which is known so often to oversweep all else of human feeling.

"Come with me, Mrs. Wilson. I have something to say to those who have been my guardians, and then I will go back with you to my husband's prison."

"Alas, poor dear! you cannot now see him. I didn't leave him till they were about to shut him up for the night."

"True! Go, then, and come for me in the morning—the first moment the doors will be opened to us."

Annabel lay as if asleep when Mrs. Ainsworth again entered her apartment. She could but feel, as she took the icy hand softly in hers, that something more than usual had given it so deadly coldness. The fair, though calm face, had a grieved look, resembling that we see sometimes in the fixed expression of a dead infant's; and Mrs. Ainsworth, after looking at her long and tenderly, only persuaded herself at last to leave her, by the resolve that on the following day she would at least probe the young heart. She sat down sorrowfully by her husband, who had come in not wholly unexcited by the events of the day, to speak of her fears. The Colonel was silent, but his look grew moody. The incident of the river, which he had forborne to mention even to his wife, rose to his thought.

"Has Annabel heard of the murder?"

Mrs. Ainsworth was unable to say. "Servants were almost always gossips, and the woman whose house had been so recently burned (as she knew from having since employed her), had asked to see Miss Hampden, and had been, some hours since, with her."

Colonel Ainsworth's frown deepened; but he had determined to keep his ward's secret, if indeed her interest in the prisoner were what he began to fear.

"She has doubtless heard it, and is shocked, of course. It's a terrible affair," said the Colonel, shrugging his shoulders; "you have never seen Ashton Grey, Marion—Annabel, I believe, has; but you would deem him one of the very last to commit such a deed."

Colonel Ainsworth's dreams were any thing but refreshing. "Have you seen Annabel this morning?" he inquired, as he entered the breakfast room. But Annabel herself entered it as he spoke.

"Are you better, my dear girl?" said Mrs. Ainsworth, her whole countenance lighting up with maternal pleasure at her entrance; but surprise and concern clouded it ere the question was wholly uttered. Perfectly calm was the face of the young ward, but it was the same calm it had worn as her anxious friend looked on it, while she seemed to lie in slumber—too still, too mournfully quiet, for ordinary feeling; yet her usually timid eye was lifted full to those that were turned with questioning kindness upon her, and her voice, mild and sorrowful, was yet distinct.

"Yes, I am better," she replied, "for I have no longer to act a part. I could no longer deceive you if I would. Kindest, best of friends, I come but to ask your forgiveness; and oh! if you will yet bestow it, your parting blessing!"

"In the name of Heaven, what do you mean? These are strange words," said Colonel Ainsworth.

"That I have but *usurped* a tenderness I have voluntarily forfeited. I am the wife of Ashton Grey, and as such may no longer claim the guardian kindness that would have shielded me from this hour of trial."

"My God! Annabel! his *wife*! Ashton Grey's wife! I cannot have heard you right."

The sad and collected look that met his gaze was sufficient answer.

"Dreadful! most dreadful!" said the guardian, turning from his ward and pacing the floor with long strides. "This is more than I *could* have feared. Marion, she is not worthy your tears."

"Alas it seems too true," said the fair culprit, whose ashen lip for the first time trembled with emotion; yet, "oh!" she added, now clasping her hands in strong entreaty, "will you in this hour of great agony withhold your forgiveness? Will you not believe that I am not wholly the ungrateful dissembler I have seemed? Heaven is my witness, that I meant to deserve your trust—that I strove to meet what your guardian care required of me. But my faith was already plighted—plighted before I had a home or a counsellor, and I came to think my vow was binding. Oh, say!" she continued, sinking at the feet of Mrs. Ainsworth, who still wept in silence, "You, in whom all the tenderness of my dead mother has been revived, will you not at least forgive me? Tell me ere I go—oh! tell me that you do forgive—that you will pray for me in my great sorrow."

"I do forgive, *fully—freely*. My poor girl!" said Mrs. Ainsworth, folding her to her heart; "my husband too will—I am sure he will—only his distress must get a little abated—and, Annabel, our home is still yours."

"Alas!" said the young wife, rising, "my home is my husband's prison. I go thither from all your kindness, but it will soothe me in my darkest hour."

Colonel Ainsworth seated himself, and drew her towards him. "You have both our forgiveness, Annabel; but tell me all that relates to this ill-starred marriage."

The frown on his brow grew somewhat lessened as she replied in detail to his questions. "Courage, my dear girl! Bad as this business is, it is not past retrieving. Forget this foolish ceremony, and we will soon, I trust, have it remedied."

Annabel withdrew herself from the arm that had been thrown kindly around her, and looked her guardian mildly but beseechingly in the face.

"If you would speak, sir, of annulling my marriage—oh! in mercy spare me! I am not able to bear it. Why should I be thus bitterly tried! You do not know me, sir—no one knows me! Even my husband, though I forgive him in his hour of anguish, has spoken to me in a cruel message of separation—of separation! as the means of shielding me from sorrow."

"In this, Annabel, he has acted well. What other means, poor child, is left you?"

"What other! would that spare me? spare me from his sorrows? Oh, sir! I cast off the blessed trust of your protection and kindness for the love I bore him; and what has life dearer, to tempt me now to a thought of abandoning him?"

"Miserable infatuation!" said Colonel Ainsworth, and again he paced the floor in extreme agitation. Mrs. Wilson came for Annabel.

"She must not go out as yet," said her guardian, taking his hat. "Take her, dear Marion, to your own room, and get her if possible to swallow some breakfast. I am going out. I will see young Grey myself, and we'll then settle what is to be done."

The gloom on his countenance was little dissipated at his return, yet he came fortified with new arguments. The prisoner did not wish to see his bride! He had penciled a few lines to her, repeating in his own strong words the wish already conveyed to her. He begged her forgiveness for seeking to link her pure life with his strange and unnatural one; he conjured her to save him from a remorse that was bitterer than death, by suffering the marriage to be canceled. What was it but a dream? and so only should she think of it—a dark, troubled dream!—Idle words were they all to Annabel. A poor reward it would be, for a love so self-sacrificing, now to abandon him.

"And do not pity me!" she said, as her friends looked more and more sorrowfully upon her young face, "do not think me mad. Whatever of degradation or sorrow may be before me, even to shame's last bitterness, I would rather share it with him, if such be his lot, than the fairest of earthly destiny apart from him."

Colonel Ainsworth had little more to say. There was something in this unyielding strength of sentiment in the child-like bride, that silenced remonstrance. He looked at her, as she stood before him in her pale and almost spiritual beauty, with a crowd of mingled emotions; but pity and kindness prevailed over all. All thought of severing the unhappy tie was laid aside, and Colonel Ainsworth himself accompanied her to her husband's prison. We pass over the meeting of the unfortunate pair—there are scenes that bear no touch of earthly coloring.

The privilege of sharing the prisoner's dungeon was of course denied, but from that time Annabel was permitted to visit him daily. The house of Colonel Ainsworth was still her home, and a tenderness, deepening with every day into a yet more trembling anxiety for its drooping object, was yet over her.

Colonel Ainsworth himself, for the sake of his ward, visited the younger prisoner more than once in the hope of eliciting something that might tell in his favor. But while with every interview some new shade of interest was developed in the young man's character, it effected little change in the conviction of his guilt. As we have already said, the circumstances that attached suspicion to the elder Grey would have passed unnoticed, but for the general odium of his character; but the testimony implicating the son, and to which Colonel Ainsworth had been a listener, was of the strongest nature. He had hoped that some explanation from the prisoner would weaken its force, but Ashton Grey, though known as of the frankest nature, seemed little inclined now to be communicative. Collected, though melancholy in the extreme,—and when the point was pressed upon him invariably asserting his innocence,—he yet declined entering with any one upon the facts upon which he had been arraigned. Colonel Ainsworth, however, did all that could be done in his behalf. Counsel was employed, testimony examined, and every effort made for evidence that might counteract what had already been given. The general prepossession was in his favor, and those who knew him best would yield their conviction of his innocence to no testimony. They thought circumstances might have made him perhaps cognizant of the crime, of which it was easy enough to suspect the elder Grey, and had at the same time involved him in that web of apparent condemnation which he could only explain by revealing his father's guilt.

As the time of trial drew nigh, and nothing favorable to either prisoner had yet transpired, the younger was strongly urged, as the only hope his position admitted, to become a witness for the State. He evidenced great discomposure, however, at the suggestion; he solemnly declared there was no one with whom he had been accessory to any crime; and as the counsel was therefore entirely idle, he peremptorily insisted it should not again be renewed. Any mention of the older prisoner, though necessarily not unfrequent in his hearing, seemed always to give him disturbance; and though he himself sometimes asked of him of the jailer, it was evidently with forced and gloomy effort. It was said the elder Grey bore the confinement of prison-walls far worse than the son. It had been known to Ashton, that, notwithstanding his ruggedness of aspect, his father's health had been some time unsound. Repeated colds had settled on his lungs, and now the confined air, to which his habits of life gave speedy effect, told deeply on his whole appearance. His wonted hardihood of manner had given way with his health; his food was rejected; he seemed not to sleep, and his look at times indicated internal conflict.

Annabel meanwhile seemed supported by a preternatural strength. Her interviews with her husband were little calculated to afford her solace. They were fraught only with passion and gloom, and, to her, fitful hopes, and fears, and agony. Even to her the prisoner spoke not of hopes, such as conscious innocence might seem to have inspired. His words, indeed, seemed all bent but lessen to her thought the terrors of death, and fix her hopes upon a union beyond its power. Her attenuated form, and wan and sunken temples, spoke mournfully of her sufferings, and more than once had Colonel Ainsworth felt almost a hope that the fading life would pass before the final trial; but she never spoke of suffering, and seemed awaiting the issue with a patience of sorrow that could but deepen sympathy.

IV.

Well may the dense throng hold their breath—
'Tis a question of life or death!
Is there no recordation of the crime,
Have that, beyond all human eyes,
In that great Book of other skies,
Not to be opened in the reign of time?

The day of trial had come. Judge, jury, witnesses, all the imposing array of court was at last assembled. The house was too small for the crowd—the whole mass of inhabitants had been called out by the sombre interest of the trial. Ashton Grey, as the first indicated, was brought forward; and at his side, supported by Colonel Ainsworth, and wearing a cast of beauty that seemed not of earth, so still, so colorless, so holy, was it, in its expression of meek submission, stood the devoted Annabel. A low murmur of sudden interest ran through the crowd as they looked at her.

The trial was opened. The testimony against the prisoner, the same that had preceded the committal, was again slowly detailed. It formed a terrible chain of evidence. A handkerchief fastened to the body of the deceased, and to which it appeared some weight had been attached that was afterwards disengaged, bore the initial of his name. A woman that did his washing, and that had been made a witness, testified, when it was presented to her, though with evident reluctance, that it was *his*. A piece of money, which the prisoner on the morning of his arrest had passed away, was identified, by a distinct and peculiar mark, as one that had been but the day previous in possession of the deceased; who, in making change to the witness, had referred to its peculiar appearance, and remarked that he always kept it for a pocket-piece. Last of all, a hunter, who was crossing the river from the opposite shore upon the night of the supposed murder, had seen through the dim haze of midnight, at some distance above him, a single individual taking a skiff into the middle of the stream. Upon reaching that part of it, this person, after some moments' delay, turned back in the canoe to the shore and the skiff sunk immediately after he left it. As the hunter was yet wondering at the strangeness of the circumstance, he observed some small floating article that attached itself to a snag within his reach. He picked it off, and found it to be a cap, which, on going ashore, he took with him to his lodgings. To his surprise he then found, written upon the lining, the name of Ashton Grey; and falling in with the prisoner the next morning as he was going to his boat, mentioned the incident to him, together with that of the sunken skiff, and was still more surprised at the sudden look of perturbation he could not have been mistaken in.

To this most appalling evidence the prisoner, through his counsel, declined making *any* defence! A sense of pain pervaded the whole assembly. No one who knew Ashton Grey could have been a cold listener. "Few knew him but to love him," and even strangers, as they looked upon the manly form, and noble and youthful countenance, felt that his guilt was beyond belief. His manner during the examination of the witnesses manifested neither indifference nor alarm, but a gloomy composure—a firmness acquired by the long discipline of a mind at last made up to meet the result. Yet, when the testimony was finally closed, and he beheld Colonel Ainsworth making his way of the crowd with Annabel lifeless in his arms, his agony, though he uttered no sound, moved every heart. He had started forward as if to follow her, and then recollecting himself, he crossed his arms on his breast, and stood motionless; but lip and cheek were livid, and the cold drops on his brow were evidently not of pressure of the crowd.

The judge, who seemed inclined to wait as if something might yet be offered in the prisoner's behalf, still delayed summing up the evidence. Some one who had just entered was in truth speaking earnestly to his counsel. An order was required from the court for a new witness; and while every countenance in the house lighted up, save that of the prisoner, an officer was sent to bring the elder Grey, who was the witness named, from his prison. It was soon understood that he had himself, through his son's counsel, demanded the permission the court had given; and more than one, impatient for his arrival, crowded to the door. The officer came up, and with him the elder prisoner; but, except by those who had recently visited him, he was scarcely to be recognized. He was but too plainly in the last stage of a disease that had been quickened from its usually slow course, into fierce and rapidly wasting ravages. A violent paroxysm of coughing assailing him as he reached the door, the officer paused, and directing him to sit on the steps for a few moments, waited till he should recover. One of the persons, whom the reader may recollect as forming part of the river group at the arrival of the young boatman, was at his side; and to this man, as soon as he could speak, he turned, with an effort to address him.

We've had our last hunt together, L' 'low, old comrade! I hadn't settled my mind to the track I should take when you was last at the jail. I didn't keer about dying in my bed—I expected it to be at some odd turn, but not where I couldn't touch my feet. But you see they must have a *spectacle*, and it has to be me or my boy. They've got the rope round his neck, but I should feel strangulation of it tighter on his throat than on my own. I twisted it myself, and have the fairest right to be benefit. It won't choke me off, no how, from such feasts as luckier men set down to. But I'll leave you a hint, comrade, and twon't harm you to remember it—'tis one thing not to keer for dying, and another to make up one's mind to be *hung*.

The strange address, to which perhaps the curiosity of the officer had extended so long indulgence, was now interrupted. The speaker was conducted forward and placed in the witness' stand. He looked at his son, and then at the vast crowd that were now intensely silent. There was a haggardness in the rugged lineaments of his face that sufficiently attested the long and fierce struggle he had, not obscurely, intimated to his old associate; and the large proportions of his broad frame were yet more apparent from its almost skeleton emaciation. Yet he stood up seemingly strong and unshrinking; his eye, with a defiant gleam that quickly passed, however, taking note of the looks of eager expectation that were bent upon him. But the workings of the yet unsubdued nature were too powerful for the diseased frame. The breaking of a blood-vessel, as he thus stood, gave ghastly evidence of the internal conflict.

The blood gushed from his mouth and nostrils, and it was some time ere the formalities of the court could be resumed. Then he kissed the Holy Book with more reverence than might have been anticipated; and when at last asked "if he knew aught of the charge under which the prisoner at the bar stood arraigned," he replied in a voice that, though slightly hollow, had yet a strength that made it distinctly heard to the remotest corner of the building.

Well, the murder was not done, as has been mostly supposed, for money. If the man had any amount, which was more nor likely, it was doubtless stowed away in his trunk or some by-place; and if so, it was sunk in the skiff with the body. He was a person that in former years was well known to me; in our young days we were townsmen. But there was no liking between us. Some matter of rivalship, as often grows out of young men's hot blood, made us enemies; but I never thought of harming him in no way. His ill will was deeper. He came forward and gave false witness against me in an accusation of taking what was not my own. I had good reason for believing he had managed himself to get me laid in the charge. I was convicted, and my good name—for it was then fair enough—was blasted to the very root. I broke the jail I was to lie in, as part of my sentence; but a skulking outlaw is a poorer thing than a jail prisoner. I got tired of what people called civilized life, and finally went to them as had no laws to be carried through by perjury. I lived a wild Ingen life for a good many years, till my mind got used to more of savage ideas than white men's. But my feelings towards my old enemy grew deeper and deeper into my natur. It never stirred me to go out of my way expressly to meet him, but I always thought we should meet some time, and then I knew we could not both of us live. Well, the time come. I found out at once that the owner of that trading skiff was the man. I heard him speak as I stepped into the craft, before I'd seen his face, and my blood took a chill like. 'Twas the same voice that had swore away for me every thing a man needed to vullie. But he didn't know me, and I didn't freshen his memory. I settled in my mind very shortly what was to be done. I kept still till I found he'd mostly sold out—that his going any how mightn't be unlikely; and then I fixed on the time. Somehow that evening I got overly restless. I couldn't stay in-doors; and walking through the streets to get myself a little settled, it brought me by one of the public buildings. It was lighted up, and with a considerable crowd in it that had been brought together by some public occasion. Some one was speaking, and thinking it might get off a portion of the time, I went in and sat down among them. Ashton Grey was there. I was used to be pleased at seeing him, but his clear handsome face, as he nodded to me then, seemed to disturb me. His kind look put me in mind how different my own thoughts were, and I got up soon to leave. He was in his boatman's dress, and his cap, which he had flung on the table with others, was of the same material as my own. I had thrown mine beside it, and my thoughts being so busy, I took his in its place. I didn't notice the change till I took it off some hour or so after, and then I thought little of it. It got time for my work. It was silent and dark enough. Not a star was on my way, and I muffled even the lantern I took, in my capote. But I knew my path well, and the skiff seemed as plain to me where it lay as if it had been daylight. I entered it without much stir. I'd had enough of Ingen training to know something of their creeping ways. I stood 'side of my enemy as he lay sleeping in his bunk. I called him by name, and held the lantern that he might see my face. It wan't from any such high notions killing one asleep, as men bloody enough minded sometimes pretend to; but I wanted him to know what debt he was called on to pay, and who gave him his discharge. I told him my name, and bid him look at me. Then he knew me, and he knew then it wan't no use to beg for his life. The deed was done, and I sat down till he was stark and still enough. Somehow I did not feel satisfied like, as I expected to; but it was necessary to get away the evidences of my work, and I'd most laid my plan aforehand. Striking my foot against a rock as I reached the boat, had put me in mind to pick it up for the purpose that I first set about. I tied it in a handkerchief that I took from Ashton Grey's cap (having that still on), and which of course was his. A kind of cowardly fear running over me, that some one might possibly come upon me, I got too hurried (as I've thought since) to make the knots secure. I however fastened it to the body, and moving it round for that purpose, a handful of silver fell from the dead man's pocket. I'd had no thought of his money—I was no robber; but this I naterally picked up and put in my own pocket. That much even didn't bring a pleasant feeling, and I wished I'd let it been; but my main anxiety was to get the body out of the way. I fastened my canoe to the skiff, and rowing it out into the river, lost little time in scuttling it and getting back to the shore. But my work had disturbed me more than I reckoned on, and in stepping into the canoe I took off my cap to let the cool air to my forehead. By some turn I let it fall into the river; I made little effort to recover it, for at the moment my attention was diverted by seeing some one crossing at no great distance below me. It was he doubtless that picked it up. Early the next morning Ashton came to me to change our caps back. He looked surprised when I told him I had lost it, with his handkerchief, so soon in the river, but let it pass with his usual good natur. Another person came up at the moment to whom I owed a small debt. He mentioned, as being in want of the amount, and I gave him the silver that I had picked up in the skiff, and turning to Ashton Grey, to whom he said he was himself indebted, he immediately handed him several of the pieces. Among them I've no doubt was the one that upon the same day was made matter of testimony at the boy's committal. Within an hour the body was taken up; whether the waves had washed it clear of the weight, or that it had to come up to give witness of the murder, no man can say; but if it was the last, Ashton Grey understood its arrant; for his cap was tuk to him, as I larned soon after, and the story of the skiff that was told him, in course must have made it all plain to him.

A hum of congratulation ran through the house. Not a face was there but evidenced an almost rapturous pleasure, save that of the redeemed prisoner. *His* was buried in his hands on the table on which he leaned, and groans that his own darkly impending fate had failed to extort, broke from his inmost heart. The crowd gathered about him. Among the few who recollected that the acquittal of the son was purchased by the conviction of the father, there were yet fewer perhaps who understood the elevated nature that made the guilt of another bitterer than his own condemnation. Yet to these few, at least, it was no shame to the manly spirit that, while he had borne his own attainder without weakness, he bowed his head to *weep* over the acknowledged guilt and utter humiliation of his doomed parent.

Colonel Ainsworth, whom we saw bearing out the fainting Annabel at the close of the accusing testimony, had shortly after returned. She had been placed in his carriage, in the arms of Mrs. Wilson, to be borne to his tender Marion; and then, returning with a heavy heart to his stand by the wretched prisoner, he had been a listener to all that followed. Ere the witness had scarcely paused in his detail, Colonel Ainsworth had penciled to his wife all that was to be told—"Young Grey is acquitted— don't let Annabel die!" Such was the note. "Speed! speed!" he repeated to the messenger, whom he followed to the door; and then pausing a moment to enjoy his own sense of infinite relief, he now turned back to draw the young husband from his not unreasonable anguish. He knew well the chord that would vibrate with softer tones. "This will be *life*," he whispered, "to your young wife. I have already sent the news that will restore her." Ashton Grey wrung the hand of his considerate friend. He struggled to speak, but his words were arrested; the hollow, yet still distinct voice of the witness was again chaining attention.

"I've told all that's needful, 'low, to clear the young man," he resumed, "but please the court, there's something more as relates to him on my mind. My time, I think, is getting short; for unless ye hurry, I shall slip the hangman, and I'd like to say all I have to, if I may be allowed."

"Say on," said the court; and the witness, after looking at the bowed down prisoner for a moment with an expression that gave a strange softness to his haggard face, proceeded.

"Ashton Grey, as he is called, has always passed for my son—he himself has no other knowledge; but I am not his father."

Again the young man lifted his head; and well might the blood rush to the veins on his wan temples! Well might he gasp for breath as he gazed at the speaker! The witness met the look with a deepening expression of tenderness.

"No, poor boy! To the last I might a' took pride in such a son; but I will not leave you the shame of either my name or my blood. You are as clear of both as the crime they charged you with. Years ago I bought you, then a fair boy no more nor two years ole, of a murderous savage. I tuk you from him when he had his fingers already clutched in your hair—your pretty, bright curls, the prettiest I'd ever seen, only one's that had been long under the dust. I give him all I had in the world to save you, and I tuk you to my bosom as a mother would. I bound up your little feet—I carried you miles on my shoulders—I fed you when I starved myself. But you paid me for it all," he continued, as the gaze so intently fixed upon him gave place to tears; "you was all the light there was for years on my way. There's no occasion for grief now, poor boy! tears aint for one like me."

"Permit me to ask," said Colonel Ainsworth, turning from the court to the witness, "what the real name of the young man is. Know you any thing of his parentage?"

"Nothing," said the other, "nothing. The child was brought in with other prisoners from the Kentuck side. But that's all I know. I was for a long time so feared he might be reclaimed, that I carried him with me from tribe to tribe. But there is a Shawanee, as I have been told by an old messmate, at this time in the place, that was one of the war-party that tuk the boy."

The witness glanced round him, and fixed his eye once more on the man with whom he had spoken at his entrance.

"One more turn for me, old comrade," he said, "after all! Go and fetch old Walk-in-the-water to the court. 'Twill ease my mind to have the young man freed for all uneasiness."

Once more expectation was strained to the liveliest interest. The old backwoodsman was not long in fulfilling his mission. The blanketed form of the red man soon stood with glistening eye before the assembly. The witness addressed a few words to him in his own language, and then, turning to Colonel Ainsworth, said, "Ask him what you want to know; he speaks English well enough, I 'low, to answer ye."

He was not mistaken—the answers of the old chief were sufficiently intelligible. The time and place of the capture, with various attendant circumstances, were detailed in a way to identify the young captive beyond a doubt. The rich color of Colonel Ainsworth's cheek paled during the narration, and for some moments he was evidently shaken with emotion. Then the soldierly spirit rallied.

"Rise, young man," he said, laying his hand on the prisoner's head, "and let me look on you as I now know you to be."

Instinctively our hero arose, and as the two manly forms stood thus together, a strong resemblance in the lineaments was easily to be traced.

"*I* am your father!" said Colonel Ainsworth, in a voice of gushing tenderness, and they were locked in each other's arms.

The immediate business of the court was at last resumed. The formula of examination and conviction was completed, and the criminal sentenced to a death that disease was evidently about to anticipate; and, supported by his guard, was borne back to his prison. Colonel Ainsworth and his son were arm in arm beside him.

"He is dying," said the latter, as he was at last laid upon his straw. The changing hues of the face but too well confirmed it; but gleam of satisfaction touched the ghastly lines.

"Kind to the last, Ashton!" he said, as the young man leaned sorrowfully over him; "so let me call you this once more. I give you that name for my little dear brother, that was laid in the ground when he was a fair as you was—just such a pretty face and curls; and it was the only holy memory I'd kept in my heart."

"My son shall keep the name," said Colonel Ainsworth kindly, and again a gleam of pleasure crossed the changing face.

"Would you not like to see some one that would talk with you of a better world?" said the Colonel.

"Yes, yes! there has been one to me more than once, that would fain a'told me of *Him that died for sinners*; and yet I refused to hear him. Can there be hope for me yet?"

The holy man was instantly brought. Deep and fervently the voice of supplication went up in that dying cell. The strong spirit was struggling now to grasp the promises of redeeming mercy; and when Colonel Ainsworth and his son shortly after took a solemn leave, it was not without hope. When the hush of night fell soon after, the heart that had struggled so fearfully with sin was hushed also.

A different scene awaits us,—we pause almost tremblingly ere we lift the curtain. We will give but a moment's view of it. The restored bride lies on the throbbing bosom of her husband, and Colonel Ainsworth, looking at them for a moment with intense delight, has turned to his Marion, and taken her tenderly in his own arms.

"My wife! my Marion! can you bear yet more happiness? You that for my sake for years have borne up under a great sorrow, will you not for my sake also be strong under a flood-tide of gladness? Marion, our boy that we have so long mourned—our precious one, whose image has never faded from our hearts,—he still lives! Bear up, my love!—he is restored to us—he is all that we could ask. Marion, Ashton Grey is our son! These," said he, bearing her half-fainting form towards Annabel and her husband, and folding them both with her in one embrace—"these are our children!"

THE END

HUGH MASON

The workings of the mind whose hidden springs,
Whose lights and shades, together strangely wrought,
And oftentimes from passing circumstance
Gathering alternate rule,—man may not trace.

"Western Tales?" repeated a traveler to his companion, as entering one of our village inns he took up one of our native legends. "'Tis a pity you western folks have become so deucedly sectional. If western literature is to have no broader field than that afforded by western history, it will need the aid of puffing. Your poets, perhaps, may find something of inspiration in the shadowy gloom and voiceless whisperings of your old forests; but the novelist, whose materials are to be drawn from life, should have other ground. He must be sadly posed in getting up a *scene* among your backwoodsmen. Events that control the pulse must be somewhat rare among a people of their simple pursuits, and perfect quality of condition.—No grandeur in ruins, no classic associations, and no gorgeous pageants. Half savage habits, and rugged and monotonous adventures, are the materials with which he is to work a spell that shall chain all the faculties of soul and mind."

"Are there then no scenes," rejoined the other traveler, "to stir our hearts but those attended by 'pomp, pride and circumstance'! No source of excitement but the glitter that arrests the imagination! Is there not always in *human* character a power, a mystery evincing itself in all conditions and under all circumstances, sufficient to awaken interest! Are there not high and holy laws controlling humans to which all the refinements of life give no additional strength, from which, independently of great events, there spring many a joy and sorrow, many a sentiment of moral elevation to call forth a sympathy and to engage our feelings! Believe me, Sir Knight of the Classic school, those whom deeds developing character in its own free strength, unshackled and unweakened by the artificial restraints of what is termed polished life, afford matter of thought deeper than mere pageantry can awaken, will find in the dull history of the West an interest quite as absorbing as that presented by a foreign and more brilliant arena. You are aware that I was one among our early adventurers, and amid the frequent struggles of which I was a sharer I witnessed many a scene. There was one at this moment come vividly to my recollection, though more than forty years have swept over its traces. The story in itself is a simple one, but still a powerful illustration of the 'marvels' with which our nature abounds; and, as from the mustering clouds yonder, we are likely to be weather bound some hours—a situation of all things favorable to a story teller—if you promise me a patient listening—so you are all attention! Well, I will go on.

"I was a sick man in the depths of a deep, untrodden, illimitable wilderness. A fever had arrested me, while accompanying a party of hardier foresters in exploring its recesses, taming my spirit of adventure most pitiably.—They were fain to leave me for some time at the cabin of a pioneer, whose name was Adam Browning. There was nothing in the character of this young man to distinguish him, perhaps, from the greater part of those who, in the season of peril when the whole boundless West was one field of deadly strife, had built their domestic fires amid its forests; yet there was much about him and his little family to interest all our better feelings. That honest pride, which scorns to yield the deference that wealth in all climes alike still claims from the poor,—that guiltless ambition, which aspires to the dominion of one fair spot of earth from which industry may reap a competence,—had brought him an emigrant from the interior. Without the peculiar tastes, or distinctive manner of the simple though warlike borderer, yet by nature gifted with a spirit of manly daring—a chivalrous contempt of personal considerations, and an instinctive facility of overcoming difficulty, he possessed all the nobler characteristics of the native backwoodsman. His young wife, whom he had led almost from the altar to his home in the wilderness, was one of those around whom hangs the perpetual charm of a fresh and buoyant spirit, with the kind of beauty that breathes like forest roses of the rich spring-tide; a complexion of the most brightness; a form, full, symmetrical and elastic; a step that as she moved through the household, told volumes of health and happiness, and an eye of clear, dark blue, beaming on all with kindness, but kindling, as it turned upon her husband or her child, with that intensity of devotedness which could alone have unnerved her to become a willing sharer of dangers by which the hearts of men, of soldiers, were at times wildly shaken.

"One could scarcely contemplate such a family with feelings of a common-place tone. Such young adventurers in so hazardous a field of enterprise, domiciled amid a solitude so vast, so fearful, severed utterly from the world of gaiety and social privilege, and yet so happy. A world themselves, each to the other, and borne on, joyful and unwearied, by the impulses of exhaustive nature. Their child too—one of those bright and beautiful things from whom the painter so naturally draws his beau-ideal of a cherub—a chubby, golden-headed boy, scarcely two years old, full of happy trust, and glee, and frolic,—to whom life itself, as it throbbed rich and healthfully through his young frame, was a gladness and a glory. As if to throw his own extreme loveliness into stronger light, the urchin was forever at the side of one to whom nature had been niggard of her most common gifts. This was a lad called Hugh Mason; slightly deformed, and possessing a manner as repulsive as his aspect; who, an orphan from his birth, had grown up a sort of pensioner upon the charity of the neighborhood, where our emigrants had also been reared. Upon their marriage and subsequent removal, he had from his own earnest entreaty been permitted to accompany them, and was still, from motives of compassion, retained in their family. With a frame, which, however illy formed, was endowed with singular strength, he might have been no inconsiderable auxiliary in the household of a forester; but that, either from a constitutional waywardness, or a strange faculty of ingenious blunders, he perpetually perverted every purpose in which he was employed. Nor did the reproofs which this indomitable dullness not unfrequently extorted from the active and efficient Browning, elicit from him either the slightest attempt at exculpation, promise of amendment, or expression of emotion of any kind whatever. He seemed a moody, uncomfortable being, whom no one could regard with other sentiment than aversion; yet the little Edward hung around him, evidently with the most trusting fondness; and the manner of Mrs. Browning towards him—invariably interposing to soften the displeasure of her husband—bespoke almost maternal kindness. 'It is not sullenness,' she would say, in extenuation of his perverse silence, and with an earnestness of defense that always called forth an affectionate though incredulous smile—'it is not sullenness. I know him so well, for he was often sheltered in his infancy under my father's roof, and though seldom welcomed by any one, yet there were times when, among those of his own age, poor Hugh was considered as an equal; and from many a circumstance I can now call to memory, I well know that had he the words he would gladly excuse himself from your displeasure.'

"At the time of my sojourn with this interesting family, a treaty with the savages had given temporary safety to the tenants of the frontier cabin; but it was for a brief season. Hostilities were renewed with yet more determined purpose. The sternest borderer troubled for the safety of the feeble ones, who looked to him for protection; and when some months after, circumstances brought me to one of the rude forts then scattered through the wilderness, Adam Browning was among those who had sought safety for his family within its walls. In three days men met upon this side of the mountains as comrades meet upon the battlefields;

and when Browning came forward to meet me, I recognized him with a rush of pleasure. But though he wore his wonted smile of manly kindness, there was a shade upon his broad open brow, that had gathered there since I last saw him; and even the tones of his clear voice, that had formerly come so cheerily on my ear, now bore with them an undeniable chord of sadness. I followed him to his room in silence, suppressing even the common-place enquiry that rose to my lips for his family. A female form was seated at and gazing vacantly from a window, but it bore little resemblance to the wife of my friend.—Her whole attitude was that of perfect self-abandonment. Some work was lying at her feet, that had obviously fallen from her hands, and her long dark hair hung in disordered masses over her shoulders. Marian, at last saw us, in an accent of tenderness; and she turned toward us. It was indeed her; but good heaven! till then I know not what changes might be wrought in the human countenance by expression. Her's was altogether mournfully changed. Her freshness, the smile, the gleam of intelligence, were all gone; and even the light that still gleamed from her sunken eye was that wild, unsettled brightness which tells of the soul's conviction of despair. My friend made an effort for general remark; but there were images pressing upon the mind of this unhappy wife, that rendered her unable to endure it. And, in a moment, and almost gasping for breath, she abruptly left us. I had looked around the apartment vainly for my quondam playmate, and now eagerly exclaimed, "Tell me what blow has fallen upon yourself and your Marian, that you are thus changed. Have you lost your sweet boy?'

"'We have indeed lost him,' was the low and forced reply; 'but we have not laid him in the safe and quiet grave. We might then still rejoice over him in hope and trust but Edward is either a captive in the power of the merciless savage or his mangled corse lies bleaching in the storm of heaven.' The image was too dreadful a one even for a father, and Adam Browning wept—bitterly wept—. By degrees, however, he became sufficiently calm to detail the circumstances.

"Danger in becoming familiar loses its terrors; and they, who had sought the protection of fortress, soon ventured forth to their fields and in pursuit of the chase, with as little fear as if the name of the savage had been a mere bugbear. Hugh Mason was constitutionally anything but a hero. His peculiar condition had led him to brave the terrors of the West, but the slightest alarm was sufficient to blanch his brown cheek, and to agitate his whole countenance, though usually as imperturbable as bronze. Yet even he, weary of confinement, gradually threw off his fears, and, notwithstanding it was a general law, that no one should venture alone beyond the immediate precincts of the Garrison, occasionally stole to the forest.

"It was one of those bright bland days of Autumn that invest a forest scene with such exceeding beauty. The yellow sunlight streamed through the branches of the immense wood, touching with deeper glory its own gorgeous coloring. The rich red leaves, glittering like jewelry on its thousand stems, had taken place of the summer flower, and with every branch, that shook the crimson and yellow leaves, the brown nut was dropping with a stealthy sound in the valley. Such a day is the festival of forest children; and Hugh Mason could not resist its influence. Towards evening it was found he had been absent for some hours from the garrison, but not alone. Little Edward was also missing; and it was evident the perverse Hugh had taken the child with him. A general alarm prevailed. A spy who had just come in had discovered traces of lurking savages; and a party of hunters, who arrived soon after, had heard within a mile of the garrison the shriek of a child, that seemed immediately to die away in the distance.

"A party, with the distracted father at their head, marched instantly in pursuit of the fugitives. Hugh Mason was soon found, concealed in a thicket of underwood, and apparently stupefied with terror. But he was now alone! No trace of the unfortunate Edward was to be found, except a fragment of his clothes attached to the brush-weed. It was at last gathered from the boy that he had left him for some minutes to gather some fruit that hung from a cliff near him, and while thus engaged, the dark form of an Indian gliding through the trees within two steps of the unconscious Edward, caught his eye. Instinctively flying in an opposite direction, he only paused to hide himself when his strength was altogether exhausted. 'God be praised' added the father, with that energy which deep feeling gives alike to all classes, 'God be forever praised, that in the storm of that moment he stayed my hand from violence. There was a strange madness upon me, but it passed with a thought, and I turned from the wretched boy, whose life I had lifted my hand to sacrifice, to pray. My poor Marian—but you have seen her! Edward, alas! Edward is not all I have lost.'

"The arrival of a strong succession of men at this time had determined us to carry retribution to the principal town of our treacherous enemy, and a volunteer party was soon organized. Adam Browning was prevented by a slow fever from accompanying us; but the deformed Hugh, who, now more than ever an object of bare endurance, moved about absolutely alone amid all who might surround him, was one of our earliest volunteers. During our march he moved on, the same thing of mere animal existence; having communication with no one, and manifesting no symptom either of thought or feeling. We at last reached the Indian town, and an engagement at once followed; at its very commencement, what was my surprise at beholding Hugh Mason, whose face, I had a moment before noted was covered with a deadly paleness, break suddenly from the ranks, and running amid a shower of bullets towards the enemy, threw down his gun and yield himself by gestures a prisoner. I saw no more of him. Night gathered around us soon after suspending further conflict; morning only revealed the flight of the savages, we returned with no other laurels than those gathered from burning the rude cabins of their village.

"I pass over circumstances that have no immediate connection with my story. It is enough, that a few months after I was myself a prisoner among them at another of their towns; lying bound and exhausted with suffering, while the important question was pending among their elders of my sacrifice or adoption. The latter prevailed; and as I was led forth to submit to its various ceremonies, my eye was attracted by a group of children who, scattered along a smooth beach, were throwing their dusky and flexible forms into every fantastic attitude. But the next moment I fixed upon one of their number, who seemed among the foremost in their merriment. It was a fair boy, whose chubby limbs though stretched to their utmost tension in the strife of society, attested him of another race, almost as distinctly as did his bright and glowing complexion. A little apart from the group stood a lad, whom I at once recognized as Hugh Mason. Between every feat of dexterity, the little urchin took his place at his side, apparently as a starting post. It was a scene that needed no explanation—it was the child of Adam Browning. The merry laugh, the broad, white brow, the rich golden curls though slightly matted, were the same. As Hugh Mason stood watching his every motion regardless of all else about him, I thought for the first time I could trace in his harsh features an expression of intense fondness, and even pleasure.

"Months passed away, and still I was a captive; but during that time I learned to look upon the condemned and unfortunate Hugh with a sentiment almost amounting to reverence. He had evidently but one aim or object in existence. His every thought and action were governed by the one sole purpose of watching over, every faculty of his mind was brought into requisition to promote the comfort of the little captive. There was famine among us—pale, withering, extreme famine. The fields of the Indian had been swept by the brand of war, and the season of the hunt had gone by. Ha! What a recollection, even now, after the space of long long years curdling my blood. Let not the man, proud man in the strength of fullness, presume to measure the fierce agonies of him that is famishing. Yet even then—then, when the mother looked grudgingly at the morsel her babe swallowed, did Hugh Mason, with a calm system of purpose, that seemed to require no effort, still lay by a portion of the putrid pittance at times meted out to us to add to that of Edward.

But our hunters again carry their furs to Detroit; and I at last obtained permission to accompany them. On the eve of my departure I enquired of Hugh if he did not want to escape. 'You are no longer watched with vigilance,' I said—'you have become a tolerable woodsman—you are swift on foot, and might easily when out upon a hunt strike a long course.' As I spoke, the dull grey eye of my auditor was lifted slowly to mine with an expression of cool determination. 'Hugh Mason,' he replied 'came not here a volunteer prisoner to return alone. There is another here who has left a dark place in a cabin where sorrow was a strange thing, and there may come a time—I have borne him many a mile before today. And anyhow,' he continued, as he threw an immense load with which he had been charged over his misshapen shoulder, as easy as if it had been a bundle of fagots; 'anyhow it is some years since Hugh Mason staggered under a small burden.' And surely thought I, as he turned from me, God will favor his purpose,—for now I distinctly understood it, and the thought cheered me, as I bade him and little Edward farewell.

"Arrived at Detroit, my ransom was soon effected; and once more I was wending my way through Western forests. Anxious to impart tidings, which I trusted would give a gleam of hope to the hearts of the bereaved parents, I went directly to the fort where they were still immured. Little change had taken place during my absence. Time had given a more settled character to their sorrows, and I felt that the tones of my own voice, rendered cheerfully as they were by the consciousness of bringing comfort, sounded with a startling discordance in that house of mourning. But I hastened to communicate my little tale; and the agitated father, to whom alone I dared utter it, ventured at length to draw his Marian towards him and to whisper, that their child yet lived, and might at some future time be restored to them. A loud cry of feeling—whose intenseness was agony, rose up from the mother's soul, and then a burst of tears, overwhelming, passionate tears shook her now sickly frame almost to dissolution. At last exhausted with emotion she lay pale and deathlike on the bosom of her husband.

"It was a stormy evening in November. The wind came with a moaning sound from the forest, and the sleet was beating heavily on the roof. Amid that stillness, which immediately succeeding the wild burst of frenzied excitement falls upon us with an appalling deadness, a bustle at the gate, which has been some time closed, drew my attention. It was followed by a murmur of voices. A strange and uncouth figure, bearing some burden on its half naked shoulders, rushed wildly into the room, and placing it at the feet of Mrs. Browning, with a hysterical laugh he fell senseless on the floor.

"But," said the traveler, as he reached this part of his tale, "the clouds I see are breaking away. I have little more to add. Hugh Mason, though spent with the superhuman efforts by which he had accomplished a flight of peril and unnatural sufferings, was soon recovered; and some years after, when the war path of the savage was grown over with blossom and verdure, the unusual strength which had stood him in such good stead, was exerted in removing the heavy covering of trees from the rich acres, which Adam Browning assigned him from his own broad domain, while Edward—but you are waiting, and the path is long before us."

BOONESBOROUGH

There is strength
Deep bedded in our hearts, of which we reck
But little, till the shafts of heaven have pierced
Its fragile dwelling. Must not earth be rent
Before her gems are found?—Hemans

"My friend Everill must live somewhere nigh here," exclaimed a gentleman, who was traveling through a remote part of Virginia. "Can you tell me, friend," he inquired of one just passing, "if Howard Everill is a resident hereabouts?"

"You have just passed his house, sir."

"Ah! Poor fellow!" said the traveller, as his eager eye glanced over the humble dwelling thus designated: "still, I see, struggling with a niggard destiny—Well, well—I must give an hour or two to old friendship at all events, though it throw me upon all the contingencies of bad roads and a dark night. Everill is the same in a hovel or a palace."

It was an early Sabbath evening, and the subject of this conclusion had gathered a young and numerous family around him for devotional exercise. The bustle, consequent upon the labors of the poor, was hushed in the holy quietude of the day. Indications of poverty were visible throughout the dwelling, but over all, there was an air of decency, telling of industry and order, though perhaps the quick glance of feeling would have noticed that *her* place, whose hand was once upon all the springs of that humble household, was now vacant. The countenance of the father wore traces of a loneliness in care; and a babe, some three years old was nestling on his bosom as if it were her wonted place of repose. Around him, however, there were gathered happy and healthful faces, and on these his eye rested with an expression of mingled fondness and delight; yet it was only for a moment—there was *one* among the group who seemed not of them, and as the glance of the father met *his*, it was at once clouded with a deepened and troubled feeling. It was a youth, apparently scarcely eighteen, and whose rich dress bespeaking high fashion and accustomed elegance was not more striking contrasted with the coarse garb than was his tall, slight figure, upon which the winds of heaven seemed not to have blown too roughly, with the chubby forms and sturdy aspects around him.

101

"Verni," asked the elder Everill at length, in a tone of affectionate seriousness, "will you hear the evening exercises of these little ones?"

"Excuse me, sir," and the youth turned away with an ill suppressed yawn, "my head is aching already." The father sighed; he bent his head over the bright curls of the nursling in his bosom, and forgetting those who stood waiting silently at his knee, was yielding to a train of busy and anxious thought, when the sound of a carriage at the door, and a moment after the animated grasp of his earliest and most valued friend, effaced every other recollection.

The destinies of man may not always be measured by the scale of human calculation. Major Worthington and Howard Everill had commenced the career of life with hopes equally sanguine.—Equally well educated—with similar talents, habits, and principles, they went forth upon the theater of action—*one* to receive the guerdon of acknowledged merit, respect, wealth, a high place in the trust of his countrymen—the other to struggle year after year with penury, to meet the "proud man's contumely," the withering pity of the prosperous, and all the heart-burning evils, that can bend the yet unbroken spirit to the dust. Buoyed up, however, by a noble nature, rising above the pressure of circumstance, he had supported all with cheerfulness, and he now met his friend with a brow as open and serene as if they had trod the same path of prosperity. True there was one moment—the slavery of the world has a strong grasp upon the soul, and he, who stands proudly in his own worth, presenting an unblenched front to the shock of fate, writhes beneath the minute evidences of his poverty—there was one brief moment as the glance of his friend denoted a pained observance of the destitution around him, that a deep glow stained his furrowed and sun-browned cheek. But it passed with a breath. "'Tis unworthy of us both," was the immediate expression of his cleared brow; and shaking from him every vestige of embarrassment, as a steed, the dust from which he has uprisen, he entered at once, and with perfect confidence, upon the minute details of his family interests. But for one absorbing source of anxiety he had little to regret. Influenced by considerations of paternal duty, from which he rigidly excluded every selfish thought, he had yielded up his first born—then a bright and beautiful cherub flinging light and gladness upon his own toilsome path, and leaving a mournful vacancy which long after years still failed to close—to the anxiously proffered adoption of a distant relative, whose wealth and generous nature promised him present privilege and future advancement. The sacrifice had, however, been vain, securing to his child only a few years of boundless indulgence and of golden dreams that were ultimately and rudely broken.

The death of his patron had suddenly revealed the utter dissipation of the wealth, upon which these dreams had been founded, and Verni Everill had just returned to the paternal roof with tastes, habits and feelings, ill fitting him to share its privations or participate in its duties. "For my remaining children," said the anxious parent, "I indulge little solicitude. He who has been accustomed only to rugged paths, treads as lightly and as securely as those, who traverse the plain; but I feel with bitterness my inability to soften the severity of the lessons this boy has yet to learn." Major Worthington was silent; but his attention was earnestly riveted upon the subject of the little detail. It was a scrutiny of interest, but not altogether of satisfaction.

Verni Everill still retained the singular beauty, that had marked his childhood; with a face of the most perfect molding and mantling, with the rich coloring of youth and health—a form like the floating vision of a dream, and that intangible grace of movement, that gives so undefinable a charm to the slight bendings of the summer reed. But there hung about him an air of *indolence*—almost palpable as a garment; an apathy that seemed the effect—not of chilled hopes—nor complexional languor, nor of a worn spirit's weariness: but of listless habitudes, early fastening upon his character, and with the stealthy and leaden advances of the incubus, chaining alike the powers of sense and soul. Over his fine features too, there was an expression of long-fostered vanity, and of that perfect self complaisance so absolutely at variance with the eternal graspings of an elevated mind, over the limitless aspirations of high toned feeling. And yet his eye—what but the radiations of intellect as you watched its occasional movements, gave to its clear hazel depths that changing light, like bright waters flashing up in the sunshine? That sudden smile too! bursting like a flood of splendor over his whole features, as turning with imperturbable nonchalance from the scrutiny of the stranger, he met and received the fondly extended arms of his infant sister.

"Pshaw!" thought Major Worthington, "is he not the son of Howard Everill,—and after all must I count the exact result—the precise percentage of any assistance I may render to the child of my destitute friend." "If," he continued aloud, "we can think of nothing more promising for this young man, I can give him immediate employment in my office. He has of course received an education that fits him at the least for the duties of an under-writer, and if worthy of his name I trust it will be in my power to afford him further and more efficient patronage."

The father's eye brightened. "Verni," he said "has been subjected to little probing, since his return; and I own I am somewhat fearful his attainments have fallen far short of my hopes. But under your eye he will have strong inducement for exertion, and most unhesitatingly—most joyfully—do I consign him to your direction."

Few preliminary arrangements were necessary, and early the following morning, Verni Everill had received the parting blessing of his father, and was on his way to the residence of his long-tried and still faithful friend. During their journey Major Worthington strove to elicit something more of the mind and character of his young acquaintance; but his own varied and animated remarks, fraught as they were with the richness of a highly cultivated intellect, called forth little or no response. —The subjects of science, of business, of general information; and the higher interests of the day, had evidently no part in the young man's thought; and the enquiries he made relative to his former pursuits, only resulted in the mortifying conviction that they had been exclusively those of pleasure and of mere superficial embellishment. "Rather an unpromising auxiliary in the line of business," thought the Major, and his imagination ran back with a melancholy retrospect over the probable capabilities and early promise, which mistaken indulgence and idle privilege had so heavily obscured.

"I trust, my dear Verni," said Major Worthington, as he ushered him the morning after their arrival at the capital, into his office, "I trust I shall find you a ready penman. These endless transcripts are to be disposed of only by the dexterity of a practiced hand, or by indefatigable industry, and I would be sorry to subject you to too irksome a confinement. Your fellow clerk," he added, as a plainly dressed and rather awkward looking youth, somewhat younger than Verni, who sat deeply engaged in copying, now for the first time looked up. An expression of momentary contempt, giving place to that of conscious condescension; passed over the brow of Everill, as he bent his head slightly but gracefully to the formal bow of the stripling.—"Before you begin those transcripts," continued the Major, handing him a statement of financial data, "oblige me by making out a little calculation. You will see"—a flush of shame deepened the polished cheek of the novitiate, as he threw a deprecating glance over the paper.

"I fear sir, indeed, I—I—have never attended particularly to figures."

"Humph—*you* will do it then if you please, James," and giving Everill some further directions, the disconcerted functionary sat down to his own labors.

"Have you finished that copy?" he sometime after enquired of the youth, who bent over his work with a still flushed and confused brow: "why, Verni, this will never do—it is a perfect scrawl—the orthography too, one, two, three, worse and worse, it is all a jargon. Why, look at this," he continued snatching the sheet from the industrious James, "not an error—not a blot—not an indistinct letter. But I forget," he added in a tone of kindness, "that *you* have not been educated at the desk.—Practice will soon make your tasks less difficult, but at present only the utmost care and attention can enable you to do them justice. Meanwhile my dear Verni, I do not wish your whole time should be devoted to the business of the office. I am anxious you should acquire that general knowledge, which can alone fit you for extensive usefulness. I will immediately furnish you with some elementary books, and by rising early you will have an hour for study before I call you to the labors of the desk." "I am glad to find him susceptible of mortification at any rate," thought the Major, as he now turned from the embarrassed and silent Everill—"if he have any dormant faculties, pride will now give them impulse." But Major Worthington was not altogether aware of the resistless power, that habit exercises over human purpose. His young dependent was indeed humbled, deeply—painfully—and many a burning thought passed over his brain, ere he finally sank to repose with the tranquillizing resolve, that he morrow should be devoted to intense exertion, and assiduous industry. The morrow's sun glared brightly through his curtains ere he woke to its fulfillment, and an immediate summons to breakfast, told him that the hour permitted him for study was added to the many, that had passed and "left no trace."

"Have you copied all this morning," he inquired of his fellow-writer, as with a cheek again painfully deepened he set down to his own appointed task.

"Why no, pray? I could scarcely have done less."

Everill mended his pen; the consciousness of being so early distanced impeded his efforts.—his first essay was a blunder—he flung it aside and commenced now—again and again his pen was reduced to a stump and flung away for another—all would not do. Blots, erasures, interlineations succeeded each other in increasing obscurity. The perspiration stood upon his fair brow. He threw up the window—a keen gust of wind lifted his papers from the table, and scattered them over the floor— "What a chilly day," he exclaimed as he picked them up—"my fingers are really too numb to write."

"How came that window open?" enquired the unconscious James, now quietly rising to shut it. "I do not wonder you are chilled," and again he was wholly absorbed in his employment.

"You possess a very enviable temperament," thought Everill, as he surveyed his coarse, serene features. Day after day thus wore away, and still new obstacles arose to impede his advancement. Carelessly as he had turned from the founts of useful knowledge, he had been far from neglecting those attainments, that were calculated to give him an early introduction upon the gay theater of youthful amusement. He sung and played upon various instruments with unparalleled sweetness—his dancing was like the wreathings of the floating vapor; and in reading the lighter works of fancy, the rich intonations of his melting voice gave them a charm and pathos not their own. From these too he had gathered many a thought of light and beauty, and in the whirl of pleasure or the occasional excitement of awakened sentiment, he flung them around him like dew-drops shaken off in the golden sunlight. With powers like these, Verni Everill was not to remain unnoticed by those, whose only pursuit was the annihilation of time; the voice of flattery and the calls of pleasure were now perpetually luring him from the sober round of his prescribed duties, and week after week, and month after month, afforded to his disappointed patron, only fresh proofs of his confirmed weakness and irreclaimable obliquity. It was in vain that Major Worthington, still cherishing in the son of Howard Everill, an interest that nothing could efface, repeatedly and affectionately remonstrated, and that Verni himself again and again resolved. He was enthralled in a net-work, impalpable indeed to his own perception, but resisting all his efforts to break from its binding filaments.

"It will not do," thought the Major, as, harassed with an unwonted press of business, he one day entered the office, where confusion and disorder were the only traces of the absented Everill. "It will not do—I must commence a new page with this boy, and if"—a letter just handed him broke off the thought. "For God's sake what is the meaning of this?" he exclaimed, starting as he ran over its contents, as if a serpent had coiled around his heart. He examined the date, and again he ran it hurriedly over.

"No, there is no possibility of mistake; it is even so," and he now paced the floor in extreme and painful agitation. To the writer of this letter, he had himself a short time previous dispatched by Verni Everill, as an express, a note enclosing a considerable sum of money, and involving business that admitted of no delay. The letter he now held had disclosed the astounding fact, that this note had never been received, and the youth in whom, despite of all his errors, he had placed an unreserved trust—whom he had indeed cherished with an almost parental fondness, was precipitated at once and forever into the fearful abyss of guilt and shame! "It is all over now," said the grieved and injured Worthington; "however I may forgive his aberrations of folly, I have only rendered encouragement to crime, nor should I have given to one thus utterly based a longer place in my household." The following morning Verni Everill was summoned to his room. "Did you not tell me the pacquet

lately entrusted to your conveyance was safely delivered?" "Well, sir"—
but the flashing eye of the culprit quailed, and there was a perceptible
tremor in his usually clear tones. "No, Verni, it is not well—read this,"
handing him the letter of the preceding day, "and see for how short a
space falsehood has availed you. Yet I called you not to reproach—that
were indeed idle—but to tell you, we must now separate. In justice to
myself, to the world, to the cause of that virtue you have outraged, all
further intercourse between us—all further efforts on my part to advance
your interests, are forever at an end. But, Verni Everill, even now I
cannot cast you from me wholly, as the thing you are. For the sake of
him from whom you inherit a stainless name, your dreadful secret shall
be guarded as closely as if my own soul's honor were forever forfeit by
its disclosure. Go—return to your father with a fame as yet unblighted as
his own. Bear him this letter; it assigns your little acquaintance with
business as the only reason for declining your further services. What
though he think but lightly of the friendship that can thus easily dispense
with its proffered trust! Be it so—better, far better he should renounce
every other tie, than that the innocence binding his child to his heart
should be severed. Once more, go—and Oh, Verni, as you bear hence no
stain upon your name that may meet the eye of the world, let me adjure
you to preserve it from the blight of *future* crime; there is nothing as yet
that need darken the prospects of your path; nothing of forfeited honor or
dark suspicion to surmount in your future exertions. Even from my own
memory, unless it be recalled by further shame, this dreadful scene"—
for upon the fixed features and moveless attitude of the wretched youth
there was a fearful expression of agony—"shall be forever effaced; or at
least only remembered as a dream of horror." Overcome with his own
emotions, Major Worthington abruptly left the room, and a moment
after, Verni Everill rushed wildly from the house.

"And what can have become of the poor misguided boy?" thought
Major Worthington, as a few weeks after a letter from his friend,
expressing many a fond hope for the child, whom he yet believed under
his protecting care, indirectly, but conclusively informed him that
instead of returning home to the paternal roof, he had thrown himself
upon the world's wide paths, without guide or support. "I cannot answer
this letter," he continued, "till I have traced him out." But all inquiry was
wholly unavailing. No trace of the fugitive, beyond a journey, marked
with indications of apparent frenzy, to the nearest town, could be discovered; and the unfortunate Everill had at length to learn a part of those circumstances from which, while delicately veiled, a mind like his, keenly
aware of the slightest moral obligation, and with every sense quickened
by paternal love to a gift of sharpened perception, must necessarily draw

inferences, if not of crime, at least of ingratitude, of folly, and of dishonor. It is happy perhaps for man, that the wave of life is forever hurrying him on—with a stormy impetus, requiring the exertion of the soul's utmost strength without pausing over blighted hopes and mournful wrecks, the Past scattered around him. The deep regret which these events left upon the heart of Major Worthington was gradually merged in new and more immediate interests. The war of the revolution, then drawing to a close, had blocked up many of the avenues of his former prosperity; while those ceaseless, but quietly-progressing revolutions, connected with the laws of the universe, and involving all things of time, had gradually undermined the remaining fabric of his fortunes. New interests had at last grown up between him and his well earned honors, and the official trust which he had supported with unblemished fame; passed, still without a stain of obloquy, to other and perhaps less worthy aspirants. For all this however, he found an equivalent in the sudden freedom, which an exemption from public cares at length afforded him of indulging the long stifled yearnings of a rich and benevolent nature. The sweet waters of domestic affection had been to him a sealed fountain, and it was only at times, when in the solemn calm which the deep midnight, with her burning stars and her hush of holiness, sheds upon the hearts of men, he stood by a marble slab dimly attesting ties long since dissolved, that he seemed even to remember "such things were." But there were those yet living, who had strong claims upon his kindness, and to them his feelings now instinctively turned. They were the two orphan children of a deceased sister; and having been consigned to the care of other relatives, they had hitherto scarcely occupied a place in his memory. "But I will immediately seek them out," he now said—"they shall give a new interest to my little house-hold, and I will transfer to them with interest, the love I once bore their sainted mother." His purpose was soon effected, and the vivid hues it had received from the warmth of his own heart, were at once deepened by his personal knowledge of his young and interesting relations.

Avoline Brentford was a slight delicate girl of seventeen, possessing in a high degree that pensive beauty so indicative of elevation of mind and saintly purity of character. Something perhaps, of visionary thought—of earthward dreaming, and the cherished imaginings of the deep, fond heart, might have been traced in the misty tenderness of her dark, melancholy eyes. Avoline's young life had passed in that loneliness of spirit, which gathers all its tides into our only current, giving it a depth and a coloring of shadowy power, unknown to the joyous and diverging fountains of sought and mingling affections. Avoline had been reared among relatives, not friends; a family of daughters whose slender claims to admiration were little advanced by the surpassing loveliness of the ward, barred her from that tenderness which her gentle virtues must otherwise have awakened; and the young orphan, whose heart, like the vines of spring, hourly put forth its delicate tendrils for support, still passed unheeded on, the only being amid a gay and numerous household admitted to no share in its sympathies—no part in its domestic councils or its tenderer interests. Such was the charge whom Major Worthington had taken to his home and his heart, and it was with a delight to which he had long been a stranger, that he now watched the soft kindlings of cheerful thought which kindness poured over her pensive features. Her brother, a noble boy of some twelve years, was a far different being, but an object of scarcely less interest. He had an untamed spirit of gladness, crossing with brightness like a leaping torrent, the paths of all around him; and the cultivation of his mind, rich as it was in native gifts, but perpetually flying off upon some wild direction, afforded the Major an abundant source of alternate pleasure and vexation.

"Here sir," said Edward one day, "is the answer to the problem you gave me last evening. Am I not a better scholar than you thought me?"

"You certainly are, my dear boy, though this is not the first time you have surprised me agreeably."

"Ah, dear uncle, if your praise now did not set on me like a stolen coat"—

"Why Edward," said Major Worthington, as he met the meaning glance of the laughing eye that was lifted askance to his, "is it not your own work? And to whose better scholarship are you then indebted?" "To your lame carter's sir; you know he is ugly enough for a first rate scholar. Almost an Esop of a fellow, save that his back is as little warped as his heart; and a whole heart he has too, I assure you. He has helped me out of more than one scrape, and to tell the truth had no small part in writing those exercises, for which I was so applauded that my modesty was well nigh overpowered."

"What, Herbert Allen!—ah! Poor fellow! I thought he had seen better days. Edward those scars which give him so repulsive an aspect, were got in the defense of our so lately freed country, and they should be even more honorable to him than the cheaper attainments of science." But the interest which the lame carter had already awakened in the mind of Major Worthington—not merely by the fearful vestiges he bore of his country's struggles—but his quiet industry—his habitual silence, and an obvious observance of the interests of his employer—was now certainly strengthened, and he sought the earliest opportunity of speaking to him alone.

"I have found you," he said "too faithful a laborer to resign your services without some selfish scruples, but let me ask you Allen, why you do not seek an employment better fitting your higher capacities?" A melancholy smile, to which a large scar on his cheek gave a kind of ghastly distortion, passed over the countenance of the disfigured soldier.

"Ah sir, if I have secured your esteem, have I not taken one step towards future advancement?"

"If my powers were commensurate with my will, most certainly; but my season for patronizing even merit is gone by. If my recommendation however can avail you aught, be assured Herbert"—

"I am perfectly content," interrupted the soldier, "with my present service; and if I may hope for your friendship as a person, I would by no means exchange it for the cold patronage of place and power."

"I have never till now regretted place and power," thought Major Worthington, as his eye followed the difficult steps of the maimed carter now resuming his labors—"but if they were yet mine, you should soon be differently employed. Still your interests shall not be forgotten, and opportunity may yet offer to promote them."

But the philanthropic Worthington had not yet drained his own cup of adversity. His health had been for some time declining, and a lingering but painful disease soon after confined him to his room. A crowd of unsettled business, deferred from time to time in consequence of his long failing strength, now pressed upon his mind, troubling even his partial intervals of repose, with a sense of probable loss and unacquitted responsibilities.

"Is there aught I can do for your relief sir?" enquired a respectful voice at the door of his apartment.

"Ah, my kind fellow, I am glad to see you—you can indeed relieve, for you shall assist me in looking over my books and loose papers while I have yet strength to take some part in arranging them," and at once and with perfect confidence he submitted to Herbert Allen, the labors of that business which had so deeply harassed him. The ready perception with which his instructions were now listened to, and the accuracy and dispatch with which they were executed, confirmed this confidence. He felt indeed relieved of a most oppressive weight, and gradually, as he still grew more and more feeble, till all other cares were at last forgotten in the inflictions of disease, the whole guidance of his somewhat complicated affairs devolved upon the soldier. Yet still amid the continued calls, to which this care subjected him, was Herbert Allen, almost perpetually in the chamber of the invalid—a sharer of the untired attention and ceaseless watchings of the devoted Avoline. The cares of both had their reward. Major Worthington at length arose from the worn couch of pain, and with the gladness of returning health, again went forth over his fields, for he had left the city for the more pleasant sphere of agricultural pursuits; and through the various concerns of his household, nothing of the disorder he anticipated was visible. There had been a watchful eye upon all the wheels of his wonted economy, and while he yet remembered Herbert Allen as a pervading presence in his own weary chamber, he found the evidences of his directing hand in every department of his interests.

"What do I not owe you?" said the grateful Worthington—"You have now indeed deprived me of the power to consider your individual prospects, for I can no longer part with you from under my own roof." "I can have no inducement," said Herbert Allen,

sufficiently strong to call me from your service while I am really necessary to you, but duties have recently arisen, my dear sir, that with the perfect re-establishment of your health will call me far hence. You are aware that a new arena of action has been opened beyond our own frontier forests. A few strong spirits—men influenced by the hope of securing a heritage for a rising family, have pierced the remote wilderness, and raised their domestic altars amid depths, where it is said that death is lurking in his most fearful shapes.

Shall *they* be left to perish while there are yet strong arms and firm hearts to which no domestic ties give other impulse? The appeal that comes from these shades is not perhaps directed to those, around whose feet the blossoms of love, and hope, and happiness, are springing; but to such as I am—it comes with a power that may not be resisted. Nor is it alone directed to our sympathies. It is a stirring call to a rich field of stormy but ennobling adventure. It offers us a home in the midst of a magnificent creation, or to confer value upon an otherwise valueless life, by rendering it an acceptable offering upon a proud and glorious altar.

Major Worthington smiled at the enthusiasm with which even the cold, harsh aspect of Herbert Allen, had become instinct, but it had awakened in his own mind a train of serious though familiar thought. Among these adventurers was the unfortunate Howard Everill, and this—a circumstance of which he was aware, had been in itself sufficient to awaken the liveliest interest in their fate. But concurring events had operated to give it increasing strength. He had himself received for early revolutionary services a grant of land in those distant wilds—this had led to enquiries resulting in many a high colored picture of that field of enterprise; and vague purposes of a removal thither, that wanted only a breath to give them form, were already floating through his mind.

"Surely," he said, "if the glory of the patriot is the guerdon of him who rushes forth to the exciting storm of battle to secure the freedom of his country, is it not equally so of him who goes forth upon the silent and obscure path of danger and death to extend its boundaries or to redeem its fairest portions from the wilderness. Herbert, my sphere of usefulness has become a narrow one, and age has not yet exempted me from the duties, which man, owes to those who must occupy his place. Why should not I also join this band of adventurers to whom even a solitary individual must be a welcome accession of strength." A few days and this query had resolved itself into a determined purpose, awaiting only his recovered strength for fulfillment. And was Avoline, so delicate, so gentle, to be subjected to the dangers of this removal? No! Dear as she had become to him, it was now incumbent upon him to transfer her to other guardianship.—Ah, how little he knew of woman's strong nature. "Think you," she enquired,

that I, who endured so long a desert of the heart shall shrink from the terrors of a forest. Would you consign me again to those, in whose glance I shall vainly seek for tenderness? No, my dear uncle, under your care only have I found a home, and your home shall still be mine, though it be surrounded with gloom, and danger, and privation.

Major Worthington caught her to his heart.—"My beloved child, in this you shall be umpire; and with such a charge surely I may feel more confidence in the protection of the Most High."

"Herbert," he said as shaking off his own weakness, with the disappearance of his niece, he turned to his young friend—"why, what is the matter? Are you too unmanned by the tears of a petted girl?"

"Nothing, Sir," and pulling his hat over his pale and agitated brow, he would have left the room. "Herbert," said the Major, a sudden thought giving to his manner an unwonted seriousness,

stay yet a moment—it is necessary we understand each other. The artificial distance existing between us a few months since, is at an end. We are going forth upon a perilous companionship, united by mutual confidence and reliance upon each other. Shall we not add to these yet another bond? I know not the heart of my child, but if, as I suspect, she has an interest in yours, my influence shall be warmly exerted in your favor—You do not answer me—am I then deceived? Is Avoline an object of indifference?

"Indifference! Eternal God!" exclaimed the soldier, and covering his face with his hands, he stood for some moments the image of passionate agony. A brief struggle however, and it passed. He took his hands from the brow where not a trace of life was now visible and turned full towards him. "Look at me!" he said in a low voice, whose very calmness told of appalling effort—"Nay, sir, not as a *man* glances at a friend he loves, seeing but his naked, unclogged heart—but as a woman, fastidious woman, beholds all of human form—and think you whether I am one to stir the tides of her soft and shrinking nature? Major Worthington, you have wrenched from me a secret, that I thought was sealed—ah! Forever, in the deepest fastness of my heart. But no matter, *you* only have witnessed my weakness; let it now be forgotten. There are other and stronger fountains that must satisfy my spirit."

"Romantic boy," thought the Major, as Herbert rushed from the room. "We will see whether he is to be sacrificed to his own sensitive delicacy, or whether Avoline Brentford is not superior to the prejudices of her sex."

"Love him!" exclaimed Avoline, as her Uncle proceeded in his unauthorized negotiation. "Think of him otherwise than as one whom you deservedly esteem!"—and the maiden gasped for breath as with the presence of some spectral vision. And this is woman's appreciation of merit?—thought the disappointed Worthington; this is the whole amount of that depth and holiness of feeling with which so many a fine sentence is rounded off. A baby devotion to pictures—a perception only of the eye. It is fitting Herbert should know it—though he condemn my violation of his trust. Passion is often fed by hopes of which we are ourselves unconscious.

But Herbert heard it all with calmness. "To the blind," he said with a bitter smile, "there is no extinction of light—you have only subjected me to another affront—Avoline must know she has nothing more to fear of importunity—Even now, as I passed her, her eye was averted, and her cheek was blanched." And with a manner of perfect composure, though the paleness of death was upon his brow and cheek he stood a few days after alone by the fair form of the trembling maiden.

Nay, do not fly me, Avoline, it is but for a moment—the first—the last your gentle nature shall be thus shocked. 'Tis but to restore to your pure spirit that wonted serenity which a mistaken disclosure has so greatly disturbed. I may not now disclaim the sentiments that have incurred your displeasure, however extorted from me in a moment of overwhelming emotion. I have loved you, Miss Brentford—*have* loved—and I must still love—no matter with what power. It is a sentiment neither presumptuous in itself, nor humbling to you. Whatever its strength, it is not of hope—the doom that has shut for ever the possibility of happiness is sealed upon my every sense—however maddening its thrillings, they are not of selfishness—and wildly, fearfully as it may sweep over my soul, and allusion to its existence shall never more give you pain. Let it from this moment be forever effaced from your memory, and the only boon I crave is, that you would restore me to that cold regard which I yet claim as the reward of justice.

Avoline breathed with difficulty. Collected as were the voice and manner of the speaker, there was still something in them that evidenced feelings, mastered only by powerful effort, and the marble fixedness of his brow was contrasted by a tremulous convulsion of lip, telling of that sickness of the heart, with which the spirit submits to the utter conviction of a blighted and irredeemable destiny. At that moment too, of deeply awakened pity, the quiet virtues and high worth of Herbert Allen rose before her, and Avoline would have given the universe to have rendered him happy. "Herbert," she replied, with a deepened cheek,

listen to me a moment, and impute not your unrequited affection to a cause that could not operate upon a just or a feeling heart. Long before I knew you, while yet a mere child, for I was an unloved and neglected one, and my desolate heart instinctively turned to some object to whom its unvalued affections might cling, there was one whose look and tones were those of kindness—on whom my whole soul's trust was bestowed. Time has but strengthened this early attachment, and though I may never meet him again, my heart is consecrated to his memory. Receive this disclosure, not made without pain, as an acknowledgment of my sense of your worth. It will enable you, I trust, to subdue stronger sentiments to the quiet tone of friendship, and then indeed I can easily and forever restore to you that perfect freedom of regard that has hitherto marked our intercourse.

When they again met, it was as those who had held no other communion than is embraced by the common interests of a household. These interests indeed, were soon more closely condensed. A short time after, and they were no longer surrounded by the engrossing scenes and mingled events of every-day life, they moved no longer amid the diverging attractions, the jostling claims and whirling interests of society. The scenes which had hitherto formed the whole world of their thought, were shut from their view, and they were moving on a path of bright waters to a world of primeval wildness. All around them was intense, limitless, unimaginable solitude. It is amid scenes like this that hearts become more closely allied. The dust of life's more common paths no longer chokes up the avenues of feeling: amid scenes like these too, the plainest practical virtues assume a cast of elevation, and confer a new ascendency upon the character. Amid the difficulties of an untried enterprise, Herbert Allen stood in a strengthened and yet more attractive light. His ready self abandonment—his inexhaustible expedients—his unwearied vigilance threw around him a kind of power by which the councils of every emergency were controlled, while the constant contact, in which they were now brought, was hourly developed to Avoline, those softer traits of mind and feeling which woman only can appreciate. Time too had been gradually softening the stern traces of sanguinary conflict upon his face and form. The contracted muscles that had given so distorted a cast to his features, had recovered their flexibility. The deep scars of his brow and cheek were becoming daily less apparent, and the halt in his gait, now scarcely perceptible, was more than canceled by a natural ease and high freedom of movement, which continual exercise and perfect health had now restored; while his countenance was at times lit up with a sudden expression of energy and passionate thought giving to his whole aspect a character of breathing spirit.

It was the midsummer, and one of those violent storms so common to that season had driven our voyagers to the shore. It passed, but not altogether harmlessly. An uprooted tree had struck the bow of their boat, and all hands were for some hours employed in repairing the injury. Avoline ascended the bank, and looked wistfully through the green arcades of the forest—a breath of flowers and the mingled hum of insects and the sound of running waters came upon her charmed sense. She felt like the captive bird suddenly loosened to the free air of heaven, and almost as unconscious of danger, she followed the windings of a small tributary, threading its silvery way from the distant hills. The *gloom* of solitude was no longer around her—all was living beauty; a slight breeze relieved the hot noon tide, and gave a stir of life to the delicate branches and clustering leaves above her. Avoline felt like one to whom a new sense had been suddenly given, and time and distance were forgotten. A quick step roused her, and Herbert Allen was beside her.

"Avoline, dearest Avoline, why are you here?" His voice was agitated, and the rifle he bore, now reminded her of the danger she had so thoughtlessly incurred.—"Come let us hasten back—this is no place for lonely rambles," and drawing her arm under his, he drew hurriedly towards the river. A shot followed by several, suddenly broke the silence of their path, "Great God I was not mistaken!—" "Avoline," he said, exerting over himself a strong effort—"do not be alarmed—our men are probably engaged in a slight fray, but I can bear you off to a place of safety till it is past," and breaking suddenly from their course, he bore her through the tangled underbrush till they had attained the bank some distance above the place of conflict. "Hide yourself in this thicket—I must join our men, but will return soon—at all events stay till you receive some signal." "Now God have mercy!" he said as having flung himself upon his face as he attained the place of strife, he obtained a view of his combatants. Major Worthington had that moment fallen, and a dark figure, whose scalping knife flashed in the sunbeams as he circled it round the head of his victim was bending over him. The whizzing of a ball and the death cry of the savage were sounds of the same moment, and as he fell back, Herbert Allen with a shout of triumph sprang exultingly forward.—"Bear him to the boats men—Bryan," he continued to one whose hunter's garb and unmoved countenance designated a veteran of the frontier, "the remainder are our work. We must dispose of these." A fierce struggle followed. There were only two of the savages, and with these Herbert and the hunter now strongly grappled. The "stormy joy" of the battle field, the excitement of its rushing impulses, and its promised guerdon of glory have no part in strife like this. It was a struggle of life and death—death without fame, naked and appalling. The sound of triumph broke from the forest, and a third savage, in whose bearing there was the pride of Chieftainship, stood gazing with a gleaming eye upon the yet undecided strife.

"Shaw-way-no!" exclaimed the hunter, with a tone of recognition, and the savage returned a sound of similar import and advanced to the combatants. A monosyllable—less a sign, and the fate of the white men was decided,—they were bound as captives. And what was to become of Avoline? Regardless of all but her, even amid the death-grapple in which he had been clutched, Herbert Allen had turned with his first power of utterance to the boats to apprize their men—now in safety, of her covert. The boats! Merciful heaven—with the first glimpse of an accession to the enemy they had been unmoored—they were already floating far on the stream and his calls maddened as they now were to frenzy awakened but the quiet echoes of the hills.

"Oh God! Oh God! These thongs! Now indeed they are unendurable. Base craven," he said, as he met the eye of his fellow prisoner turned on him with a kind of careless pity. "Is life, in the hands of these monsters so very joyous to *you* that you have bought it thus instead of selling it for all we might of their blood?"

"Wait man," said the other calmly. "We may sell our life in these parts, a most any day of the week! As for buying one, I reckon there is a heap of difference, so you may just as well make much of your scalp while you have it. After all I have seen many a yellow sun set upon a stormy day," and again turning composedly to the Indian Chief, he pointed where he had deposited a large bottle of his own favorite liquor. The snaky eyes of his victors glistened. It was a spoil of no ordinary value, and with their prisoners in their midst, they again struck into the forest. Night came—their encampment was pitched and the bottle reserved to dissipate the fatigues of the day was speedily exhausted. The artificial exhilaration it produced passed into heavy and deathlike slumber; and no sound was now heard among that outstretched group, save the bursting groans of Herbert Allen.

"And this man sleeps," he exclaimed, as he looked at his fellow captive, in whose deep drawn breath there was every indication of sound repose—"mysterious God, of what pulseless clay has thou formed some of thy creatures." There was a slight stir—the hunter was drawing towards his feet with a knife dropped by one of the savages, and on which the waning firelight shed a dull glare. It was achieved—his own thongs and those of his companion were cut in breathless silence, and the philosophic hunter stood upon his feet with a countenance upon which every trace of its wonted character of indolence had given place to a dark expression of deadly hate and ferocious purpose.

Herbert, though no longer a stranger to the peculiarities of the western borderer, looked at him with surprise. It was not a moment however for idle speculation, but of stern necessity, in which no compromise might be made with the fierce dictates of self preservation. Blood—the blood of unconscious sleepers whose lineaments were yet those of humanity, though in the exterminating strife waged with their race they were shut from its communities—was yet to be shed, and it was only for Herbert to obey the look with which his companion now stood between two of the swarthy slumberers. With the instrument of death already lifted over each sternly assigned him his part in the sacrifice. It was consummated—no word was left in that encampment when the coming day might awaken to retrace their steps, and our liberated captives were at last, silently, but joyfully threading their course through the forest. The morning sun looked brightly upon the scenes of the previous day's contest, and near it upon the long wet grass lay the senseless Avoline. Beside her knelt Herbert Allen, and at no great distance the carefree figure of the hunter again restored to an appearance of imperturbable contentment, stood leaning upon his rifle.

"Avoline, my beloved Avoline!" exclaimed the agitated Herbert. "God be praised you are safe" and with the sound of his impassioned accents the wandering senses and the strength of the maiden, which had alike fled before that night of horrors, were at length recalled to a full conviction of life and safety. "And so," said Bryan,

the life you would have flung away but yesterday sets mighty comfortably on you this morning—well, well, jist mind it for the future, and don't ever fling away your rifle because you do not see no tracks. But come, we must be going, it is some years since my last hunt hereabouts, but if I don't disremember, I can strike a pretty strait course to Boonesborough: yet it will take us some days to reach there if this young woman's strength don't fail, why it will be only a change in the mode of traveling.

Herbert shuddered as he looked at the almost ethereal figure of the scarcely recovered Avoline, and thought how utterly frail was such a being to the exertions so imperiously required; but who shall measure the strength even of the frailest form in the soul's deep purpose? Amid those trodden depths of that far forest, and through the long and sultry hours of the burning noon-tide, our little party passed on, and still the cheek of that delicate maiden lost not its coloring, nor her smile its brightness. The brow of him who noted every variation of her countenance, as the mother watches those of her sick child, was occasionally clouded. The tenderness, into which the excitement of the recent events had betrayed her, had given place to silence and reserve, and as he sometimes bore her over the difficult passes of the hills in crossing an intervening stream, an expression of conflicting emotion and passionate despondence wrought his features with a strange power. As the day declines, the preternatural strength that had supported Avoline gave way to the feebleness of humanity, and the travelers, after preparing a rude supper from the spoils of the hunter's rifle, raised a tent of branches for her repose. The hunter flung himself on his gun. "We must keep," he said, "an alternate watch through the night"—his cares were the next moment forgotten in a peaceful slumber. The full moon shed a flood of light through the forest; a cloud of odors rose on the breath of the evening, and the eye of Avoline was lifted to the scene of beauty—so wild, so solemn, so impressive—it met the fixed gaze of her preserver. That gaze was full of tenderness and painful consciousness of an unnatural, but entire dependence, so utterly at variance with the cherished scruples of a pure and delicate mind, colored her pale cheek. "Avoline," said Herbert Allen, and the solemnity of his tones fell upon her heart like the sprinklings of the baptismal cup; "I do deserve your trust—sleep only can restore your exhausted strength, and let your rest be as hers over whom brother keeps vigil." The unsettled light in the troubled eye of the maiden, gave instant place to a look of ratified serenity; and a slumber as tranquil as moon-light that lay on the closed flowers around them now fell on her weary spirit. The voice of Herbert, who was yet walking near her, fearing to sleep through the whole night's watch, was the first sound to which she awakened. She uprose from her couch, and extended him her hand. A grey light of early day heightened the paleness of fatigue and watching, and Avoline felt how deep was the interest that had supported him through such exertion. Her own strength was indeed restored, and their journey was resumed with the elastic step of renewed hope. The consciousness of the dangers on their path, blunted the sense of privation and fatigue, and perhaps the gentle spirit of Avoline drew something of its strength from the conviction, at all times soothing to the soul of woman, that her slightest suffering was noted and felt with all the depth of intense and passionate sympathy. But whatever were her sources of support, their path of peril was measured with but little delay from the feebleness of the lovely journeyer, and the rude but massive walls, that promised them security and repose, were at length before them. The fortress of Boonesborough at that time presented an assemblage of stern men—men, who stood prepared and girded up to encounter suffering, to grapple with dangerous adventure, as with a pastime, and to meet with death as a familiar and unappalling presence. Some of *these* were doubtless thus served by the desperation attending conscious crime; and there were others, who with a nature framed only for the smoother paths of life, had been strengthened for their present field of stormy action, by the deep, though silent appeal, that reaches a father's heart from his own circle of loved ones, doomed to a life of penury. But by far the greater part were men accustomed from infancy to deeds of high though obscure daring—borderers, reared upon the frontiers of the different states, and unused to other paths than those of the savage or the game of the forest. Some of the better feelings of our nature are, however, far less affected by rugged and even ferocious pursuit, than by the artificial distinctions of refined life; and beneath the harsh aspects, assembled in that garrison of the wilderness, there beat many a pulse of kindness and hospitality. There was joy too there with the arrival of our little party—such joy as is felt amid the desolation of the deep, when meeting ships exchange glad greetings. The fugitives announced the approaching accession to their strength, and a party was speedily fitted out to meet the boats, and assist them in ascending their own picturesque and romantic stream. Our harassed voyagers stood indeed in need of this support: a fever, the consequence of his wounds, had rendered all a chaos to Major Worthington, from the moment of his rescue from the scalping knife, and in Herbert and Bryan they had lost all other efficient resource. Our little band of veterans was consequently met with the most animated welcome, and even the suffering Major seemed suddenly recalled to recollection as the voice of his beloved Herbert, now soothing the half frantic Edward, with assurances of Avoline's safety—now enquiring with almost equal incoherence after his own wounds, met his ear. Herbert had indeed cherished the most painful apprehensions for his friend, and as he now learned that with the care and repose, which safety would afford, he would probably recover, he approached his couch with a countenance telling of deeper feelings than language may utter.—Nothing more occurred to mark the remainder of their voyage. The navigation of our streams was at that time a monotony of fatigue, but it was then shared by strong hearts and nervous frames. They reached Boonesborough in safety, and even the pallid features of the Major lighted up with pleasure.

"Is not Howard Everill," he enquired, as they bore him to the fort and laid him on a couch that had been prepared for him by the hand of Avoline, "an officer of this garrison?" Some one broke through the surrounding crowd as the friends were the next moment locked in a deep and mutual embrace.

"You are much altered," said Major Worthington, when, except Herbert Allen, who sat with his face buried in his hands, in an obscure part of the room, they were at length left alone—"Yet it is but a few years since we last met." "Alas!" replied Everill, evidently unconscious of the presence of a third person, "the branding impress of shame had not then passed over my brow. Tell me,"—and a purple flush stained his sunken and sallow cheek, "tell me if you have ever heard aught of my wretched boy?" "Nothing—though my enquiries have never been wholly discontinued." Everill was for a moment silent—his eye was restless and bloodshot, and his breast heaved with obvious effort. "Major Worthington," he at last said in a low voice, "I owe it to your friendship to acknowledge that I know its extent. The guilt and shame of my unhappy boy are no secret to my withered soul."

"How," exclaimed the Major, shocked beyond the power of disguising his extreme embarrassment, "what mean you—is it possible—who can have dared—to whom indeed was it,"—"Accident"—resumed the unfortunate father in that forced tone of stifled calmness that tells the depth of suppressed agony: "Accident threw me in contact with some one, a stranger to me, but who seemed to know you familiarly, who was at that moment detailing to another of your friends some failure in a matter of considerable moment to you in consequence of a messenger's base purloining a sum of money you had entrusted to his care. 'And was there no redress for him,' enquired the other. I listened attentively, for whatever involved your name was to me a matter of interest, and the reply came with a horrible distinctness on my ear that has left an eternal ringing in my brain, rousing me even from the heavy sleep of labor— from the quiet of midnight. 'Oh no,' was that reply, 'he never even disclosed who the wretch was; and instead of seeking redress, covered the affair entirely up. The truth is, I believe the money was taken by one of his clerks—a young Everill, whom you may remember. An idle—ignorant fellow, whom he could only have kept about him on account of an old friendship with his father, and for whose sake, I suppose, the affair was not disclosed—at all events he absconded at that very juncture.' Worthington," continued the unhappy Everill, as the large drops now broke from his furrowed brow with the dreadful effort he had made, and the features, grown rigid with suppressed suffering were strongly convulsed; "Worthington, even now give praise to Him, who in taking from you the wife of your idolatry, took also the babes through whom only you might have learned the extent of the soul's deepest agony. Since that hour of terrible conviction, I have seen fathers standing over the mangled and bloody corpses of their sons, and have looked at them with a withering and criminal envy. What were the traces of the tomahawk on the fair brows of their boys, to the disfiguring blots on the soul of mine." Major Worthington was affected even to tears. He felt it impossible to offer consolation, and only extended his hand to him in silence. But Howard Everill had learned the hard lesson of mastering his own individual sorrows, and he was soon able to speak with calmness, and on other subjects. "I have but just," he said, "returned from a hunt of some days, and have not yet learned the particulars of these wounds." Major Worthington gladly detailed the minutiae of their voyage. In speaking of Herbert Allen, to whose opportune rescue he owed his existence, he alluded to his many virtues with no small degree of enthusiasm. "Come forward, Herbert," he now added, looking toward the young man, who yet remained in an attitude of apparent torpor, "come forward, my dear Herbert—he who is to me as a beloved son must not remain unknown to him, who has been the friend of my whole life—Why, what is the matter, Allen—have you"—

But the surprise to which Herbert's still immovable attitude gave rise was at once suspended by the bustle attendant upon bringing in at that moment a wounded man—a soldier of the garrison, who in venturing alone too far beyond its walls had been fired upon by the savages. He was laid upon a mattress in the same apartment, and his dying eye, for it was evidently glazing with death, almost immediately caught the features of the Major, beside whom he was laid. "Major Worthington!" he exclaimed, or is it only a resemblance to remind me at this terrible moment of my crimes?" "My name is Worthington," said the Major, leaning compassionately towards him—"do you then know me?"

"Ah, but too well—and I must divulge and acknowledge my sad account. I have no blood upon my hands—no perjury of guilt that is so very fearful, but there is a thing that still weighs heavily upon me. My course of action, Major Worthington, has been a short one—since you first knew me, idleness has been my path." "Poor fellow—I have no recollection of having known you—when or where?"—"I was formerly in your neighborhood, but not indeed one much noted by such as you were.

Still I injured much more greatly yet, I fear, a youth belonging to your household, one Verni Everill, to whom you recollect giving a sum of money to take on a day's journey. I met him early on his way, and he offered me some reward to take it for him. I undertook its conveyance, and a momentary impulse to crime led me to break the seal."

"Hear you this?" interrupted the enthusiastic Worthington, turning to the gasping Everill, who was listening to the tale with a breathless intensity—"hear you this, my friend?—but go on poor fellow, you broke the pacquet, and"—"And took the money it contained. I afterwards learned that Everill had left your house and gone into the army. My guilt rested heavily on me." "God be praised!" exclaimed Howard Everill upon his knees; and Herbert Allen, now sped forward, stood with clasped hands before him—"My father! Look at me, your son—the son who had fallen from your name—God has withdrawn this lie in his own due time." "And is it even so?" murmured Major Worthington, as his benevolent gaze now radiant with joy, rested upon the locked forms of the father so strangely ransomed from dishonor.—"Ah fate has been drawing its misty fingers through these relations, or I should have discovered this earlier. Those disfigured features there have still been regaining their former brightness." But Verni at length added, "am I to have no share in your redemption? Is losing Herbert Allen to lose the son of my affection?" "Oh, no, no!" Everill now sprung to the embrace of his friend—"to you I owe it all. But for your kindness, I had been a blasted outcast, stricken alike from fame, and ambition, and from hope. My father, let us go to a more quiet apartment, and there I will explain what has led to the present moment."

It was a brief, but to the parties interesting explanation. At his last interview with his patron, Everill had rushed from his house only to seek the youths whose projected amusements had induced him to transfer his mission. It was of course a vain attempt and then came the consciousness of having cheated that high trust of character, which could not support his unattested assertion; this burst upon him with a maddening power. Nothing now was before him but despair and shame—no anchor was left him so that his soul might rest in this hour of tempest. A company was levying for the reinforcement of the army, and he entered it as a volunteer. Called almost immediately to the field, he was conveyed from it a mangled form to the environs of a hospital. Here he felt bitterness and agonizing, yet he had a salutary thought. When he at length arose from his bed of suffering, it was to behold himself as the repulsive remnant of what he was. A vague dreamlike thought gradually assumed form and stole over his soul. "For the sake of my father," he mused, "I have been cherished in folly and grown in shame. I will yet stand redeemed by myself. Amid the very household where I have forfeited claim to respect—beneath the very eye of he who tolerated my follies and my debasement, I will yet rise in confidence to esteem." With his earliest return of strength, he devoted himself with an intensity of purpose that overcame every obstacle, to those branches of knowledge in which he had been found most palpably deficient, till a perfect restoration to health enabled him at length to seek the dwelling of Major Worthington. No one recognized him, and assuming the baptismal names of his two brothers, as talismanic, as well as familiar sounds, he obtained the servile employment from which he trusted to his own efforts for future exemption.

"Your purpose has been more than fulfilled," said Major Worthington who had found in the happiness of the past hour a more efficient medicine than the proudest attainment of the healing art; "and now as you see I am quite able to bear all of joyful agitation that earth can afford, you may certainly permit me at last to see my beloved Avoline. It is fit, my dear Everill, that you should have a share in my children, as I do in yours." With a countenance, which if not altogether restored to its original beauty, was instinct with high feeling and the better radiance of recent joy, though an occasional shadow still told of some unquiet thought, Verni Everill conducted Avoline to her uncle's pillow. Major Worthington presented her to his friend with all the pride of paternal affection. "Avoline," he now said, as he drew her fondly towards him,

Edward once told me that your early life was spent in the immediate neighborhood of Verni Everill—that he was the favorite associate of your childhood—your champion at school—and that you indeed owed your life to the intrepidity with which, at the risk of his own, he snatched you from a lake of ice that was parting beneath your feet. Is this so? Ah, that blush is sufficient answer. I suppose then, my dear, you will find no difficulty in regarding this, his father, as your own. Verni Everill, who has followed him to this new world, yet regards you with affection, and it only remains for you to subscribe to a covenant that shall unite our families by yet another bond.

Avoline's color went and came, but her dark eye was lifted with a full and serene expression to her uncle's face. "Verni Everill," she said in a tone of mild solemnity, "was once exceedingly dear to me: and I shall ever think of him with gratitude and interest; but, my dear uncle, in seeking longer to veil affections, that have a deeper fount than the partialities of childhood, I should be unworthy of your trust. From the idea of a union with Herbert Allen I once recoiled, but time has taught me far different sentiments. To his virtues I owe this solemn and free avowal; and to him," she continued, as her pure soft eye was now turned timidly toward him, "to him to whom I owe your preservation, dearer even than my own—if he yet value the gift—do I now proffer the heart which you my more than father but lately wished me to yield to him."

Verni Everill spoke not, but in the look with which he clasped the hand that was half extended towards him, there was the utterance of a joy, mocking the power of language, while Major Worthington caught her delightedly to his heart. "All is now consummated," he exclaimed; "I have nothing more to wish of earthly happiness. Avoline, my child, your feelings are too sacred to be tampered with. In this devotion to real worth you have no cherished memories—no once-bright visions to sacrifice. In him to whom you now pledge your faith behold the object of your attachment—in Herbert Allen recognize and acknowledge Verni Everill!—Here, Verni, bear her to the air—you may choose your own manner of explanation. You will recollect I am an invalid, and the conversation of lovers is any thing but strengthening." "Verni Everill!" murmured the bewildered maiden, as her betrothed, pressing her passionately to his heart, bore her from the apartment. "He, whose image was for long years perpetually at my side—whose memory I have indeed cherished with love, that but for the strange resemblance you occasionally bore him, had scarcely yielded to virtue not his. Verni—Herbert, whichever you are—Oh! Solve this dream of mystery!" Hours rolled away, and still our lovers had retraced but small part of the eventful Past.

Major Worthington slept calmly and refreshingly—and in the apartment of the dying soldier, whose path no human eye had marked with interest, Howard Everill spent the long watches of the night in seeking to administer hope and strength to the parting spirit. The morning light at last broke upon that forest garrison, and with the shadows of night passed the struggling soul of the soldier—if not in that rejoicing faith to whose eye the glories of heaven are already unveiled, in that trembling hope with prayer and penitence pour over the spirit. And while those around him were wakened to the varied excitements of the new day, Howard Everill, alone in that chamber of death, now lifted up the voice of thanksgiving with a joy, only less holy—less ineffable than that of the *just made perfect*, exclaiming in the beautiful language of the parable, "My son was dead but is alive again—he was lost but is found."

SKETCHES FROM LIFE

In a certain valley, overshadowed by the wing of peace, and bestrewn with gifts that attested one of nature's most prodigal moods, the inhabitants had to busy themselves only in the various devices, by which enjoyment is diversified—inventions, to which, in the absence of all need, man is still driven to charm his soul to quiet. And among these devices they made themselves gardens of pleasure, and called upon genius, and taste, and fancy, to direct and assist in their embellishment. Whatever, from the wide fields of fiction and enchantment, or from the exhaustless resources of art, could delight the sense, or minister to the soul's capabilities of enjoyment, was brought thither. Invention was wearied in striving to give *them* variety as well as beauty, and industry was overwrought in laboring to bring them to perfection. Flowers and fruits of intoxicating sweets were trailed over their bowers, and a dreamy and delicious languor was sent through all their shades. Rich shadows lay upon their walks, and mellowed the golden light that streamed through the foliage—fountains sparkled in their recesses, and the fall of cascades came lullingly upon the charmed ear. The young, the gentle, and the lovely, to whom these gardens were especially consecrated, rambled through them with a bewildering delight, yielding themselves up unresistingly to the seductive sorcery of the influences of the place.

But the dwellers of that valley, who were watchful observers of all the diagnostics of human weakness, and who were familiar with the arcana of natural science, became aware that these influences exercised no healthy spell. They found, by analysis, that the waters that so sparkled to the eye were possessed of no power of refreshing, or of quenching the heart's thirst—that the odor of those gorgeous flowers, though ravishing to the sense, was blent with miasma and stupefying vapors; and the fruits so lovely to the eye and pleasant to the taste, were imbued with a slow and insidious poison, which, to those who fed often thereon, resulted not only in an utter prostration of their strength, but a morbid loathing of all that gave health or vitality. And they who marked the feebleness of others but to pity and support it, looked upon the fair crowds that resorted to these deleterious shades, with an earnest and sorrowing interest. And they said,

125

Let us plant for them yet another garden in which there shall not be a single plant or shrub that will not sustain and invigorate. They who are charmed *here* to repose, need exercise rather than slumber—they are to be nurtured for other realms! How is it that we leave them thus, where the faculties we should seek to strengthen are drugged to utter inaction? Let us prepare for them other and healthier bowers. There are shades that send up no dank vapors—there are trailing vines, and goodly and umbrageous trees, whose fruits possess no poison. These let us plant. There are waters, not only bright and sweet to the taste, but full of strength and of healing. We will dig deep for these, and they who draw from *our* pure, cool wells, shall be indeed and essentially refreshed.

The suggestion was not lost. The garden was forthwith laid out. From the east and the west, the north and the south, plants and "trees bearing fruit" were brought hither, and all were of sustenance or of healing. Its paths were cleared and its gates flung invitingly open. Pure and bracing was the breath exhaled from its bowers; and they who entered and ate of its fruits, found themselves soothed without stupefaction, and strengthened without excitement. But, alas! Of the throngs that had pressed to the gardens of pleasure, how small was the number that was drawn hence to this place of health! Those who had resorted *there* so rarely as to be little enfeebled by their influences, or whose stronger taste had become sated with their sweets, turned hither with delight; but the young, the gay, the sickly, the feverish and thirsting crowd gave but a glance at its quiet and somewhat grave shades, and hurried past to their wonted and favorite haunts. They who had labored in the new garden, and who looked with an eye of tenderness upon those for whom it had been prepared, mused upon the cause. And they remembered that gaiety, to the heart of youth, is as the warm sunlight to the butterfly, and that they turn with instinctive revolt from the shades where no summer beams play. And they said,

The boughs which bear our precious fruits fling too heavy a shadow for the eye of youth, or the nerve of the feeble. They should have been checkered with plants of lighter form and hue. The wells we have dug are too deep for the feeble or the indifferent to draw up their waters. Neither do these wake their thirst. It is the stream that gushes musically over the rocks—not the founts that lie so still and deep—that arrests the careless, and bids them pause and taste. Would we draw *these* within the influences of our medicinal shades, we must accord something of indulgence to the eye and the fancy. Our founts *must all be pure*; but we will lead some of those summer streamlets hither whose sparkling and not unhealthy droughts may be tasted without too great an effort. Among our rich and strengthening vines and fruit trees we will plant some simple shrubs bearing blossoms, such as the young eye loves to look upon, rather than fruit. What though in themselves they be of little worth. See only that they are innoxious, and they shall not be valueless. They shall lighten the depth of foliage that wears so repellant a solemnity to the pleasure-loving eye, and lure within the circle of our healthful walks some who would never otherwise be drawn from the Upas bowers of our rival gardens.

There is a moral to all human tales; and what is the moral of this our little allegory? Simply that, in like manner, we would draw the young, the uncultivated, and the volatile, within the influence of *The Repository*—we would lure to its pages the eye in whose depths the world of thought has not yet been stirred—that turns for all its interests to the unintellectual paths of life, or, to the cloud-land of imagination. How shall we effect our purpose? What shall we bring for the gay, the thoughtless, the pleasure-seeking, the sensitive, the dreamy, and the romantic? How are *these* to be lured to the grounds consecrated to their nurture? Our range is circumscribed by the law of moral health, which the founders of these grounds have established as the rule of their arrangement. We may not go into the fields of fiction; for our offering is to be *innocuous*. However varied, or whencesoever the droughts we bring, their founts must be *one*—their sweets must be of truth, their glitter of reality. We may not mock those who taste with ideal claims upon their interest. Tell us, then, our young, or gay, or sentimental reader, how are we to interest you? You have found a luxury morbid though it be in laughing over the pictured and labored scenes of humor, or still more in weeping over those of perhaps guilty passion. The sweeping chords of romance stir all your treasure of feeling—awake all your capabilities of intense emotion! And this is luxury! But has real existence no tones of sufficient power to call them forth? Is there nothing in breathing, acting, feeling, suffering humanity to thrill the deep places of your sympathy? The ear whose fine sense has been quickened by cultivation rather than deadened or perverted by fictitious sounds, will turn with interest to the great mass of actual human beings—it will listen for the "still sad music of humanity." The world is not *all* vulgar rush, and din, and coarseness, and heartless jargon. Through all its common-place sounds of tenderness, and trust, and love, and joy, and hope, and sorrow, and suffering, and all that make up the material of the novelist—not as coming fitfully from theatrical halls, or the bowers of romance, but like the sound of a living stream, to be heard ever, ever by the heart that listens, and feels its burden. But *thou*, young creature, whose soul is full of colored dreams and fond imaginings, tender though thy real nature may be, and full of sympathy, thou hast yet no ear for this—it wakes no echoes in thy heart.

When life—as assuredly it will—shall have corrected the hallucinations of thy fancy—when its teachings shall have shown thee how bitter may be its ordinary sufferings, and haply, how pure its real happiness—when thou hast learned there are interests in its common paths deeper than all thy busy fancies contemplated, then the voice of wide humanity, with its many tones, shall come with interest to thy ear. Thou shalt then understand its language; for thy own heart will have become a faithful interpreter, and thy quickened sense will gather sounds thou canst not now hear. But in anticipation of this, which we foretell with more than sybilline authority, wilt thou not go out with us and look for a half hour upon life, even now, under the chance aspects which the palpable world around us may afford? Trust us, it shall not be wholly bootless. What though we call thee from Elysian rambles? So much the better thou shouldst bear *us* company. We call thee from haunts that are sapping thy mind's strength—we are drawing thine eye from colors whose glare is weakening its vision. In some sort, too, it shall afford thee hints preparatory to that practical teaching of which we have spoken, and which is generally of harsh administering, and often of most anguished endurance. We would fain amuse thee as a weaning child; but the toys of the infant must be chosen as to be safe in their handling, and leading to no further disquiet.

And now where shall we turn our steps to look our half hour upon the stir and action of life's drama? The city spreads before us a world at once. Shall we enter it—the crowded, bustling, jostling, hurrying mart, with its mighty mass of being, swaying to and fro with conflicting interests, like a forest with adverse winds? We may gaze upon its throngs long and earnestly; but we strive vainly to fix upon a single point. They sweep past us like river waves—identity mocks our grasp, as in the pageant of a dream—we feel only as we gaze that *we* are alone. Ah, well-a-day! We must change our stand. Our city *environs* will afford more favorable prospect—we may there possibly individualize. The *dramatis personae* pass before us with better distinctness. Yet, no! We eschew the city altogether—it is a most unsatisfactory point of observation. Its faces are all masked with the immobility acquired in constant contact with the throng. We would look into the *heart* when we go out, "a chief among our fellows, taking notes." The country, then, with its pure, delicious atmosphere—its fields of verdure and of bloom—its homes of independence, and abundance, and love, and trust, and quiet? No! not now there. We would hie thither when we would babble of the sentiment that is felt in the wary shadow of the leaf, and the odors of the twilight hour—when we would seek the *repose* of life; but now we would look upon its front and action. We have come forth to be amused—inferentially, we hope, instructed, (for what of life hath not its moral?) We must seek yet another position. And what, then, of the village? Ah, yes, the village! Where we shall feel ourselves a part and parcel of those about us, and shall have a sense of the individuality of being rather than of its mass. That is our true arena, with enough of action for interest, and of simplicity for truth—pleasant little communities, growing up like green islands in the sea through our whole happy land, dotting the margins of our rivers with points of light and cheerfulness, and carrying life and its energies into the heart of our wide forests. And here we have *one* for which we ourselves have some especial preferences; and so—as there is some alloy of selfish feeling in the spring of all human movement, albeit it may seem of *purest gold—here we will settle us*—to observe or moralize as best we may; for in default of incident, we may not chase but eke out our time with our own reflections. But we despair not here of discovering manifestations of character and feeling; nor shall these be less impressive that they are gathered from the humblest actors that meet our gaze. Meanwhile, let us look if *our village* has aught in its outward aspect to distinguish it from the hundreds that might have claimed our regard. It hath certainly something of the picturesque, if not of the distinctive—the undulating circle of hills, almost embosoming it, with the ancient trees upon their still wooded summits, and which are thrown into broad relief against the sky—the deep ravines between them, from which clouds of mist are at this moment wreathing in graceful folds, and which mark the channel of sundry streamlets, that are seeking their way somewhat noisily, with their little tribute, to the far-off sea. Then there is its broad square of tufted green-sward, and the *planted* shade trees, which spring hath just touched, as with a pencil, into the brightest of verdure; and above all, here is our own Ohio—la belle riviere—associated with a thousand romantic legends and thrilling recollections, sweeping its mighty volume by it, and bearing away from it, in many a shape and fashion, the trust of its merchant citizen. Various crafts, from the feathery skiff to the deeply laden flat-boat, are floating from their moorings, at its landing; and in these latter, how many and deep are the hopes invested! They are freighted for our southern emporium. Some of them have completed their loading. And here, amid the rough call of rugged and exciting labor, and the ungentle slang of river craft, the voice of nature may be heard in her very tenderest and most hallowed moods. Not one of these boats but bears from the bosom of some family, for what, to the heart of love, seems a long period, son, brother, father, or husband. And the domestic affections, which in their wonted flow seek the sheltering concealment of the home sanctuary, now in the hour of separation, forget their shrinking reserve, and all regardless of the vulgar gaze, hover to the last moment around the beloved adventurer. Two of these boats seem upon the point of departure. "A hand" is standing ready to slip the moorings; but one of them yet awaits the presence of one of its owners, a brother of the young man now standing in the prow, and whose singularly open and manly brow, had we no other data of speculation, would afford us most pleasant conclusions. A shade of thoughtfulness has settled upon it, for all is now ready, and the call to action no longer interferes with the mind's engrossment of whatever image or train of images the heart has in its keeping. But for the brief space we have previously observed him, he seemed instinct with spirit and energy—not the mere flingings off of the superabundant tides of animal life, but the quiet out-going of character. He is young—we should deem not more than one or two and twenty. Yet his eye, in its quick and comprehensive glance over the various arrangements of his floating store-house, evidences both forecast and decision. And our favorable augury of his success is nothing owing to the reply of one at our elbow, to some misgiving spirit, who is croaking of bad markets and the lateness of the season: "Never fear, I tell you, for the boys; they know how to coax sunshine out of a rainy day." But the brother included in this assuring reference is now at hand, and we are gratified at seeing in face, air, and manner, the same indications of character as in him we have so satisfactorily studied. But he comes not alone. He is accompanied by those who give a new interest to the scene—two fair young sisters, who are clinging to him with an intensity of fondness and an earnestness of grief rendered them all unconscious of the pertinacious impertinence of our gaze, together with the mother, who, among the other particulars which we have managed to elicit, we have learned is their only parent—a pale woman, something past the middle age, and with features of thought and meaning. And now we have the key to the early and distinct formation of character which mark the bearing and countenance of her boys; for not a particle of maternal weakness can we detect in that grave and quiet face or manner. She has been their sole guide and counselor, and she hath trained them as she has now disciplined herself—by moral power. All about her is calmness and settled feeling. She glances at their little *final* arrangements, and her serious smile betokens satisfaction and approval. She speaks to them of the probability of their detention by slow sales till the approach of the sickly season of the south may require personal caution. She has looked the danger in the face that she might counsel accordingly. She points them, in a cheerful voice, to the last minute, and fond provisions of a mother's love, for their individual comforts. And all this is done as quietly as if there were no effort in those tones. Yet is theirs an enterprise to stir a mother's fears. It is their first adventure, and their little all, embracing but a narrow competence, is staked upon the precarious result.

But we have as yet taken but little note of those belonging to the boat "along-side;" and now these others have afforded us so much of interest, we will observe them more closely. The owner is a young man, also, with a dark but high handsome and frank countenance, and that high freedom of limb and muscle bespeaking familiarity with action and emprise. This is not his first *trip down the river*; but even this circumstance seems scarcely to account for the perfect nonchalance, the unconcern, the entire want of any interest beyond the "bound and circumference" of the craft he manages so adroitly, which mark his whole appearance. But a bright, girlish form, though with a babe upon her fair breast, appears from the interior of the boat; and we smile at the instant and pleasant solution of our marvel. His young wife accompanies him! And to him, at least, no world is left behind. Yet what an enterprise for the delicate and inexperienced mother! She has never been beyond the bounds of her native village—she is all unacquainted with peril or difficulty. Yet now, with her maternal responsibilities new upon her, she is about to become at least a *passive* sharer in the rugged accommodation, the incidental exigencies, and rough encounter of a river trading voyage. Yet who that instant doubt her perfect happiness? It seems a matter of unqualified *mystification* to a sturdy ferry-man in the scow that is just landing; and he expressed his surprise, half soliloquizing, half addressed to some one beside him, in a phraseology peculiar to his caste,

Now that takes my eye, to see that little skeery woman a-starting to Orleans! Why I tuk her wunst across the river here when a bit of a gale come up; and she'd no more blood in her face than the white caps popping about us.

But were our honest ferry-man something better versed in the mysteries of woman's heart, and had he marked the glance of fond and all-confiding reliance with which that young wife looked upon her husband, we should probably have lost his most characteristic remark.

And now our boats are at last unmoored. The young men, with many a whispered promise of speedy return, and of many a gift, brought from the pleasant south, have kissed the tears from the cheeks of their sisters, and received the kiss and blessing of their mother. Her voice has not yet faltered—its tones are full of encouraging assurance. Were she of Spartan lineage she could do no more. The boats are rounding out into the current—the men are at their oars—the "little skeery woman" is standing smiling in the prow; and, though she presses her baby to her bosom somewhat more closely, as she looks upon the glittering waves beneath her, yet doth she dream of no possible danger for herself from which the arm of her husband may not shield her. We might smile at her weakness, yet in it we behold the law of nature; and in view of its merciful amelioration of her woman's lot, we regard this unquestioning reliance as of something holy.

And now they reach the current—they are floating rapidly on—they are melting into indistinctness. The mother has gazed upon them till her eye has grown dim. She turns slowly and in silence away—she draws her daughters with her, and ascends the bank. But tears, big tears, are now flooding her pale and worn face—she fears no longer to unman her boys. Nature at last asserts her supremacy, and her tribute may be withheld no longer. She hath sunk on the bank, and folding her weeping girls to her bosom, gives way to the long suppressed passion of a mother's tears. Yet we fear not for her. She who, from principle, hath at need held her feelings in so strong control, hath her help from above; and we doubt not that she will rise from that brief prostration tranquilized by prayer, and faith, and the full committal of her beloved ones to *Him* who shall hold them in the hollow of his hand.

But are there none but scenes of parting sorrow here to wake our interest? Does not the returning steamer, bearing back to the broken circle of home the object of nightly prayer, and of daily, hourly watchfulness, also touch our shore? And how many a rapturous welcome, how many a silent but "full-of-soul" embrace may be there witnessed! How often, among the crowds from the various interests of labor, business, amusement, and curiosity, are scattered along the shore, may some lingerer be distinguished, whose eye, averted from all within its immediate vicinity, is bent with a fixed gaze upon the wave in the far distance, straining with trembling, perhaps vain expectancy, to catch the first approach of the boat in which the heart's best hopes are centered. There is a young woman at this moment standing upon the verge of the water. A moment or two since we saw her emerging from a miserable dwelling near us, bearing a bucket on her arm; but we noticed that her step was languid, and her look as of one debilitated by long illness, and we felt that necessity had driven her to an exertion to which she was unequal. But she is now standing absorbed in some interest that makes all else forgotten. The bucket of water, which she seemed to lift with painful effort from the wave, is standing beside her, and her eye is upon the distant stretch of the descending river. Her dress betokens poverty; and now, that we look upon her face with more scrutiny, though much is changed since we last beheld it, we recognize her. We know something, too, of her little history. She is the wife of a young man who left here some four months since as a boat "hand;" and we recollect, for we ourself witnessed, the simple pathos of their separation. They had married very young—little more than children—and had begun life with literally nothing but their hands. But they were full of hope and joy of health. To her the tie that had given her one whereon to lean was especially a bond of flowers. Her childhood had been spent in the most abject poverty— her riper years in servitude—and now a *home*—a home where the voice of too often dissatisfied exaction would no longer direct her labors—was to her, however humble, a place of rest—of untried delight. Love, too, was in their hearts—young, warm, trusting love, and what was there for them to fear? So hope whispered. A few months in the dream of happiness passed, and reality began her bitter course of lessons. The autumn fever, so frequently prevailing in our western country, prostrated him for many weeks; and when he arose, the incubus of debts necessarily incurred in their progress was upon his efforts. The *pressure of the times* had narrowed the field of labor, and to go down the river as a "hand" was the only resource left him. He must leave his young wife, now a mother, alone and destitute; but the elastic spring of her woman's heart made of this but a light matter. She could manage to get along the few months he could be gone—*she* could get labor in a variety of ways. What though his own heart echoed but faintly the springing hopes of hers? Necessity overruled him, and the young mother turned back from the shore, where she long watched the receding oar at which he labored, to wrestle as she best might for her bread. But disease was now in her veins, also. The exposure to which she had been subjected during his illness, and her great efforts to procure him comforts, had told upon her nature. Chills and fevers settled upon her system; and little was she able, during their brief remittance, to labor for supplies for the winter that gathered around her. Still she struggled on; and so cheerful was her temperament, so averse was she to complaint, that few of her neighbors were aware of her lapsing health and strength. Ah, how little note does the vulgar eye ever take of the silent tokens of uncomplaining suffering? "She is a hardy little soul," said one in our hearing; "I often see her gathering driftwood from the river, when the shore is lined with ice." But had he marked the heaviness of her eye or pallor of her lip and cheek—had he followed her to her humble shelter, and watched the convulsive shudder of her frame, as she bent, perhaps a half hour after, in strong ague, over that wet fuel—had he marked the anguish of her eye, as it turned upon her child, whose wants she might not relieve—but it needs not to elaborate the picture! Disguise poverty as we will by the cold interpretations of philosophy, or in the glittering frost-work of the poet, it is still, in the language of one who applied the term to a different drought of suffering, it is yet a bitter drug. Poor thing! How would our own heart thrill if the boat, for which her sunken eye is fixed upon that vacant stretch of wave, were indeed visible! Yet *must* her husband arrive within a few hours. Letters from his employer arrived within have advised *his* family of their being on the way; and we take comfort to ourselves in the assurance. Yet hath she stood here too long. The paroxysm of a *chill* is upon her, and shaking her whole frame. She looks as if her very heart were yielding to its icy curdle. How ghastly is the expression of her purple lip, as, turning with an eye of anguish from the river, she lifts it wistfully, as feeling herself unable to reach it, though so near to the house that affords her its poor shelter! A ragged boy, who we learn is her brother, has been playing near her, and we are glad to see him by her side, as with a deep shiver she slowly reaches and enters it.

But a sudden revulsion of interest withdraws our gaze—a steamboat is in very earnest at hand. The jar of its mighty impulse, as it ploughs its path of strength against the current, is felt through the whole village. It is already within our view. How, with the speed of a leviathan, it comes over the waters! What a pageant it affords, with its rushing wheel ploughing our quiet river into turbulence and foam—its crowded deck—its volume of smoke! What an array of life—of action—of power! But now it nears our shore. There are deeper interests in it than as a *pageant*. A crowd of our village citizens are springing down the bank. It is the boat so anxiously expected! It bears back to *our village*, from an absence of months, more than one of its native and familiar citizens. Whose blood so sluggish as not to be something quickened. Hats are waving, the signals are interchanged. A person is standing in the guard whom all seem to recognize with pleasure. It is the well known trader whose letters have advised of their approach. He is in all the flush of health and successful enterprise. Neighbors and friends crowd the wharf to greet him. At a little distance his family are gathered in a group, passive, and silent with deep gladness. Hath the scene no shadow? Upon the deck some two or three of those who accompanied him as "hands" are recognized; but where is the young husband? Our heart has turned again from the more cheerful interests of the scene to *her* within that wretched dwelling. Where is he whose presence we trust will soon restore life and health to the youthful sufferer? The ragged boy we have noticed is suddenly in advance of the crowd. He is the first to greet the citizen, who steps with such buoyant spring upon the shore. Why does *he* falter? Why that sudden shade upon his animated countenance? But he has at last answered the queries of the boy, and has passed on. He is surrounded by his family—he has forgotten the mournful intelligence he has given. But it has been caught by more than one ear—it passes through the crowd. The young man is dead? He has died upon the passage, and they have given him a grave upon the shores of the Mississippi! A thrilling shriek breaks upon the ear—it comes from that hut of sorrow! The boy has broken from those who would have compassionately detained him, and burst upon his sister, now feverishly slumbering upon her pallet, with the deadly stroke. And that scream of woe is followed by another, and yet another, curdling our heart with their prolonged agony, as if the poor sufferer would pour out her life in the succession of these wailing shrieks.

And this is reality! This, young sentimentalist, who hast accompanied us thus far, is a scene of common, real life. Hast thou no feeling to bestow upon its actors? We have given it no coloring to cheat thee of thy sympathies—we have thrown no fictitious spell over thy senses. The obscure and nameless sufferer we have brought before thee yet lives and suffers. Wouldst thou linger with us yet longer? But our half hour is elapsed. We claim for ourself no further courtesy. But for thine own sake, now that thou hast entered our sober garden, hasten not carelessly from its shades. Taste of its more *precious* fruits, and of those fountains of higher and holier truth which have been prepared for thee by skillful and *hallowed* hands.

HISTORY OF "OUR VILLAGE," PART I

If our last month's look upon real life's real stage afforded ought of interest to our young reader, she will, perhaps, vouchsafe us a second glance upon its scenes. The actors will no longer be the same. Like the figures of the magic-lantern, they have passed from the view, and others, and yet others, claiming in turn a brief tribute of notice, have taken their place. Our especial instincts have taken us to the precise point of observation we last occupied—the same green, tufted bank where the shriek of the young wife came upon our ear. The village is again spread out before us, which, but for loitering so long upon that bank, we had purposed to ramble through. And now we may fulfill our purpose; for the shore offers little at this time to claim our interest. The river—the ever glorious river—is stretching its interminable mirror, rich with the reflection of spring's abundant garniture, away upon our vision; and, would we indulge the dreamy reveries with which we have sometimes gazed into its glassy depths, a multitude of busy forms might perhaps arrest and hold us in durance. But such is not our purpose. We have come forth eschewing the world of shadows, and seeking interests of a *weightier* and less "questionable" shape. To us even nature herself, in all her lovely forms, and with all her ministries of power, has less of interest than *one human face*; for *those* shall pass away—the green earth, with her mountains and floods, the skies, with their gorgeous drapery and their burning fires, shall pass as a scroll; but that human face, no matter how common—how unattractive—how debased even—yet it speaks of eternity. And though the soul struggles but feebly and darkly with the immense conception of that imperishable nature, of which those lineaments are the seal and token, yet have they *thence* a power over it—an ever operative and still existing claim upon its interest, which nothing else in the whole universe of matter may assert. Man meets his fellow man hourly, perhaps momently, upon some of the paths of life, and still he looks in the *stranger's* face with an inquiring earnestness—a strange observance—which, but for that *power*, would be wholly inexplicable.

But our shore is not quite deserted, though we are thus running into the speculative mood we are so prone to indulge in. That single passenger in that single skiff, shooting so like an arrow across the stream, is beyond our ken. But here is a group of uproarious urchins to claim our notice, laughing, shouting, and dabbling in the wave. Nor can we pass them without a moment's pause, unconscious as they seem of our observance. We can never look upon children without a feeling that grows into melancholy—from the fair waxen form upon whose softly closed eye the mothers turn with so watchful a tenderness, to the sturdy boy who has either furtively or by sufferance escaped her gentle surveillance. Yet might the latter seem little calculated to awaken such a mood. The merry rebel! Who looks the very impersonation of mischief and frolic. Of such are these before us—the little miscreants!—upon whose rosy faces the broad laugh gives such rich effect—or perhaps it is *vice versa*—to the dirt that, 'mid "moving accidents by field and flood," they have contrived to accumulate upon them. Little do they care for our gaze, as we watch their feats of prowess; but smile though we may—and most infectious is that gleeful laugh that breaks ever and anon like a gush of spring music from some effervescent spirit—yet is a feeling widely apart from mirth, and which we would gladly suppress, stirred deeply within us. Young wrestlers! Growing up for the future arena of life's *strong* struggle! How *should* we look upon them and not give up our whole soul to the surging floods of thought that come upon us? Those fresh, and pleasant, and happy faces! Upon which that laugh shall become less and less gladsome till the heart's free gushings shall have passed for ever from its sound as has already faded from the face the tenderer smile of infant trust and joy—over whose glance, too, where every thought is now mirrored like gems flashing up through clear waters, a *mask* shall be drawn—all insufficient though it shall be to veil the harsh lines of thought, and passion, and suffering that may be traced there beneath it. Alas! Alas! But why linger here? Or rather, why turn our glance so fearfully toward their unveiled future? A better trust should be ours—a single thought should chide our solicitude to peace. They are thine, almighty Father! and shall we not trust thy own to thy keeping?

But our village. How quiet it lies beneath the softening and brightening touches of sunlight and shade! It has enough of stir to tell of all life's busy and cheering impulses; but to one accustomed to the condensed mass of action presented by the city, its aspect is that of perfect repose. One would deem that sorrow and suffering had never found entrance there—so calm—so pure—so cheerful, seems the atmosphere hovering over it. But man is still the same in the simple village as in the crowded city. Everywhere the law of change and the subjection to stern and mysterious influences mark his existence. We once beheld it a wide scene of suffering unto agony—a place of terror, and despair, and death. The streets where the quick tread of industry and the impulsive call to action may now be heard on every hand of us, were then as silent as the grave. Scarce a vestige of life was to be seen, except when the slow opening of a door revealed some worn face, wan and haggard with watching—or yet more appallingly marked with the deep ghastliness of recent disease—looking out despairingly and wistfully into the hoary and tainted air, or perhaps emerging into it with a group of some four or five to follow the ill-supported coffin, in which, husband or wife, parent or child, was borne to the fast-peopling place of the dead.

Such is a portion of the early history of this now peaceful and happy village—scenes with which we were ourself familiar. We traversed its streets while yet the shadows of the forest tree lay heavily upon them, and we tell no gossip's traditionary tale. *Thirty years since!* Why that to the young—though to the actors in those scenes they are but as things of yesterday—yet to the young and the romantic it is already of the far past. Hope we, then, *their* interest in the annals of that date, plain and prosaic though much of them be. Well do we remember when, to our own young fancy, *thirty years since* imbued all things with that mist that gives a character of romance to the most common events. The aspects of time to the young and old are, in their relative proportion, though reversed in the order of their change, like the noontide and evening shadows. To us the rise and growth of our village is a reality whose somewhat harsh coloring is little mellowed by the lapse of years; but we can hardly forbear smiling at the illusions it once presented. A new town in the far west—the land of all the habitable globe "the pride!" and this the fairest—the very fairest portion of that land—situated upon the border of the river of rivers—embracing all felicitous "combinations of circumstance"—impressed with indubitable marks of nature's particular favoritism. Brighter suns and fairer moons than ever shed their light elsewhere rose upon it—purer skies o'ercanopied—softer winds fanned it. Such was our *town* as we first beheld it—a diagraphic square of lines and angles—in the newspaper of the day. And, albeit, the world *is* infinitely wiser than of yore—yet were there hearts, even at that late date, just as needful of hope, as willing to believe, and as prompt to act, as when the slumberer of the olden world smiled upon his pillow over "bright glimpses" of El Dorado. And so the *new* adventurer embarked for the *new city*; and the freighted broadhorn is floating quietly onward—its passengers nothing doubting the realization of their dreams. And now, as our boat rounds one of those fairy isles that lift up their green heads from our river, we at length fairly behold it—or rather its site; for as yet it is only a *deep brown forest*. The town! How ludicrous the term! We gaze upon the location before us, and think sympathetically of the *well known* little boy who could not see the town for the houses—though *our* perplexity has certainly a different source. Not a house is to be seen—nothing but the gray old woods, that had "stood and perpetuated themselves from century to century." But, courage, our messmates! That lumbering and ponderous fall gives "heavy and startling note of preparation." A giant tree, with all its arms of pride, is lying prostrate— and now another—and yet another, frightening the echoes from all attempt at imitation; while, like a merry interlude, the click of a dozen axes, as if in rivalry, fills up the pauses. Woe for the towering forest! Woe for the silence of its ancient shades! How irreverently are its honors scattered to the dust! How rudely are the vulgar ministers of *sound* breaking into its depths! But the laborers are looking cheerily up to the broad patches of blue sky; and the sun, that has hitherto been seen but as a veiled god through those cloistered shades, is breaking in, full and glo- riously, through a dozen openings. The checkered-off domains are speedily appropriated—lines and limits are drawn, and specific rights duly designated. The clink of the hammer, and the forced rush of the saw, come next upon our ear, and cabins are going up with no tardy operation. The infant community is gathering from the north and the south, the east and west, and it seems instinct and absolutely breathing with impulse. If there are any in it who have hitherto been the victims of mishap and disappointment—the bankrupts of fortune—hope has raised its altar anew in their hearts. Every man is the lord of his own tiny domain, and (let the man of princely acres smile if he will) in the honest pride of that thought, many a nature, that had sunk under the paralysis of disastrous effort, is re-energized to exertion. The little spot of earth, with its newly erected cabin, is made a holy place; for it has become a *home*; and on every hand there seems a strife who first shall have that spot pre- pared to receive the pleasant and patient trust of the gardener's seed; for it is yet the early spring time, and many a "pale spring flower" is taken up from its wild bed by some young votary of taste to re-plant in the rude domestic garden. The twinkle of the fire-fly is lost in the myriad sparkles that go up at evening from the ruddy fires of the log-heap; and round these many a group of happy children is gathered at the merry twi- light, "piling on" the withered vegetation and the dry faggot, and shout- ing with joy as the leaping flame flings its glare upon their elfin forms.

Meanwhile we were not without interests beyond the little sphere of our new being. We were not a people altogether isolated and cut off from the larger world. The wilderness was about us, but not *wholly* around. The natural thoroughfare between our embryo state and her older sisters was sweeping evermore past us, and it bore us frequent and exciting tid- ings—news from kindred hearths—from political halls, and the marts of commerce. It brought us, too, frequent accessions to our numbers; and such accessions formed a pleasant era in our history. It is in such com- munities that the social nature has its freest play. The simplicity of their condition communicates itself to the character. The heart seems restored to its original freshness. The superincumbrances acquired amid the conventional formalities and cold refinements of a more artificial state of society are thrown off. The avenues of feeling are left unchoked. The bandages that have stopped the circulation of its warm currents are loosened, and the rich tides flow out again. So it was with the denizens of our forest town. Distrust had no place among us. The new-comer was hailed and welcomed with a familiar kindness—an immediate and kind of family adoption by one and all. And how lively was the interest—or perhaps curiosity, we will not pause to analyze the term—with which we marked the newly arrived emigrant, striving at the first glance to read the whole history and character. But though all were welcomed, all were not equally satisfactory in this study. Some repelled—others, independent of our relative position, afforded interest only as unique modifications of humanity. Some there were to whom our affections went out with a ready and instinctive embrace; and *their* faces, though many of them are dust, rise still upon our memory just as we then saw them—trustful—open—beaming. But none were so repulsive or so common place but their arrival was a source of excitement; for it extended the narrow limits of our social world, and at least afforded matter of pleasant speculation as to the amount that each one would be likely to contribute to our fund of social enjoyment.

The steamboat was then a rare pageant upon western waters; but the flat-boat gliding so noiselessly down the current, was an object of almost equal interest. The approach of the humble and quiet ark was hailed with quickened pulses, and earnestly did we watch its course, from the moment it appeared, a speck upon the wave, till it had either brought its freight to our shore, or dwindled again to a speck in the receding distance. How busy memory becomes as we recall these scenes! Every minute point, every faint shade is touched into life and freshness.

We stand again upon the bank we so recently left, but we are now surrounded by primitive wildness. How wide upon the stream lie the shadows of the forest, that upon the opposite shore reaches the very margin of the wave, deep, dead, unbroken! How darkly it stretches away in the distance—an immensity of solitude! But our foreground hath objects of life; and we forget the glooms and the grandeur of the wilderness. We are watching the boats that are descending the stream—we have no eye for objects of mere visual interest. Here is one at hand that has been heralded by some half-dozen "out riders"—a store-boat! Laden with fancy merchandise—an exciting array of red, and green, and yellow, now quiet for the hearts of the demoiselles both of our town and our backwoods. Why, look! The stirring rumor has been out upon the wings of the wind. They are already hurrying, in not silent groups down the bank—the young—the fair—the guileless hearted. Beshrew the heart that would scorn their simple vanity! May every little purse (and well we ken they are light enough) prove sufficient for the favorite want! For hardly have its contents been earned, and carefully have they been treasured, doubtless for such destination. But another boat has landed—it is moored to one of the sycamores that fling its white arms like gigantic specters over the stream. It seems stirring with life. A dozen forms are crowding forward—they spring on shore—they look around them with the most animated interest. Why, what is this: Such a *troop* of young and smiling faces! They are but one family! A father and mother scarcely past the meridian of life, with their eleven children, from the ages of six to twenty-four, all in the very flush and fullness of health and action—most of them, too, of exceeding loveliness. They bring with them comparative wealth. Their boat is heavily freighted. Everything about them evidences habits of industry—of business—of energy. There is that in their manner not to be mistaken—the very earnestness of their glance, as they look about them, bespeaks character and purpose. What an accession to our incipient community! Yet does the first words of the father, as our citizens welcome him to our shore, stir a feeling of still deeper interest. He asks anxiously what are the religious privileges of our place—has it a people devoted to the Lord? Alas, for the negative that is given! But so it shall not remain. Our emigrant is a humble laborer in the cause of our Lord and Master. He has been a class-leader, and a devoted one for many years. He is not one to remain inactive in his present sphere. He passes on to the cabin erected for his reception; but already has he spoken of a meeting for prayer beneath its roof. Peace be to that dwelling! From that lowly sanctuary the voice of prayer shall not go up vainly. The few who will gather there for worship shall become many; and the corner-stone shall be laid of a church that, though it shall come through much tribulation, shall finally triumph in the fullness and power of faith.

But here is a boat that has been floating from its moorings some days. It contains a family, too—a young husband and wife. They have availed themselves of its shelter till the cabin that is being prepared for them shall be in readiness. They are standing in the prow, and looking out upon the wild scenery before them in rather a musing mood. We have managed to gather some items of their history, and our interest in them has a touch of sadness, as what we have gathered of them has of romance. They turned from the hymeneal altar to seek a home amid our wilds. They are indeed *strangers* in our forest land. Their views of life, their habitudes, their tastes, have all been formed amid the widely different influences of the eastern states. They know little of rude companionship or rugged encounter. They have brought no wealth; for their little all has been lost in a voyage of singular peril and disaster. We "cannot choose," but fear for them; and fain would we gather from the study of their lineaments somewhat to re-assure us. They "have not renounced the land of their fathers, the scenes of their childhood," without many a dream of promise, many a glowing vision of the future, that will be scarcely realized. And how shall those young hearts suffer as their eager aspirations meet the biter chill of disappointment! The husband, it is true, should be strong to endure; and now, that we mark his countenance particularly, we are inclined to think our misgivings for *him* are altogether idle. His face is difficult of study. His nature—it may be cold or deep—the indices are not always to be distinguished. There is nothing in face or manner to afford us access to its real character; but the surface, at least, is unexcitable; and from the stern compressure of his lip we cannot be mistaken in deeming him one but little likely to indulge in day dreams—able, at all events, to repudiate them at will, and to meet, without any wreck of feeling, whatever of difficulty or trial he may be called upon to encounter. But so we read not of the wife. On that young face— young to extreme girlishness, and commonplace, too, in all its features— there is yet something to move a fear of her special appointment to suffering. It is not the expression of *sentiment*, for that is not there. The face has not a shade of the *pensive*. Neither eye, nor lip has any thing of possible association with the *melancholy* of romance. It is simply a face of health, freshness, and hope. The manner, too, is in perfect keeping with it—not exactly perhaps a *dash of the romp*, but indicating a spirit particularly untamed and gleeful, subject to impulsive outbreaks, and by no means duly regardful of all staid and seemly observances. Her eye, which has been busy with the scenery of shore and river, is now turned to her husband, and some thought has wakened her merriment. How gleeful is that laugh—how full of heart! Scarcely is it checked by the rebuking glance of her graver husband—rebuking even in its want of sympathy. Yet all this is to the contrary notwithstanding, accustomed as we are to read *life* rather than romance, there is something in her look and manner that bespeak unwonted capacity to feel and therefore to suffer. Rue, our "reading" is assisted by various other data of conclusion; but so our interpretation is not a fault it does not matter. We are assured that this buoyancy of temperament belongs but to the surface of her character. Her manner hath its shiftings, and through these we catch occasional glimpses of an under current that is flowing strongly and deeply beneath it. We learn that her life has been spent in a singularly rigid seclusion; and the tendency to sentiment, to which such seclusion is calculated to give rise, has been probably overruled by complexional elasticity. But with this there was a tendency to strong feeling—an undue ardor of character that her position was also calculated to foster. And it has been fostered to enthusiasm. The bias of her mind, which might or might not (for it is difficult sometimes to determine between original bent and that of early circumstances) have been slightly imaginative, has been borne out to excess. She knows nothing of the world—its wearing cares or oppressive responsibilities. Her companionship has been with books, birds, and flowers. Among the latter she has dissipated the over-flowings of her joyous nature. From the former she has gathered aliment for her ever busy and vagrant thought, and learned to create images, upon which, from the want of tangible purpose, she has poured out the fervors of her character. Over these has she thought and pondered till they have become realities—bright—glittering—Eden-like. The sun-shine of her spirit has imparted to them its own glow, and they have not a shade of somber coloring. The *west* has been to her a land of romance. She has dreamed, not of its privations, its difficulties, its rugged hard-ships, its want of the refinements and elegances of life, but of its primeval forests, its mighty rivers, its broad and green savannas, its summer skies, streamed over with gold and crimson—all of the wild, the imposing, the gorgeous and the picturesque. What to her have been the dangers and disasters of the journey hither? What marvel they have left no trace upon her brow, now that they are past! Life is before her, new, fresh, untried; and through the mist of uncertainty that lies upon it her fancy shapes our forms of strange and surpassing beauty. Ah! Pity for the dreamer! Yet it is high time she awaken. That undisciplined heart is yet to have its *schooling*. Her morning is lapsing fast. Let her wake to the lessons that her immortal nature needeth.

HISTORY OF "OUR VILLAGE," PART II

The panorama of our wilderness village life melted from our view with our last month's sketch. Yet, as memory has again brought it before us under some of its subsequent phases, we will glance at it once again. Some few years from the date last referred to, its appearance and character were greatly changed. A business-like aspect had taken the place of its picturesque wildness, and the early simplicity of its inhabitants had become lost in the avidity of speculation, and the bustle of incipient enterprise. Houses of brick and frame had risen upon the side of the low-roofed cabin, and wild grass and flowers no longer sprang up under the foot upon the streets they occupied. It has become a shire-town, and a court-house and jail rising from its center afforded gloomy evidence that crime was already abroad even in our forest land. The community that had seemed like a single family, so closely drawn were the social ties that united it, had, in its extension, lost much of that pleasant relative character. The petty and absurd distinctions of life had crept in to poison the pure currents of friendship and feeling that of erst flowed through it like sweet and healthful waters; and the uniformity of appearance and condition among its members, that had characterized it as a whole, was gone. The artisan and laborer were met upon their paths by those whose dress, air, and manner betokened pretension and conscious superiority. There were now among them the merchant, the lawyer, the professor, the speculator, and the officers of *the bank*, whose establishment in our village had been matter of no measured gratulation, and which had given it present impulse as the meed, some thought, of prospective ruin. But among these might have been marked faces of far deeper anxiety than any we had seen at the earlier date of our history. There were now among them *men* around whom unsuccessful speculation or enterprise had drawn the heavy and iron chain of debt. We recollect, at a particular season, when one of those re-actions which always follow great excitement in business without a correspondent support, had taken place, having met with a half a dozen of those who were in legal durance— prisoners for debt—having the bounds of the corporation assigned them as the limits of their freedom. From the general want of wealth among the citizens, and the sparseness of the population in the country immediately surrounding them, there was little to justify the emprise into which many adventurous spirits, with narrow capitals, were led by the rapid growth of the place itself. Failure on every hand was the inevitable result. How strongly did the appearance of these men, as with listless and objectless step they now strolled around the environs of the village, contrast with that of the humble and unambitious laborer who went whistling past them. His dress might have been something poorer, but his step and countenance were cheerful—their look was care-worn, anxious, harassed. They had failed in schemes into which they had thrown their dearest aspirations—his wishes were bounded by the avails of each day's labor; for this was sufficient for the wants of his family, and beyond such supply he had no vain dreams.

There is one of this latter class now fresh in our memory, whom, at the time we speak of, we were led especially to notice, from having accidentally become interested in his family. They were recent emigrants from an eastern state, and were of that class of respectability which habits of industry and of decent pride create among the most indigent. The mother was a pattern of domestic gentleness and quiet order, and her children, as we saw them daily passing and re-passing to our village school, attracted our attention, from the uniform and exceeding neatness of their humble garb. We are now led to speak of them from their association, in our memory, with a portion of our village history, to which we have already alluded—the prevalence of a pestilence that swept off, as with a besom, nearly a fourth of the population. It was in this family it commenced. Just without the environs of the village and under the shelter of one of the hills embosoming it, was a small cabin, which was their home. Would our reader stroll with us to the field of tall grass that is now waving over the spot in the richness of deep summer, we could point out the very spot; for the blackened hearth-stones around which that father gathered his family at evening might still be found. There we were suddenly summoned to the burial of our neighbor, even before we knew that sickness had entered the dwelling. That exemplary wife, that tender mother was dead! For two or three days we had noticed that the father passed not, as was his wont, to his labor, nor the little ones to their school; and while we yet mused what was the cause the summons came. A fever of three days had for ever darkened that home of peace. The two eldest children lay scorching with the same malignant disease, and all unconscious that the still and shrouded form which lay stretched near them was all that was left of her upon whom, in their childish dependence, and amid the ravings of frenzy, they were momently calling. The father stood by them as one paralyzed, turning only from their convulsed faces to look upon that of his dead wife, now, alas! *Fixed* in its marble tranquility, and utterly incapable of the least effort. Truly was it a scene of woe. And why was the funeral so scantily attended? Not from the humbled position of the departed; for changed somewhat though our villagers might be, they were still, as a community, feeling alive to the claims of suffering humanity. But *they* were absent whom we have been wont to see especially in the house of mourning. We inquired the cause. Sickness was in *their* families also. What could it mean? It was yet but the close of summer; and though autumnal fevers were common to the newer settlements of the west, we looked not for them thus early. The fever, too, was of a more malignant character than we had formerly experienced. But whatever the cause, whether the result of natural laws, or the immediate visitation of a chastening God, its present threatenings were fearful. It soon became general throughout the village, and the progress of the disease from that hour gradually accelerated, till at last every house in the village had its sufferer, or rather sufferers; for in many cases whole families were stricken down almost simultaneously, and the instance was rare of a *single* victim from a household. The friendly sympathies—the neighborly attentions which in seasons of individual suffering are so readily extended in all small communities, soon ceased to soften the scene of affliction. One by one, they who visited the early sufferers ceased their visits, for they themselves became of the smitten, or their cares were engrossed by the sufferers of their household; and at last every house was an isolated dwelling—communication had ceased among us!

The disease manifested itself under various aspects. In some instances the victim survived but in others the struggle of life and death was long protracted. Some, after lingering for weeks, recovered—others, after partial amendment, were at last taken off by sudden and deadly relapse. The bereaved children, of whom we have spoken, lay long and dangerously ill, but the disease was finally overcome. They were slowly recovering, and the father was driven forth, by the necessities of his family, once more to labor. We can never forget a little scene which we witnessed near that dwelling. We had been confined to the pestilential breath of sick and dying chambers till we were literally gasping for fresh air. We escaped for a brief space from our duties—we took a path that led to the hills, and hurried along it as if our speed would enable us to outstrip the unwelcome reflections that accompanied us. We approached a ravine where a summer streamlet was tumbling in a delicious coolness over the rocks, when a childish, but faint and hollow cry, lifted up in continued wailing sounds, struck our ear. A moment after, a small figure appeared upon the verge of the ravine, from which she seemed to have risen, and ran feebly, but with an action of the extremest excitement, toward us. It was one of the children we have mentioned—a little girl of some eleven years old; but we could not have recognized her, had we not been aware of her condition. Had she risen from the grave, her appearance could scarcely have been more unearthly. They only who have witnessed the ghastliest ravages of disease upon human lineaments, can form any conception of that deadly, though childish face, or spectral figure. Her eyes were wild and sunken, her lips and cheek of an ashen paleness. Her hair, which was singularly long and dark, but now all matted and tangled, hung loosely around her shoulders; and her little arms, yellow and emaciated, were thrown up with an expression of passionate anguish, the more impressive that it was unnatural to one of her years. We sprang forward to meet her.

"Fanny! Dear child, what is the matter?" "O my sister is crazy!—she will kill herself—she has flung herself down on the rocks in the ravine, and I can't get her away." We ran down the bank that descended to the place. The little girl, the younger of the two who had been ill, had been for some days apparently convalescent, so that her father, as has been remarked, had under the pressure of strong need ventured to leave her for the day to the observance of the elder one, the latter being so far recovered as to sit by her bed. But a sudden relapse brought on a paroxysm of the wildest frenzy, which no effort of the poor feeble sister could soothe. The fever gave the child strength; and springing from her burning pillow, she bounded up the ravine, at whose opening the cabin stood, till she reached a spot where the stream, that was nearly hidden below, gushed over the rocks. And there she now lay among them, with her cheek pressed upon their moss—her feet, cut and bleeding with their points, in the stream—her little chest heaving with the hot breath of the disease, and laughing wildly, as we approached her, with the unnatural, but exulting excitement of the hurried powers of life. We lifted her, not without a struggle, in our arms, and carried her back to the cabin. Alas! There was no one there to whose care we could commit her. The elder sister was utterly exhausted, and sunk, like one dying, on the foot of the pallet, where we laid the other. A babe, not two years old, with its little face stained with the tears that had dried upon it, lay asleep on the threshold. Two others near it, of three and five years, with a look of stolid patience, were eating a crust of coarse bread. Could the daughters of luxury have looked upon the scene! We turned back from it to the chambers of sorrow we had left. Our heart had gathered no refreshing. Alas! There was no place for us to turn where there was not woe!

Just without the edge of the village there was a spot yet covered with forest trees, that was marked by some indications of the town boundary. A narrow path led back from it to a cabin, with a small opening, in the edge of the wood. There was something about this dwelling, humble though it was, that contrasted pleasantly with the forest scenery around it. A garden, into which a multitude of flowering shrubs had found their way, was kept with great neatness, while a honey suckle had clambered to the low eaves of the building, and sent at evening its rich cloud of odors out upon the air around it. From this cottage, we saw for several successive days, a young woman walking with a hurried, though evidently feeble step, to the spot we have mentioned; and there was she met by a person whom we had noticed for some months preceding with an especial interest. He was one of those whom the duress of debt limited to the bounds of the village, and the *line* upon which he was met by his wife—for in that relation they stood—was one that he might not pass. We had regarded his position with more than ordinary concern, from having learned that he had become thus enthralled, not by debts personally incurred, but in a matter of surety for another, in whom he had too confidingly trusted. We had an interest in him, too, of an earlier date. These were the young emigrants whom we brought before our readers in another number, and the fears we then expressed for them had been all too truly realized. Nor had the angel of the pestilence now passed their dwelling by. That wife's hurried step, so at variance with the languor of her countenance, had its meaning. She *would* come herself to meet her husband; but she might not linger from the bed-side of her suffering children!

Ah! How fully had our predictions been verified of that once light heart. How greatly had a few years changed her appearance. It was not merely that present affliction had touched it with sadness—a deeper work had been wrought upon it than that of the mere anguish of the hour. The whole character of the countenance was changed. The whole aspect was sunken and heavy and toil-worn. The play of hope and feeling seemed to have passed from it—not by sudden woe, from which the elastic spirit might hereafter spring to its former bias, but from the long and surely effacing wear of bitter discipline. That joyous face! So full of freshness—of hope—of rich expectancy—of glad enthusiasm—of ardent thought! There is no trace left there of the existence of aught of these. Alas for life! How do its rugged influences mold and warp the early character. Yet are they, doubtless, necessary to fit the heart for the operation of that sublime and holy influence, whose breathings upon the soul are of eternal peace—as the fire which seems to scathe the fresh green soil, and the plough-share that tears up its bosom, prepares it for precious seed, and must prelude the blessed dew and sunshine that call forth the germ and ripen the fruit to maturity. Happy, most happy was it for her of whom we speak, if the extinction of her earthly dreams—the utter falling out of the bright visions—the gorgeous hallucinations of her early years, left her heart in its deep desolateness at last accessible to the hopes that are of another world. But we might not at that time withhold from her our compassion, for the "iron that had entered her soul" pierced it harshly. She was passing an ordeal of no common endurance. Even the husband, whose usually unaltered countenance and changeless manner had evidenced the truth of our early impression of his stronger nature, asked for his children, as morning and evening the poor mother came to tell him of their state, in a voice that had lost something of its firmness; and when his wife, with a step faltering with weakness, at last turned back to their home of suffering, he looked after her with an expression (though not a muscle moved) that bespoke anguish. But these interviews of sorrow were interrupted.

There was a morning when the wife came not, and the husband paced that spot of ground with a look he had never before worn. But another messenger at last came. His *children were thought to be dying*, and something further was yet added. What was that line of legal restriction now? The trammels of the law were broken asunder as flax and the father strode over the disregarded boundary with a step that brought him as it were with a single stride to his dwelling. Did his wife meet him at the door? Or at the bed-side of his children? No! She was lying in the same room; but she was unconscious of their state, or of her husband's presence. She was raving in the wildest delirium of the fever—she was unconscious even of the existence of her own new born baby that lay, a thing of scarce perceptible life, beside her.

But why linger over a single scene? Suffering and death were all around us. Within view of the window where we are penning this most inadequate sketch, is a building that was then our village hotel. In every chamber of that building, through the long watches of the night, burnt the flickering taper that betokened the sufferer within. How fearful—how sad was the passing of some of those spirits. Many of them were young men whom the wide arena of western enterprise had lured from the parental home; and no familiar voice, no kindred face now met their wistful gaze or ear when dying. Among them we recollect a young man of that abiding interest of character which genius and talent in youth especially create. He was a member of the bar, and had just entered a career of singular promise and high distinction. He was betrothed to a lovely girl of congenial mind and station, and envy might have looked with a baleful eye upon the morning of brightness that seemed opening before them. But death had marked him for other than the bridal chamber. He was ill but two days. Even she "who was all the world to him" had not been called to his pillow when the summons came. At the hour of midnight he sprung suddenly from his bed, and stood strong and erect upon the floor, calling upon his *Maker* in a loud voice of unimaginable agony. His watcher took him by the arm—a change came over his features. He was laid back upon his bed without resistance—the conflict was over—the form of youth and beauty and pride was a thing of dust.

In the same row of buildings there was one that, though a private dwelling, had always been open (for at that time we had no public sanctuary) to the worshipers of our faith. There was a small people among us professing Christ, and here had their meetings been most generally held; for it was the dwelling of *one*, of whom we have formerly spoken—him whose first inquiry as he touched our shore had been, hath the Lord a people here. How often had we knelt under that roof as that devoted follower of our Lord poured forth his earnest soul in prayer for the extension of that small and most humble Church. But *whom the Lord loveth he* chasteneth—his hour of earthly trial had come. He had been eminently prospered—he had acquired wealth, and his large and interesting family had grown up around him amid the comforts and privileges of abundance. But of all he possessed, nothing now availed him, but his trust in God. Day after day a small funeral group emerges from that door. Three lovely daughters in the prime of womanhood, and these followed by a brother in the flush and spring-time of youth, are borne, one after another, to our silent city.

But who was there to take note of the mourner? The horrors of the pestilence were hourly deepening. The mourners themselves had to fulfill the rites of the dead. Mothers laid out their children, and children their parents. The wife wrought her husband's shroud, and the husband himself laid the form that had slept upon his bosom in her coffin. Yet were there woes bitterer, perhaps in the endurance, than even these; though, except by those who have felt the *might of need,* its agonies may not be understood. In our devoted village there were some dying of want! Many a family among us were dependent for the supply of their immediate necessities upon the daily labor of their head, and the blow which deprived them of this resource left them utterly destitute. There were children who lifted up their little hands, at the bed-side of their parents, vainly for bread; and parents who watched over their families, night after night, without the sustenance necessary to support them under their painful vigils. In many instances, too, where the disease itself yielded to medical skill, or the mastery of nature, (I should rather, perhaps, have said, where a mightier than death staid *his* power,) the convalescent sufferer awoke from the torpor or madness of fever, to experience the consciousness of the keen gnawings of protracted and terrible want.

But amid these scenes of heart-rendering trial, we became yet more sadly schooled in the appalling philosophy of human depravity. We had read that in those fearful visitations of the plague, which almost depopulated the thronged cities of the older world, at a season when it would seem that madness itself must have paused before the dreadful chastisements of Him who had "loosed the seals of the pestilence," there were those who abandoned themselves to every excess of licentiousness and mirth. Yet had our utmost credulity accorded but slow belief to the proof such fact afforded of the possible grossness of that nature which in its better attributes is "allied to angels." But even in our small and simple village, and amid scenes that, however deeply and darkly colored, necessarily afforded but slight parallel to the horrors of those cities of the plague; yet were we taught, from what we did witness, a most fearful lore. We learned how revoltingly callous the human soul *might* become to the deep rebukings of an offended God, and amid the most terrible manifestations of his chastening power. In the later stages of the disease, the awful sense of the calamitous visitation, which had for a time prevailed, gave gradual place to a spirit of strange and even profane recklessness. They who ministered to the sick—not from kindred claims, or those of duty, but from the hope of reward, indulged in frequent and unhallowed excesses, and the light jest and the heartless remark were heard in the very chambers of death. "Are you seeking some one to lay you out"—"Are you going to bespeak your coffin?" Such were the remarks which, in allusion to the ghastliness of their appearance, were addressed to those, who, for the first time, went forth from their chambers of suffering. One was borne to his grave by bearers who staggered—not under the weight of their burden, but with the unholy drought they had swallowed ere they "took up their mortal load." Nor did they finish their task! Upon the verge of the yet unfilled grave, into which—not without many an awkward effort—they had at last lowered the unchiding dead, they poured off the remainder of the flask they had brought with them to cheer their labors. And then, unable to fling their kindred dust upon the poor remains, they left them to the dews of night that were already falling, and returned to the village in the revolting merriment of inebriate carousal.

But let me be just. If, amid the revealings of nature, to which a season so calculated to destroy conventional restraints necessarily led, there was many a trait from which memory recoils, there were also those upon which it dwells with delight. Many an instance was there of active benevolence—of unguerdoned vigils—of generous self-abandonment—and of the faithfulness of friendship unto death. Though the common offices of neighborly kindness, as has been remarked, were for a season suspended, yet it was but for a season. The deep sufferings of want and destitution that followed, were only unheeded where, for the time, they were unknown. There were those who testified their faith in our Lord, by ministering to the needy, and those who were hungered. Then, too, did we witness the fulfillment of the promise of him who has said, "Leave thy fatherless children to me." From several large families in circumstances of absolute penury, both parents were swept as by a single stroke. Yet were not these orphans in a single instance left unprovided for? A way was opened out for them. Does the unbeliever regard it as a circumstance of change?—those numerous little ones whose helplessness drew heavily, even upon the now sealed fountain of paternal love—without claims of kindred—without those attractions which, in the home of wealth; childhood deserves from the fostering hand of care and culture, in a world essentially cold and selfish and full of cares; yet was a way opened for their support—not the stinted and humbling allowance of county charity, but for their being reared with kindness, with watchfulness, and with respectability. To the feeling reader, who, from an interest in all the children of sorrow, may wish to hear something further of those we have individualized, we would add, that *the little girls of the ravine* (if that be not a term too much savoring the phraseology of fiction,) were among those *doubly* bereaved orphans. The tender father who had seemed so illy pared from his motherless little ones, for the labor necessary to procure them bread, was in a few weeks after the scene alluded to, called to leave them, to return no more. His labor and his paternal cares alike ceased, and he slept by *her* side, whom he had so deeply deplored. The stricken flock was scattered, yet were they all provided with homes of comfort and decency. That of the elder of the little girls was *more*. It was a home of affluence— of careful instruction—of estimable example—of sheltering tenderness, and enduring and steadfast affection. But we may individualize no further. Our village history has been insensibly drawn out far beyond our purpose. Yet have we *later* scenes to depict. We may not pass over them, though it is here we feel how all-inadequate is our pencil.

If there are any among our readers, to whom the cup of suffering has been sanctified to the healing of their soul's deepest malady, they will, perchance, have mentally inquired ere this, whether this season of unwonted calamity were followed by no general awakening to the interests of that world, where sorrow and death are not. And truly, to the dim eye of reason, the obduracy of the nature that could resist the deep rebuke of the commissioned pestilence, would seem unfathomable. But we recognize in this, the overruling delay of that mysterious, but questionless wisdom, which still deadened the ear of the oppressor of Israel, to the deep cry that went up from his smitten land. Not through the ministry of gloom and terror, though sent upon us as tokens of his chastening power—not in the season of dread excitement and fainting dismay, was it the will of Jehovah to make himself clearly revealed to us. In the season of subsequent prosperity, in the protracted hour of calm and sunshine, in the supineness of gay security, but in the possession of all its functions, was the secret soul at last shaken by the small still voice, that bespoke the awful presence of Him, who can alone behold its depths. And then might the stranger in *our village*, have stood still and beheld the salvation of the Lord. Incomprehensible and unutterable power of redeeming love! How was it manifested in its utmost fullness, to the needy dwellers of our at last awakened village! There, where instead of prayer, the frequent strain of pleasure came upon the ear—where the things of time seemed the sole object of general desire, and the deep poison of infidelity was infused through many a heart—there at last were heard the loud wrestlings of the men of God, agonizing for a people suddenly aghast with the sense of sin, and moved like waves in a tempest, by the power of the Spirit. For many days, the stranger among us would have vainly sought for a public door open to his entrance, save those of the sanctuary, which had been but recently erected. The stores and shops were all shut. Not a stroke of the anvil or hammer was heard. Not a sound from the haunts of traffic or of pleasure. Not a voice even in the street, save at those hours when its eager throngs were pressing to the house of the Lord. It was a long continuous Sabbath. Day after day came and went, and still that protracted assembling for worship was prolonged. On the early air of morning, at the hour of noon, amid the stillness of evening, the sound of prayer and praise, the cry of the suppliant, and the strong assured voice of faith and trust went up from that temple. And yet the interest deepens! They who have expostulated from the pulpit, and ministered at the altar, have become exhausted. They cry for help. From the Churches of a neighboring city their mightiest intellect, their strongest laborers are summoned. They come to assist in the harvest. Our very temple seems shaken with their power. The aisle no longer affords a foot of space. It is filled with those who make haste to the altar. They are of the old or the middle-aged—of the poor, the humble, the stricken, and the sorrowful—yes! Yes! And of the low, and ignorant, the condemned, the vile, and the debased; for all these have been *bought with a price*, and they are now called that their names may be enrolled on the book of ransom; but with these are the young, the gay, the distinguished, the wealthy, the talented, and the proud. All are alike thronging to the foot of the altar, and prostrating themselves in the dust, as mourners for the sins that have crucified their Lord.

Within the precincts of the village, there is a small settlement of foreigners, from the land of the Alps and the vine. They brought with them the customs, the gaieties, and the religion of their forefathers. They have been strangers to the peculiar doctrines of our fervid and simple faith. National preferences and habitudes have kept them measurably isolated and apart from those around them. But they, too, are among the crowd. In more than one *foreign* accent, we hear the inquiry, "Which is the way to Jesus." Their way is led by one whom we mark with peculiar interest. It is one whom we have long known. She has been the daughter of sorrow. United after a long betrothal, to one worthy of all her woman's trust—a native of her own still beloved country, young, gifted, amiable, and chivalric—she was early widowed by a stroke of terrible bereavement. Mid a festal hour, the discharge of a field-piece at an unguarded moment, closed forever the career that had opened so brightly, and left the young and thrice happy wife, a blighted and stricken being.

But upon that face, where the seal of hopeless sorrow has been so long set, there is a new expression. A deeper than earthly interest has been stirred in her soul. Holier and stronger affections than those subject to death, are awakening in her heart a peace that shall give a new coloring to the whole sad world around her, and is already settling on her pale brow. More than one of her own country are kneeling beside her—the fetters of early prejudice are dissolved. The *witness* in their hearts attests the simplicity and lowliness of the religion of Jesus. The triumph of the little church, whose corner-stone was so many years since laid in our wilderness village, is at last arrived. The prayers that went up for it in that lowly cabin, where its first converts knelt, have been finally heard. Why do they cease to press to the altar? Why is the call of initiation at last disregarded? The fold is gathered in—the warfare is accomplished. In all our village, there is scarcely one who has not named the name of Jesus. Peace, be still, to all! and the steadfast faith that brightens to the perfect day. Within our view, and beautiful in the quiet moonlight, that is now flooding through our window, rises the simple, but neat church where, but a few seasons since, we beheld them rejoicing with that exceeding joy for which earth has no language. We gaze upon the now silent and empty temple, and the whole scene is again before us. We seem again to hear the glad hymn of redeeming love rising in the rich swell of a hundred voices, and floating away to the distant heaven. But it is only the voiceless hymn of the stars, as they wheel on their eternal round, that is now upon the night. The earth is at rest and we may no longer indulge in retrospect of the past.

A FAMILY HISTORY

It is not so easy a matter to write a story as one would think. We intended to give our readers something absolutely transcendental—a tale for the Journal!—for the thrice three thousand readers, who we trust are impatiently awaiting its advent. The young, the sentimental, the imaginative, the—why, what a tale it should be! And forthwith we summoned the spirits and ministers of romance to our aid, and made sundry demonstrations of marvelous beginnings. After all, we were but reminded of a bright-haired boy of some two years old, whom we once saw elevated upon the top of an immense block. He had managed to surmount it by the help of an inclined plane attached thereto, but he made a show of springing from it by a Sam Patch leap. There he stood upon its verge— one of those chubby, rosy forms that want nothing of the cherub but the wings, swinging his round arms in most gymnastic style, and calling out "hurra! hurra!" at the top of his lungs, lifting his eye too occasionally as he shook back the golden curls that shaded it, with a sidewise glance and a disdainful smile struggling about his lips to see if attention was directed to his feat. At last, in a very quiet manner he settled himself down upon the block and slid from it to the ground by the plane aforesaid. Just so, after all the demonstrations in our case, did *we* finally slide down from the topling height of our intent, relinquishing the purpose of leaping up into the empyrean of romance, as wisely, as quietly and as smilingly as our baby hero did that of leaping *down*.

An old lady opportunely at our elbow afforded us far safer resource; and turning to her with our very blandest smile, we begged she would furnish us with some downright narrative:—some affair growing out of the just common affection and minor currents that are flowing on always and everywhere.

"Let it be Western, however," we added; "we go in distinctly for consumption of home material." The old lady removed her spectacles, and lifting her eyes from her work, directed them somewhat musingly to an old-looking house across the street. You who are going to read our story, look at it also. Here I mean, not a hundred paces from the center of our queen and queenly city: (don't be fancying that a Western story must take you into the vast depths of some primeval forest). In that range of handsome and fashionable looking houses, don't you see one bearing the impress of time? not the moss and mould of another century—it is but a touch, and we can't exactly define it. "Would that it were" thought we, as our eye followed that of the old lady; "would now that it were a bona fide ruin, all aged and green, all eloquent of antiquity, but it was simply an old looking house."

"Why," said the old lady—(she was a grave but kind-hearted matron somewhat in keeping with the house itself, being rather out of date than in decay, and like many dwellings we have seen of better aspect inside than out; the memories and feelings that had been gathered by years of intellectual thrift and benevolent observance being still in good repair)—"why there," she said, "in that very house there lived, some thirty years since, a family by the name of Ellesly: emigrants from New England whose history had a good deal in it that was interesting."

"Ellesly," we repeated, "did they afterwards remove to one of our newer states, and had they a son, Ned Ellesly, as he was called, who was somewhat distinguished in its legislative councils as well as at the bar?"

"They had. You know them, then, it seems and are probably familiar with the circumstances to which I allude?"

"I knew a part of the family and something of their later history sufficient to feel an interest in the whole. Pray tell me all you know of them. From New England you say?—the land of classic shades and ultra observances. Did you know them there?"

"Yes, I was a distant relation of theirs, and in the days of my early girlhood (that season of vivid and ineffaceable impressions) was a frequent visitor at their house; yet my recollection of them is rather a picture left on my memory than a detail of facts. Mr. Ellesly was a proud man, and I remember that at that time I had a little shrinking from him, always turning with a sense of relief from his lofty figure and aristocratic expression of countenance (handsome though it was) to the soft and placid features of Mrs. Ellesly. The latter had great refinement of manner, and gentleness of nature, but her character, further than her affections and sympathies gave it tone, and was wholly negative. Upon those who loved her, and whom she understood, she poured out a whole world of tenderness, but these engrossed the entire wealth of her feelings—though this was rather the effect of her position than of the want of more expansive capabilities of character. They who have a world of flowers growing around their feet rarely think of the *duty* of planting them in the yet barren places.

Mrs. Ellesly had two children, a son and a daughter of nine and seven years, who might well fill any mother's heart. The little Isabel was one of those dark-eyed, sylph-like children that make you think so of poetry and all that; and Edward—the Edward of whom you spoke, with a face of great beauty and the air and bearing of a young autocrat—had a mind and manner precociously ripened by all the appliances of hot-bed stimulants. But with the recollection of his bright face at that period there always came upon me for years after the remembrance of one widely different under the same roof. It was that of a boy some year or two older. I saw him in the family only at one of my visits, and he certainly added little to its interest, and yet somehow I could never forget him. Even now I can almost fancy him before me. Poor fellow! with his always averted and stupid face—seeming amid all the interests of a gay household to have no more part or portion in them than if he had been of a different order of being; and yet was he Mr. Ellesly's eldest son—the child of a former marriage. Some circumstances connected with this boy will perhaps give you a better idea of the family as I first knew them, than mere description. At the time I speak of, he had been but a few weeks an inmate there, having been from his birth under the care of a natural aunt in very humble life. Mr. Ellesly, though constitutionally proud and with a fastidiousness of taste and a devotion to talent that separated him from the vulgar even more widely than his pride, had yet married out of his caste. He never alluded to his first union; and it is probable that he soon awoke from the dream of passion into which at a very early age he had been lulled by the extreme beauty of the young girl he married. But his fetters were also early loosened. *Her* life passed with the gift of life to her child. She survived that event only long enough to obtain a promise from her husband to whom at such an hour her appeal could not have been vainly made that her babe should be left to the care of her sister till it was ten years old. This sister was settled, as I have before remarked, in very humble life, but was without children. She was many years older than Mrs. Ellesly, had the care of the latter in her own orphan infancy, and the dying mother knew from the tenderness with which *she* had been watched over, that her child would be tenderly cared for. But George, as he was called, had now reached the age at which he was to be reclaimed and had been consequently brought home. Most unfortunately he seemed to have inherited nothing of his mother's beauty; still less, if less could be, of the patrician elegance and high-bred manner of his father. He was large of his age—shy, awkward, and rustic to uncouthness; and the pride of Mr. Ellesly was hurt whenever the child met his eye. The contrast afforded to his other children could but be painful, and it was perhaps impossible that he should regard them all with the same feelings. Edward, with all his acquirements, had a tameless flow of busy glee that sent him through the house like some leaping stream, all as sparkling and gladdening. But George moped or skulked through it like some conscious delinquent—never lifting his eye to meet yours—never answering when spoken to, but the monosyllabic *yes* or *no*, from which he could not escape, and meeting the stern reprehensions of his father for his perpetual awkwardness with an aspect of stolid immobility. And yet I have since remembered something in its expression that, to a kinder and more experienced eye than was mine at that time, would have bespoken the bitter swelling of a young heart unable to plead its own cause, rather than sulkiness and stupidity. But whatever wrought in the depths of that childish heart, there was nothing about him to wake an interest in its study. He put forth no claims upon any one's sympathy or tenderness; no one dreamed that he ever felt. Mrs. Ellesly's manner towards him was always gentle: she could not have been otherwise towards a wilful offender, but even the quiet smile, which was all the notice she bestowed, upon his blunders, evinced indifference. She would hardly have known how to win her way to his feelings, had she deemed him possessed of any; as it was, she thought not of the effort. Meanwhile, the poor boy was subjected to contumelies of which she was wholly unaware. Some juvenile relatives of Mrs. Ellesly were at that time her visitants. Children are not exactly the angels poets and painters choose to make them. The veriest little elf that can fashion a jeer takes upon himself all the insolence of superior advantage in whatever shape it exists. Edward's fashionable cousins were not slow to discover in the country-bred boy a fit subject for malicious merriment. Even the young Edward, though possessing a more generous nature, gradually caught the tone. His own high breeding gave a keen sense of George's deficiencies. He felt that he was gawky and uncomely, and he thought him ungracious and unloving. There had been nothing awakened in Edward's heart of better feeling toward his unlucky brother to counteract his own love of mischief. George had a bird, for which his engrossing care, had we thought it worth our while to notice such manifestations, would have given us some clue to the affectionate susceptibility of his young nature. Claiming no notice for his favorite, or rather shunning it from others, he would steal away to its cage in silence, and unless bidden from it, remain perhaps for hours, intently watching its movements and apparently regardless of every other living thing.

"I would not have a bird that was too stupid to sing, George," said Edward one day as the former stood feeding its little prisoner; "stand away," he continued, pushing him aside, and taking the bird from the cage in no very tender manner. "Come, George I'll give it to the cat, and Pa shall get you a canary."

"Don't take it from the cage, Edward," said George anxiously and even earnestly. It was the first time I had heard him speak so much: "You'll let it go, and something will happen to it."

"I'd be glad if there would," said Edward; "I'm tired of seeing you fuss with it—and such a splendid cage too! I wonder Pa let you bring it here; Lydia shall take it to the kitchen for kindlingwood."

"I heard your Ma say," said I, touched to something like interest for the aggrieved boy, "that she must get a new cage for George's bird."

"I don't want another cage!" exclaimed George; "I like this best; aunt Mary got uncle to make this for me himself, and I won't have another. But you'll kill the bird, Edward, handling it in that way! give it to me, I say!" continued he anxiously, at the same time approaching his brother, and striving vainly to take it from him.

"You'll wait till I'm ready to give it to you, won't you? If you *are* bigger than I am, Mr. George, you'll not get it till I'm done with it;" and the young tormentor sprang into a chair and held the bird as high as he could reach. George still pressed upon him, and in the eagerness of resistance, Edward lost his balance and fell. His grasp upon the bird had been unconsciously tightened. "You've killed it," cried George, "I knew you would." Edward loosened and looked at the bird with some anxiety. It gasped as if dying. George took it from him, for he no longer resisted, with a look of anguish. It gasped once more and then lay motionless in his hand. It *was* dead! Edward thought it expedient to be badly hurt with his fall.

"What is the matter," inquired Mr. Ellesly, who happened that moment to enter. "What ails you, Edward?" Our young visitants explained.

George had knocked him out of a chair because he had taken his bird a minute, and killed the bird itself, getting it away from him. Mr. Ellesly looked at his first-born with an expression bitterer than anger—it was of dislike, of distaste, almost to loathing.

"Your incorrigible boobyishness hardly needs the act of ill nature, sir." His tone was severer than his words. Then turning to Edward with a look wholly changed, he drew him fondly away, as if unwilling to trust himself to say more.

Some hours afterwards I passed George sitting upon the hall steps with his dead bird upon his lap. His eyes were yet riveted upon the little stiffened thing, and the tears were coursing silently, but in large drops, down his face. My heart smote me for not having defended him—"Never mind your bird, George," said I, touched at last to even painful compassion. "I'll tell your father that you were not to blame, and he will get you another."

"I don't want another," said George, "I liked this because it liked me and always hopped to meet me when I came towards it; and when they brought me here it was all they'd let me keep, and now I han't nothing in the wide world to care for."

"Well George, I am very, very sorry for you. I wish I could so something to give you comfort. If there is anything you want—"

"I don't want nothing now," said the child sobbing, "but to go to Aunt Mary's once more."

"Why don't you ask leave to go then, George?"

"Oh because—because whenever I talk of Aunt Mary, Edward and his cousins laugh, and when they see any body that looks poor and mean, they always ask if that is not some other of George's relations."

I felt that I ought to turn informer, but the duty was an unpleasant one, and I strove to find some commutation of it. "Well, George, I will ask for you; you shall go to see Aunt Mary."

Impatient to fulfill my promise, I took my time to ask, indiscreetly, not even waiting till the bird scene—which I had not yet the moral courage to explain to Mr. Ellesly—was forgotten; nay, still worse, at the moment of a fresh displeasure. I did not see Mr. Ellesly till the evening when I met him in a stroll I had taken with the other children and in which for the first time, I had drawn George along with us. But at the moment of meeting with him, George had started from our path to speak with a coarsely dressed man laboring by the wayside. It was his mother's brother, and Mr. Ellesly's countenance darkened. A little discretion would have taught me better than to speak at that moment of all others; but an impulsive girl of fifteen is a bad diplomatist.—George's glad face, glad for the first time that I had seen it as he met the affectionate greeting of his uncle, reminded me of my morning's promise, and I proffered my petition at once. Mr. Ellesly gave a stern and decided refusal, and he added to George, in a low and bitter voice, as we now turned homeward, that the society of the Rawsons (that was his mother's name) was not particularly calculated to improve his manners.

Some days after this, Mrs. Ellesly deputed me upon an errand of charity a little way from the city, and once more I called upon George to accompany me. I had noticed since my ill-timed petition that he was more moping than usual. His cheek had become sallow, his step more heavy. He would sit for hours upon the door steps with his eyes fixed upon the vacant distance. He obeyed my summons, however, and I strove during our walk to draw him into some childish confab. The effort was wholly bootless. A morbid inertness seemed to have taken entire possession of his faculties. Yet I noticed as we reached the outskirts of the city on our return that his languid eye settled on the road that led from it in a certain direction with a kind of troubled interest.

"Ah, George, you want to get out into the country," I said, "and no wonder. Who does not pine for the old shady trees and the mossy brooks when pent up as we are in the hot city." But I was all unheard. A decent but humble looking woman, who seemed to have been on some errand to the town and now to be hastening homeward, was approaching us. George's gaze was fixed upon her with an earnestness that absorbed all other perception, and he at last sprang towards her with a loud cry of joy.—"Aunt Mary, Aunt Mary!" The boy absolutely trembled with excess of delight as he was folded to her bosom. The woman sat down by the roadside and took him in her arms. She kissed his lips, his cheek, his eyes, and then folded him again and again to her with a fondness even of passion. I could almost have cried to see them. No wonder George's little heart had frozen in his removal from the warmth of such a love.

"George! my blessed George! my own dear little boy! but you have got so light; and your eyes that used to be so bright are all dead and sunk in your head."

"Aunt Mary! Oh, Aunt Mary! take me home with you. I can't stay here. Let me go and see dear Uncle once more, and stay with you again, always."

"Dear! dear!" said Aunt Mary, with that pathos of tone and manner which impassioned feeling calls forth from all ranks alike—"That I should hear you ask that and not take you! God knows how dark the house is since they took you away, and your little bed looks like a coffin to me, but your Papa, you know, would not hear of it now, and surely all are kind to you, dear, ain't they George?"

George did not answer.

"To be sure they can't in nature be cross to you, for ain't you your own Papa's son, and your Mamma that is now, don't look like one to be sharp with a dead woman's child?"

"Mrs. Ellesly," said I, for my genuine sympathy got the better of my girlish shyness, and I made myself a party concerned, 'sans cere-monie,' "Mrs. Ellesly is very kind and tender to every one, and Mr. Ellesly must, of course, think much of his son, but George, you know, is almost a stranger with us yet, and 'twill take some time to make him feel quite at home."

"Yes, yes," said Aunt Mary, "that can't be helped, but then I thought they meant to let him come and stay with us now and again, and then he would not take it so hard."

"Let me go with you now, then," repeated George, sobbing.

"Not without leave, dear; I can't take you without their leave, but you go home and ask, George, and I will wait here for you," she contin-ued, glancing at the sun, "if it makes dead night before I get home."

"They won't let me go," said the child bitterly. "They don't mean to let me come any more at all. Father scolded me for stopping by the road to speak to poor old Uncle John." An expression of honest and indignant pride crossed Aunt Mary's face, and she evidently struggled to suppress its rising utterance.

"Ah well, I suppose they'd have you forget your dead Mamma's relations now, and it may be it's all for the best. You are getting older, George, and will have to learn new ways. Good bye, my dear boy," she added in a choked voice, as she tried at last to put him from her. She had obviously striven with her own feelings for the sake of the child. "Good bye, George; you've got such a fine home now and such fine clothes, and they'll make you such a grand scholar."

"I hate my fine clothes," said George, "and they all laugh at me at school, and I'll never learn as much as Edward knows now; and nobody loves me any more at all."

Aunt Mary's tears burst forth afresh, and she wept over him long and bitterly. But the scene had at last to be ended. Aunt Mary had given him her final kiss and turned from him; he was wholly passive. Young as I was, I was certainly to blame that I did not try to make an interest for George in Mrs. Ellesly's feelings by telling her of his griefs. It seems strange to me that in our world of "suffering, sad humanity," there is so little skill in binding up each other's wounds and so little tact in perceiving them, or in appreciating their anguish. Had George had any more palpable woes, had he been beaten or overtasked, or stinted in food, or clothing, or pleasant privilege, my sympathies would have been all in arms. As it was, I deemed his sorrows but things of the moment, and when his tears were dried up, I forgot as I supposed them forgotten, for they were griefs of which I had no real conception. Most children, apart from the large endowment of parental love, are objects of fond interest to all around them, and perhaps there is no sorrow so little understood as the desolateness of a childish but sensitive heart under those disadvantages of person or manner, which shut them out from that common interest.

"Mother," said Edward the morning after our walk, "George is not up yet, and it will soon be school time. I believe he is ill, too, for he is very pale and has eaten nothing these three days."—Mrs. Ellesly rose to go to his room. Her gentle nature was somewhat stirred. She had herself observed for some time that he looked thin and sallow, and she hastened to his pillow. She found him indeed ill. A low nervous fever, superinduced, perhaps equally by habitudes to which he was unaccustomed, and the deep dejection that had settled upon his young nature, had wrought upon him for days, and he was now reduced to almost infantine weakness. Advice was called, and Mrs. Ellesly saw that he had the most careful attendance, but his disease was of too quiet a nature to awaken any special alarm, and for some time it made little interruption to the gaiety of the household. At last, however, as from time to time the family looked in upon the little boy, his appearance roused our fears. We gathered around his bed and looked upon him in sorrow and silence. Even the father stood and gazed upon his disregarded child; nature, though perhaps faintly, was at last stirred in his heart.—Emaciated, motionless and corpse-like, the child lay with closed eyes and a seeming unconsciousness of all around him. His father, for the first time, took the little yellow hand in his; the pulse scarcely moved. "George," said Mr. Ellesly, "my poor George! What can we do for you? I fear you are getting worse." The child did not speak, nor open his eyes, but a single tear forced its way through the closed lid and lay for some time like a drop of dew upon his ashy cheek.—Mr. Ellesly turned away and sighed heavily. "If we could only *rouse* him" said the physician, "if we could stir any chord of interest in the child's feelings." That tear had been unobserved.

For once, I acted with some tact, or rather *impulse*, directed me aright. I pressed my face to George's cheek and whispered, "don't you want to see Aunt Mary?" He opened his eyes and looked with a ghastly earnestness in my face.—"Has she come," he spoke in a voice of even startling loudness. The father turned back to him. "Who, my dear George?" "Aunt Mary," I now unhesitatingly replied, "he wants to see his Aunt Mary."

"All right—he shall see her. Let her be instantly sent for."

Aunt Mary came. He had sunk again into the most deathly quiet; his breath had become momentarily slower, and the beating of the little worn heart was scarcely perceptible. We stood back from his pillow as Aunt Mary approached. Not a soul was there that did not feel the sacredness of her claims. For some minutes she looked upon him in silence, though her tears fell fast and bitterly. At last she stooped to kiss the faded cheek. She whispered his name. The sunken eyes were again opened; he raised himself from the pillow, and flinging his wasted arms convulsively around her neck, exclaimed as before in a hollow but distinct voice, "Aunt Mary! take me home with you."

Every effort was of course made to tranquilize him, but in vain. All promises for the future were unheeded. Soothing entreaties or expostulations were alike unheard. One sole idea had buoyed up his sinking nature again to life and was all that had any power over him. The physician at last determined it. "Let him be indulged," he said, "it may save him, and it is all that can."

The seemingly dying child was lifted from his bed and, supported upon Aunt Mary's arms, was borne to her home. It was a long struggle. Months elapsed before the powers of life, so nearly spent, had fully regained their functions. The child at last recovered, but he never again returned to the paternal roof. The interest excited by his immediate danger passed away with the apprehensions that had awakened it. The demonstrations of tenderness that had been elicited from the family at the crisis of alarm were all insufficient to efface the sense that had been burnt in, as it were, upon the child's heart of the mortifying position he had previously held. The awkward avoidance with which he had hitherto shrunk from their approach, the dull immobility of his aspect and manner in their presence, were now nothing changed at their occasional visits; and if he had been heretofore unattractive, the querulousness and imbecility of sickness were little calculated to render him an object of better regard. The consequence was that all solicitude in reference to him had shortly abated. The indulgence necessarily accorded to his feeble state, with the probable benefit to be derived from the country air, were sufficient reasons, for the time, for permitting him to remain where he was. But it was hardly to be doubted that Mr. Ellesly felt it as a relief when the child that had so deeply mortified his pride and revolted his taste was no longer before him. And even Mrs. Ellesly, occupied with her own children, and the heart-deadening claims of fashionable life, had little thought to spare for one who had neither made nor sought a place in her feelings.

Meanwhile Aunt Mary availed herself of George's protracted feebleness to press a point which, though it embarrassed and even pained the father, found yet a too ready accordance in his secret heart. "Why can't you," she said at one of his cold and far-between visits, at which I had chanced to accompany him, "Why can't you give me little George for good? You'll never raise him if you take him from me again. This is the second time I've got him up from nothing, I may say, for you know that life was hardly in his little bit of clay when I took it from his dying Mamma. Many was the long night I watched over it that sleep did not come to my eyes. It was not just a hired nurse that would have restored him; for though you would have been mighty generous with me, it was not money that would have kept me up through it when for weeks I did not know what rest was; but it was the love I had for him when I saw his Mamma's look that gave me the strength."

"He has nothing of his mother's look," said Mr. Ellesly, abruptly, though in a tone scarcely audible.

"Oh dear heart! yes—not so much, to be sure, as he had then; but if you'd see him smile once, the look is there yet. And his eyes, too, when he looks right into yours like—but, as I was saying, he'll never keep his health long if he gets it ever so well, if you take him from me again. He's just used to our ways now, and he has got a hankering like, for his dead

Mamma's people, for it is natural they should make much of him, being *her* child, who was herself the pet and pride of us all."

The subject to Mr. Ellesly was excoriating.—It stirred up memories that were no small degree humbling and perhaps a little tinctured with remorse. The claim of poor George upon his paternal character was a robe of thorns to him, which these conversations pressed more closely around him. With time, perhaps, he might have rendered those claims less annoying, but it was easier to fling them at once and forever from him. So he at last decided it.

"Truly," he said, "it may be better to give him up altogether. Had he pride, or character, or intellect it would be, probably, doing him a wrong. But stupid as he is, what can I make of him? His tone of mind is decidedly low, and doubtless he will be infinitely happier in the class for which nature seems to have intended him." Thus the matter was philosophically settled.—George was given over to his country tastes and his cottage-home, and Aunt Mary's heart was relieved of a weight that had told upon her strength more than the labors, heavy though they had been, of her maternal cares for the invalid. The little interest that George had created in his father's household was soon utterly forgotten. He had won there no "golden opinions;" he had made himself necessary to no one's happiness, or convenience, or vanity. There is no tenure in memory feasible without some of these bonds. When a year after, Mr. Ellesly removed to the metropolis of another state, they hardly deemed a ceremonious farewell to George incumbent. From that time, I saw nothing of the family till some months after their subsequent migration to this, our western city. I was not then a resident of it, but a brief sojourn here, at that time, brought me once more a guest under their roof. That house, yonder, which I told you was their residence, though now flung in the shade by the more modern ones that have risen round it, was then distinguished by its elegance and taste. How fresh seems that visit there! Were it not for the faded look that has gathered over it, the changes that have taken place about it giving it so different an aspect, I could fancy it still the dwelling of my friends. Though separated more than ten years, I found little other change in the family than that which a month of spring time or of early summer brings to the garden—a change from the bud to the flower—from the flower to the fruit. I spent a week with them of delightful sociality, of the full out pouring of renewed friendship, and all the pleasant ransackings and overhaulings of "Lang Syne." Such a week is a bright, green spot as your scribblers say—not in the *desert* of life. The pen or pencil that makes a desert of our bright and busy world is always dipped in spleen. Happy and pleasant it is, despite "the trail of the serpent," to all whose hearts are tuned to concord. *Old* ladies you perceive, must be allowed to moralize, though not always very complacently listened to. I have little more to tell. As I have said, the family was little changed in its general aspect. A proud man, like Mr. Ellesly, is the very one, if he welcome you at all, to give you a rich welcome. The warm smile upon such a face, so habitually dignified, so aristocratically grave, is like the sudden opening out of unsuspected treasures, and no one could be more pleasant than he among equals or in the bosom of his truly lovely family. Mrs. Ellesly's character had deepened. Its habitual softness had more of *feeling*. The death of two sweet children had touched it with a shade of *thoughtful* tenderness. During their illness, which had been of a protracted nature, she had looked upon life in another phase; she had learned that it had duties.

Isabel, whom I had last seen a thing of fairy playfulness, had grown into a lovely and accomplished woman with form, features, and bearing, upon which her fastidious father and her brother, every whit as fastidious, looked with an exceeding and exulting pride. With those, too, her mind was in perfect accordance, refined, high-toned, intellectual, rendering her in all matters of literary acumen, and poetic taste, a match with her brother Edward, whose naturally fine mind had been cultivated with assiduous care and under high scholastic advantages. Years and close study had tamed the exuberant spirits of his boyhood, and amid the refined and classic circles in which he had moved, he had acquired rather an undue sensitiveness of nerve, and delicacy of taste, and a too exquisite polish of thought and manner; though the question of their excess was, perhaps, referable to his future position in life. For the present, to a lady at least, not then an old one, this poetic refinement, this sentiment of character was delightful. Then our flights to cloud-land were relieved by the frolic gambols of a young sister, a child four years old, privileged without limit, as are all the youngest children, and pretty and wild as the wildest and prettiest fawn in all our ancient hunting grounds. There was a sweet girl, too, in the family, whom they called "cousin Alice," an orphan niece of Mrs. Ellesly, whom you would have instantly loved. She had a figure of *embonpoint*, rounded and polished to all the symmetry of the Medician Venus; and her movements were those of a mist wreath with a face too of exquisite softness, quite wanting in color, but with perfect features and large, dark, loving eyes that told the whole character at once—a fond, trustful, gentle and happy nature—happy in itself and constituted to remain so. For nothing could have made her unhappy but unkindness, and this she could nowhere meet.

Wherever the chances and changes of life might have flung her, unless into some abode where human infirmity had found no place, there would Alice have made herself friends. Nobody about her ever had a want that she strove not to obviate—a weakness that she did not seek to favor—a sorrow to which her unobtrusive sympathy, like some soft ministry of nature, did not afford solace. Yet Alice had no accomplishments, no talents, no literary pretension. Her father, till his death, was considered a man of wealth; but he was a man of speculation, and engrossed in visionary projects, which finally left him a bankrupt, he thought not of educating his child. Perhaps he deemed her sufficiently lovely without adventitious aid; and in this he was not greatly wrong. Had you known her, you would no more have thought of any deficiency in Alice than of the want of a language—a learned one, for the zephyr that fanned your cheek. She had a natural refinement of manner that satisfied even the Ellesly family, and they regarded her with a fondness that manifested itself in every look and accent. Such was the family thirty years since—a little circle of high polish and cheerful and varied interest. I frolicked with little Ella—talked with Mrs. Ellesly—looked with her husband at his pictures, his garden, his library—watched Alice, as she hovered round whatever luckless wight most needed her, and listened to Edward and Isabel as they scanned over the dubious meaning of some classic line. There was a young man too of the name of Brown, an inmate with us for two or three days with whom I could not but be pleased, though of a humbler order than might have been looked for in an Ellesly guest. But he had become known to them as a fellow passenger from Pittsburgh in the large flat-boat that had borne them down the Ohio; for at that time the steamer had but in a single instance, I believe, ploughed through its waters. The voyage was consequently one of comparative peril and positive inconvenience. The young man was a denizen of the West, and somewhat familiar with river voyaging, and by dint of a hundred little courtesies and attentions to their comfort, for which under other circumstances, the personal knowledge of a lifetime in their distant positions, would hardly have afforded opportunity, he had won their gratitude, if not their familiarity. A recent accident had deepened this sentiment, and thrown them under an obligation that could be cancelled only by personal attention.—A carriage in which Mr. Ellesly was taking out his little girl with cousin Alice had been run away with by a horse of unmanageable muscle.—The animal had been arrested by young Brown at the point of especial peril, by an effort that deprived him of the use of his arm, and of course they insisted upon his becoming their guest until it should be restored. This is an accident that I am aware belongs to your story-telling craft, so chivalrous and all that sort of thing, but horses you know actually *do* run away, and somebody stops them every day of the week. But Brown was young and good looking enough anyhow, for a hero—very different, it is true, from the tall slight figure and elegant proportions of young Ellesly, but nevertheless a form in the full perfection of active, healthful, vigorous and youthful manhood—one of those which the garb can neither add to nor subtract from. There was character breathing throughout it; you felt it at once in the free movement of the muscular but lithe limb, and the careless arrangement of the simple dress. His countenance too was frank, open, and manly, and his brow, broad and cheerful, was thrown up with an expression of habitual self-reliance, and a quiet air of conscious equality with those around him in all that *should* distinguish man from man. But for this, his introduction to the patrician circle of the Ellesly parlor would have been altogether an awkward concern. Truly grateful to him as they all were, cousin Alice was perhaps the only one whose manner was wholly free from effort. Yet Alice was silent as well as the constrained Isabel, for maidenly delicacy held them alike in reserve. Mrs. Ellesly was silent from habit—her husband and son for want of subjects of common interest with their guest. He was wholly a stranger to Edward, for the latter had followed, not accompanied, his parents, having waited for the completion of his college term; and to him it was an especially irksome task to acquit himself of the requisite courtesies. He had no interest in the ordinary topics of the day. He was fresh from the rarified atmosphere of classic halls; the tangibilities of life were out of his line, and he believed that every thing belonging to mind and feeling was left "beyond the mountains" and far away. He essayed a passing remark to the stranger, and then plunged again into his books or started some moot point of criticism of taste with his sister that generally led out into a train of thought upon which both were carried off into utter forgetfulness of their guest. Yet, embarrassed as was the position of young Brown, he freed himself from its awkwardness in much the same manner he would have done from a spider web drawn across him—by a single turn and all unconsciously—the simple power of character within him evidently counteracting the restraints of circumstance. When a remark was addressed to him, he replied somewhat gravely but always with freedom; when withdrawn, he took up a newspaper or strolled off to a window, or entered into a low but embarrassed chat with Ella. I have always observed that in an ill assorted circle, where interregnums are apt to occur, a lively and interesting child is a most efficient auxiliary. And so it was now. Ella was in perfect friendship with our backwoodsman—she sat upon his knee—slid her fingers through the crisp and dark curls of his hair—talked to him of the peril from which he had rescued her and cousin Alice, and told him that his eyes were "more handsome even than brother Edward's."

"Don't untie Mr. Brown's bandage, Ella," said Mrs. Ellesly, during one of their chit-chats; but the interference was too late. The busy fingers had already loosened the knot of the sling that supported the arm, and now the little meddler tried in vain to refasten it.

"Cousin Alice, come tie this for me!" and Alice unhesitatingly obeyed.

"Will you loosen the bandage a little, Miss Alice?" Alice touched it with the tenderness of a sister—the bandage needed considerable adjustment. Brown lifted his eyes to her face; no wonder Ella had called them beautiful! Literally were they pouring upon her a stream of deep, thoughtful, passionate expression. Alice's were veiled by the long heavy lashes that fell over them, yet did something of that expression seem to reach their gentle depths. It might have been the reflection of the rosy clouds that were flooding the sunset sky; but Alice's usually marble cheek was, at that moment, tinged with crimson.

"But what of it?" said I, mentally, as I watched those flitting shades, "tis but a brief and soon to be forgotten passage in their young lives.—They part in a day or two to meet probably no more. They belong to different orbits!" And then a crowd of matters and memories, connected with those paltry distinctions of our little life, gathered upon my mind. Among them came the recollections of little George, and I turned to Mrs. Ellesly to enquire for him. They had not heard from him for years; they were even ignorant if he yet lived. The last intelligence they had received was that Aunt Mary and her husband were both dead, and George, still a lad at that time, had gone, no one knew whither.—Mr. Ellesly had made every possible enquiry, she believed, but without avail.

"Poor fellow;" she added feelingly, "it always pains me when I think of him. I am afraid we were wrong in giving him up as we did. I wish he had been sprightlier. Mr. Ellesly was so hurt by his dullness, and even yet he looks miserable whenever he is mentioned." Fortunately, I had timed my question when he was out.

But my visit was at last ended. Mr. Brown had already left. He was anxious to return to the interior, having left it only for a trip or two on the river and could not be prevailed on to remain longer. There was much about this young man to leave an abiding interest on the memory: the open brow, the simple manliness, the youthful, but well defined character. There was a dash of sadness, occasionally in his manner, at variance with its usual tone that bespoke latent feeling. It seemed more than once called out by the prattle of Ella and particularly at the moment of his leaving us when she hung around him with inquisitive fondness and asked him a hundred questions about himself, his home, and his friends. It was evident from the sad smile with which he replied to them that they jarred upon some chord of sorrowful tenderness.

"I have no particular home, Ella."

"And no brothers nor sisters, neither?"

"Yes, I have a little sister much like yourself, whom I love very dearly. But I shall perhaps never see her again. Brothers are sometimes great ramblers, though it grieves them to be forgotten; and so, Ella, if you have one whom you should never see, you must sometimes think of him and love him still."

"Well I never met one of that pleasant circle again! So, the friendships of the day pass! A year or two after I learned that a great change had taken place in the Ellesly family. Some of those sudden turns which the wheel of fortune is every day bringing up had stripped them of their wealth. Mr. Ellesly, unable to endure the change amid the scenes of former prosperity, had plunged into the new country yet further West. Edward had exchanged poetry, sentiment and the classics, for Blackstone and Coke, and had settled himself as Attorney, Counsellor, Etc. at no great distance from the family in one of our far Western towns."

Our kind narrator had reached the point at which we were able to take up the story *ourself.*

"Yes! yes!" we exclaimed, "and little fitted he was, poor fellow, for the atmosphere of such a place!" And so now we went on with the old lady, comparing notes and filling up the outline of the whole story. Alas for our young collegian, alas for the place where he had located himself and his hopes! A new town! You see such a one through whatever portion of our still extending and newly settled West you may chance to pass; a village risen to the dignity of a country town with some two hundred or less houses, the better portion of them confined to a single street, and the remainder sparsely scattered over a wide area of bright and rich green sward—a court-house of rather ambitious pretensions, rising from the center and near it a jail, from which you of course turn with a shudder of somber associations. If you have an eye for the picturesque, it will be apt to wander to the dark outline of forest by which it is surrounded and sundry other wildernesses in the background. But if your speculations tend business-ward, it will rest upon the principal street, aforementioned, and take note of the demonstrations thereon of the stir and vitality of the place. Here upon its entrance is the forge of the smith, as attested by the heavy stroke of the hammer within, and the smutty faces occasionally peering out. Further along, the strip of flaunting merchandise fluttering in the breeze assures you of articles in the *fancy line*—and here is *the* Hotel! with Washington, Jackson, or Lafayette ingloriously suspended between heaven and earth and looking down upon all below with some indifference. Among the half-dozen boarders ascending and descending the steps you may distinguish the doctors, lawyers and professors, "gentlemanly and melancholy alike," who with nothing in their pockets but their diplomas, have come to our Western arena but to learn, perhaps, the fading of hopes all too sanguine. Across the street is the village grocery where a fair representation of indigenous backwoods population affording divers startling specimens of humanity are congregated, from the lineal descendant of Boone or Leatherstocking, lounging apart upon his gun, to the busy trader, bustling forward in the very face and action of the crowd. Here do they all gather to talk over matters and things in general: commerce, politics, legislation, and to pour forth those bursts of accidental eloquence with its magnificent metaphors and figurative brevity, so properly in keeping with the ample features and nerve of the country. Thanks to Western legends and Crocket memoirs which enable us to imagine these, for truly we have not time "to tak' notes."

Over the way from just such a scene as this, was the sanctum of Edward Ellesly. There he sat from day to day, looking like some fine vase on a kitchen shelf among a goodly array of stronger and more serviceable ware, or rather he shoved back in a corner near them, for Edward could not bring himself to mingle with those around him. The nerves which education and circumstance had wrought to a most useless fineness were now morbidly quickened by a sense of his changed position, and wholly isolating himself from those whose patronage he virtually asked, he found they were content to leave him "alone in his glory." Striving indeed he believed himself, shut up as he was amid tomes of legal science, to increase his professional capital, but in reality, wasting his very soul away in dreamy reverie, and idle regrets.

Day after day, and week after week wore on, and still our young lawyer was without a client; yet he had, absolutely, no resource but his profession and the pressure of positive need was in close prospect. The reveries of sentiment deepened into the reflections of bitter necessity.— Idealize as we may, the greater portion of our nature is wonderfully *human*, and when its wants are upon us like the grasp of a strong man, we must needs come to a parlay. He had one day flung away his books with a most theatrical gesture and was pacing the floor with the strides of a much stronger feeling than "melancholy." The hilarious sounds that came from the street in a variety of tones, jarred tauntingly upon his ear, but as a quick, lively tread passed his window, the sound of his own name attracted his attention.

"Why don't you employ Mr. Ellesly in the matter you told me about?" said the person passing to another whom he met at the moment. "I take him to be a whole team." The voice seemed familiar to Edward's ear, and yet he could not identify it.

"Why," said the other, "he looks as if a fellow in a linsey coat could not get to speak to him nigher than a set-pole's length."

"Pshaw! If he wears a better coat, it is a sign he has pocketed good fees."

"Irrefragible evidence!" thought Edward, half laughing, half bitterly. But it seemed conclusive. In a few minutes the man to whom it had been adduced, knocked at his office. Edward would have enquired of him who it was with whom he had just been speaking but a feeling of pride suppressed the question, and he turned to the matter of litigation. It was one involving no great amount, but luckily for our friend, a mass of contradictory testimony. Luckily, I say, for this at once gave it interest. Court was at hand, and Edward found himself drawn out of the "horrors" in which he had been plunged for the last half hour and busy with the merits of his case. When it came to trial, he found himself opposed to a lawyer of long established practice and of no trifling celebrity. The perfect plainness of his manner, however, and the unimposing good nature of his countenance, upon which thought seemed never to have written a single line, satisfied our tyro that he had nothing very formidable to dread. As he rose to address the jury, he distinguished one among them whom he instantly recognized. It was young Brown, and with the first glance of that ingenuous face came the recollection of the voice he had so vainly striven to recall. The conviction brought with it a rush of grateful feeling and a glance of recognition, that even, on his part, had now something of soul, was exchanged.

He opened his case. The witnesses, contradicting each other in a singular degree, had been examined and the pride of strife, that pride which gives interest to the combatants in the poorest cause, roused him to exertion. His argument was polished, labored, classic, and he felt that it must be successful. Alas! it was borne down at once; demolished— annihilated by the blended humor and strength, the off-hand sarcasm and matter-of-fact manner of his opponent. It was like the smashing of a Grecian urn by the fist of Hercules. Our discomfited advocate felt himself a thing of shadow. Yet was his rival no erudite counsel; his allusions and illustrations were all of home material; his knowledge was of men & *things*. It was certainly a matter of curious speculation to our scholar, but at present he was not in the mood to investigate. His mortification was intense. The jury went out and an immediate verdict was anticipated. But hour after hour wore on, and they did not appear. The crowd wondered, waited,—dispersed. It was midnight when the verdict was at last presented; Edward's client was the victor! A passing remark from one of the jurymen as he left the Court House explained the marvel. Young Brown's pertinacity had been the pivot upon which the decision turned.

He had overruled the eleven! Of the whole jury he was the only one whom the tact of the opposing counsel had not won over.

"You must have had a very strong conviction of the justness of our cause," said Edward as he drew Brown home with him to his room; "or had you a particular interest for my client? or shall I impute your verdict to a friendship for myself? "

"A juror, I believe, is bound to act only upon evidence."

"True. But *ours*, as you Western folk say, was *mightily mixed*. Nothing but oracular wisdom could have decided which was the aggrieved party."

"We might as well suppose it your client then, might we not?"

"*Suppose*! Why you hung for him as if it had been a matter of assurance and involving life and death. Well, well! I understand it; you had sent me my client, and you had a generous interest in my success. I feel the full kindness of your motive. I appreciate its value, too. Not only has it saved my present feelings, but it will doubtless bear upon my future practice. I am in need of friendship too, Brown, for I am poor— positively poor, though perhaps you are now aware of it;" and Edward, fairly warmed out of his usual manner, into that of unreserved feeling went on to detail the change of affairs of his family. The cold formality that had existed between the young men was melted away. They conversed long and freely, and Edward listened to the young backwoodsman with surprise and interest. There was not merely the raciness of native humor and of a vigorous mind in all he said, but through the plain outpourings of thought and feeling that had been trained only in the rough school of the world, there were frequent gleamings of a rich and deep nature. "Yet after all," thought Edward as the young man took his leave, "perhaps I have been unnecessarily free;" and his strongly biased mind regained something of its ordinary contraction. What if Brown should presume upon his present freedom to press a troublesome familiarity? The thought was unworthy of his own grateful nature, but the prejudices of education are woven through the whole inner man. He was soon aware, however, that no undue claims upon his regard were likely to ensue. Except by accident, he saw little more of Brown for some time. Yet as if to give a narrower character to these misgivings, continued instances of some friendly office on the part of the young man still came to his knowledge; it is true, of a very slight nature, but attesting a uniform and unobtrusive interest in his behalf. He found, too, that the influence which was thus at all times exerted in his favor was by no means a light one. Brown's character, as he was led on to observe with greater and warmer interest, was gradually developing itself to his perception, and he felt that he was one to be popular to a certain extent in the most aristocratic sphere. There was that entire abandonment of self about him that must have been the perfection of ancient chivalry. He was generous, impulsive, fearless, and had a freedom of manner and a sunny light of eye that were calculated at a single glance to bring the proud down and the humble up to his own standard. Such a one in our backwoods community could scarcely fail of being *king of hearts*, and such he emphatically was.

Edward became ill. Our unacclimated emigrants have usually to become naturalized through a course of fevers and chills. For some weeks he was principally confined to his room, and then for the first, his young friend became a frequent visitor, tasking all his powers to cheer, to amuse, to cater for the capricious appetite, and the invalid learned to listen for his inspiriting step with the querulous impatience of a sick child. But at last he was restored.

The professional practice he had been slowly gaining had made him known to a few who were capable of appreciating the refinement of intelligence. All are not coarse minded even among illiterate backwoodsmen; nor are all backwoodsmen illiterate. Here and there throughout the neighboring population there might be found a family of cultivated taste and education, and among these Edward became favorably known; the rich stores of his mind and the polished gentleness of his manners gradually making them his friends. At length he was spoken of by those who wished to elevate the tone of popular favoritism as a suitable candidate for their forthcoming election for the legislature of their infant State. The proposal at first met with a cold response, and Edward was unaffectedly reluctant to be brought forward. It was certainly a matter of most unpromising issue. There was a candidate in the field—a man of wealth and influence.—Edward's friends were of the intellectual few, but they were urgent and importunate. Some under-currents of private interest set in his favor, and young Brown, unsolicited and unspoken with, had managed at once to throw the whole weight of his own popularity in his favor. Edward could but eventually acquiesce. Then came the toil and "the tug of war;" the excitement and the *joy of strife*. Our backwoods population was all astir and effervescing with the leaven of *patriotism*; and our gentle collegian, upon whose nerves the touch of coarseness had jarred almost to agony, was ruled to *come out* and mingle with the crowd, ay, and to thank God for the grasp of the rudest hand, to turn a pleased ear to the roughest protestations of support, and to listen gratefully to the counsel of intellects that in those days of anti-temperance were often grievously *obfuscated* by the libations they poured out "like rain" to his success. Then, too, came the *swift encounter* of the stump with his doughty adversary and the sharp play of weapons with which he was all unfamiliar. Still he got along. In all these several and severe trials, Brown was still at his side, seeming, like our heroes of romance to have a gift of ubiquity that enabled him to be at all points of exigence. If Edward was occasionally mystified by a phrase of concentrated Western-ism, he always interpreted. If the candidate's answer seemed unsatisfac-tory at any time to a question upon the several points of his political creed, Brown, by some dexterous interposition, expounded for him, by an off-hand cut that was always perfectly satisfactory to the catechist. But he was also abroad, securing interest, and giving tone to the prevail-ing sentiment in the remoter parts of the community. Not a *gathering* through the country but he was there, now mingling with the crowd— now engaged in private colloquy; and his wake could be traced wherever he moved, by the commotion he left in favor of his party. He had that peculiar dictation of manner, a taking-it-for-granted sort of way, accom-panied by a hearty and bland courtesy that always gives their possessor an ascendancy over the multitude.

If our candidates harangued, he stood with a quiet air by the speaker's stand, lifting to his face, if Edward was the occupant, an occa-sional glance of merry humor that could not fail of communicating some-thing of his own spirit to the speaker. If his opponent was on the stump, Brown listened with great gravity, but commenting ever and anon to the bystanders, and giving, by some quaint remark, a turn of ineffable ridicule to the positions advanced. Meanwhile, he had acquired an influ-ence over his friend of which the latter was perhaps scarcely aware. Edward's whole character was undergoing a rapid transmutation. A new channel had been opened out to his thoughts and feelings; new interests had given him new perceptions, and called out faculties and energies that had long slumbered. His distastes had been overruled, his sympathies enlarged, his morbid tendencies corrected. The companionship of Brown had reconciled him to scenes which he had considered unmitigatingly revolting, and the contact of life's rough play had strengthened his nerves to meet it. He was rapidly acquiring, too, the tactics of border politics and prowess. He was catching, unconsciously to himself, the tone and spirit of Western population. He was, in fact, *'coming it.* "Remember now," Brown would say as he mounted, "that you can't row up Salt River with a carved and filigreed paddle; throw out a strong pole and push along."

"I know—I know," Edward would reply, laughing, "never fear me now; I have done with the philosophy of the schools forever and a day. You shall think me 'half horse—half alligator.' I will use no comparison, as Sterne says, less than a mountain."

But the canvassing was at last over; the Ides of March were at hand. a close strife and a strong strife, and Edward Ellesly had the victory!

"Come," said he a day or two after to Brown, "I have for months succumbed to your domination; it is now my turn to rule. Prepare yourself to accompany me in an hour to my father's. It is little more than an afternoon's ride. They are your debtors of old and are aware of their increased obligation. Nay then, you can't be off now—but I'll say no more of obligation. You'll allow me at least to speak of friendship. My parents are anxious once more to see their young friend. Ella has her choicest flowers reserved for you, a bouquet; and next to her own lover, who is solemnizing at old Harvard, Isabel will give you her very warmest welcome."

The young men were speedily on their way. It was a ride to be especially enjoyed. Their horses were fresh and fleet, and all the exhilarating influences of a bright afternoon and a succession of the most picturesque forest and prairie scenery, in the wane of summer, were around them. Edward felt his whole nature expanding—his feelings kindled to enthusiasm.

"What a glorious world this West of yours! what a prodigality of creation—what a magnificence of scale—what gorgeousness of coloring! your population too—your generous, full-souled, back-woods population! how falsely I estimated them—how little I understood their character! But, Brown, I owe my better appreciation wholly to you— nay, even my enjoyment of your scenery. You have aroused me from a languor that was curdling my very being; you have unlinked the prejudices in which I was encased; you have taught me that a warm, rich, confiding nature like your own sheds a thousand times brighter light than the cold moonshine glitter of intellectual refinements!"

"Ah, dear Edward!" (it was the first time Brown had used so familiar a term)—"there is no occasion now for any extra republican rants. You may put your gloves on and touch hands as gingerly as you will, till the next campaign. But look! who would trust to appearances, even in the skies! Shall we make up our minds to a thorough drenching and a few ague shakes on your part or a yawn of some two hours in the next cabin?"

Edward chose the latter. A heavy rain of some hours succeeded. When they remounted, the day was far spent and the night gathered round them while they had yet some miles to travel. But the "cold round moon looked brightly down" upon their path, touching the wild features about them into extreme beauty. The influences of the hour deepened; the air, purified by the passing storm, was full of odors, and a stillness fell around them like a palpable sense.

"I feel myself," said Edward, as an opening in the distance at last met their view,—"I feel myself a very child when I near my father's dwelling. There is such a sacredness in the paternal home—such a sense of rest associated with it from the weary strife of the world—so many fond and tender and joyous recollections!"

"I have been many years an alien from *mine*," said Brown.

"Ah, but you are so little needful of support—so sufficient to yourself."

"We are none of us sufficient to ourselves," said Brown in a tone of great feeling; "we can work for our bread and meat and a place to stretch ourselves on to rest for new toil. But love is not an article of trade, and that is just as strong a need within us as bread. It comes upon me with such a gnawing craving that I could fairly weep for it. If the whole world was mine there are times when I would give it all up for a parent's, a brother's or a sister's embrace."

"You can never be without friends," said Edward—"warm, devoted —but my God! what is that light?"

The wood from which they had just emerged opened upon a small prairie upon the border of which Mr. Ellesly had built his cottage home. It was a small building but evidenced the taste of its owner. He had expended upon it and the pleasant acres around it the small remains of his fortune, and it was a home to be marked by the traveler. Beautiful did it lie in the quiet moonlight with its deep embowering of vines and shrubbery, but well might Edward's face blanch with agony as it met his gaze. A strong broad flame was pouring from the roof; the windows glared with light, and yet all within were evidently hushed in slumber. Edward gasped for breath, but Brown's deep voice as he plunged his horse forward rose in long and repeated calls of superhuman strength. Terribly did those sounds come upon the stillness of the placid night; but they reached the slumbering and imperiled family. They walked amid the roar of flames, but rescue was at hand. The young men reached and forced open the closed doors, and the voice of Edward was now also heard.

"Father! father—but you are safe; you will all be saved; mother! Isabel! Ella! Great God! are you all here?"

In the delirious terror of the moment, they rushed instinctively to the door, but all were not there; Ella had slept! But a strong form rushed past them. The father had yet calmness enough to direct his way, and the moment after Brown had placed her in her brother's arms. They were indeed *saved*. Amid the glare of the burning dwelling and with no shelter but the skies, Edward folded his mother and sisters to his bosom and thanked his maker with that passionate devotedness which bursts from the heart of even the irreligious when the hour of fearful peril has revealed to them their entire dependence upon the *dreadful God*.

A few only of their valuables and those wholly by the calm energy of Brown, were saved. But the family bore it with much fortitude. The tenderness of Edward, and the efficient and cheerful exertions of his friend were not lost upon them. Of the latter Mr. Ellesly remarked with a sad smile that he seemed "the better portion of his family's destiny." So they all seemed to regard him. He had become to them a support upon which they all leaned.

It was but a thin settlement, yet hands were nevertheless rallied to their assistance. Brown's own vigorous arm was foremost in whatever was to be done. A cabin was thrown up, and the family had once more a shelter. The exertions of the young men gave it an aspect of cheerfulness. The laugh of Ella, as she sat on Brown's knee, rang through it; and the smile, though somewhat faintly, came back to the lips of Isabel and her mother.

Mr. Ellesly had been calm through it all, but a fever, common to the country and the season, had threatened him for some days previous. His exertions probably confirmed and gave it deeper malignity. He was at last confined to his bed, and in less than two weeks, despite medical skill and the efforts of his family, it was evident that he was hastening to the "far off countrie," where earthly cares cease. How insignificant, how less than nothing to the dying man were now the strong interests of his life! The pomp, the pride of wealth, the splendors of intellect,—where were they now!

An itinerant minister, meek, humble, and illiterate, opened out to his view visions brighter than them all. In the conversations he held with the man of God, the faith which had hitherto been but a cold belief was kindled into fervor and vitality, and Mr. Ellesly became reconciled to death, not as an escape from a *weary life*, but as the valley and shadow through which his Lord had passed. Yet did his affections yearn over his beloved family, so as at times greatly to darken his spirit. At last he spoke of his first-born.

"My poor George!" he said, "how coldly I have neglected him! Edward, 'tis my dying charge that you rest not till you find where he is and make him feel that you are indeed his brother. And you, too, Emily," he continued to Mrs. Ellesly, who sat with face hidden upon his pillow, "will you not, for my sake, should you ever meet him, make up to him the tenderness I should have shown him? Give him my blessing; it is all I have to leave my children."

Young Brown, who throughout his illness had scarcely left him, manifesting by his sleepless care a solicitude of singular intensity, slowly approached the bed. Tears were coursing fast over his manly cheek. He took Mr. Ellesly's hand and pressed it to his lips.

"Father, bless me now! *I am George Ellesly!*"

We have intended no surprise to our readers. If they have read our story with any interest, they have doubtless anticipated the result. *Brown* was the name of Aunt Mary and, sharing her home so many years, he came gradually to be called by it. She wished him to retain it, and aunt Mary's wishes in life and death were to George a law.

But what a scene was that dying bed! Truly we know not how to get on. George was folded to the heart that had so coldly spurned his earlier claims with a fervor that seemed for the moment to rally back the full strength of life. Again and again, as he put his child from him to study the lineaments which nature now exultingly acknowledged, the dying man would press him back to his bosom and pour over him the long withheld blessing for which his soul had so yearned.

"Yes, the bitterness of death is now passed; my outcast boy will close my eyes. The love that unites my children shall shield them all from sorrow. And felt you now that he was our brother, Edward, during all his loving kindness? And I too! why did I not know my boy? yes!" and he gazed long and fondly upon his face; "yes! he *has* his mother's eye; and his smile—why did I not see it was hers!" The memory of other years had come back upon his vision.

"And is he our very own brother?" said Ella, as Edward and Isabel knelt beside him and wept, and George himself took his feeble and exhausted stepmother into his arms and mingled his tears with hers—"Is he our very *own*?"

"Pray for us and return thanks!" said Mr. Ellesly to the minister who just then entered; "Pray that we may have yet one more meeting in Heaven."

Soothingly did that prayer come upon the hearts of all; for the strongest emotions of earth are tranquillized as we turn to the vastness of eternity. But when they rose from their knees, they saw that his hour had come. A smile of that peace that passeth show settled upon his features. He kissed his family one after another, but George's hand was retained in his, and his eye rested upon him for some time with an expression that George never forgot. Consciousness soon after left him, but its last glance was upon his first-born son; and hours after, when the pulse was at last still, George yet imagined that he felt the pressure of that stiffening hand.

"Do you remember my cousin Alice?" enquired Edward, a day or two after the interment. "*Remember her!*" George lifted his eye to Edward's with a look that told volumes. "But how is it," he added turning to Mrs. Ellesly, "that your niece is no longer with you?"

"We thought her too lovely for our wilderness home," was the reply; "she had other friends who proffered her a wealthier home, and we sacrificed our more selfish feelings to our interest for her good."

"Yes—but mother," rejoined Edward, "you made a sacrifice of her feelings also; and that is rather an equivocal good. Here is a letter from her which I shall answer immediately. Read how she begs to come to us, and I shall tell her mother that I shall come for her as soon as I can get our domestic arrangements a little settled. Shall I not, brother George?" A smile almost played upon Edward's saddened features as he spoke.

Some four or five years after this, I had become intimately acquainted with the family. Isabel was united to her betrothed and had forgotten her former sorrows.

"My brother Edward," she said to me, "is making himself a name—winning his way to wealth and eminence. I am proud of his success, and he is extremely dear to me. But I love my brother George with a passion. There is something about him that stirs up my heart from its very bottom. My mother too leans upon him more fondly, I sometimes think, than upon any other of us; and my cousin Alice! Oh I've no words to tell you how happy she is, nor how her husband doats upon her. Truly, she who has seen George Ellesly's look, as his young wife leans upon his breast, must be very happy herself, if she be not envious."

AUNT HETTY

Yet still she filled life's task, although a part
in its glad sunshine was no more her own,
Toiling with busy feet—the while her heart
Gave out a voiceless but unceasing moan.

The instances in which I have been called, since journeying on your western waters, to witness the mortal grasp of the Asiatic destroyer now among us, has more than once made me sick at heart. But I have just returned from the burial of one of its victims, with feelings so like the music of Carroll, that I cannot resist the impulse of sitting down at once to give you the story (for story it is) in detail.

I am alone, in the principal hotel of a village on the eastern bank of your great highway of waters. It is September, and the day has been the very blandest; but when I landed here, last evening, the weather seemed to have the breezeless sultriness of a southern August. On recognizing the place as the stopping-point of my voyage, I was struck with its appearance. I had spent a night here some two months previous, and it was then all astir with business life. Now there seemed to hang over it a quiet like that of perfect desolation. I was not permitted, however, to dwell on the matter, my attention being drawn to an object of more immediate and most painful interest. Beside me, as I passed from the boat, two or three of the hands were carrying from it the stalwart but convulsed form of a young man, who, knowing as I did that the cholera was on board, I saw at once was struggling with the fierce agonies of that terrible malady.

But what time was there to mind the death-throes of a mere fellow-being? Action and emprise are the only influences to get a hearing on our great highways. The poor fellow was tossed on the wharf, with evident satisfaction to the bearers at getting rid of their burden. The rush of steam, the voice of command, the plash of waves, mingled in one stirring sound, and again the boat was ploughing on her way, as if the principle that impelled it were the very lord of destiny. I had myself approached the sufferer with no light interest, but was unable to make the least personal effort; being not only in great anguish at the moment, but moving with extreme difficulty. A severe sprain in my only efficient foot, some few hours previous, and want of attention, had caused it to become violently inflamed. But some three or four men, of that well-known class that haunt the river purlieus, were lounging about the wharf, and to these I applied to have the sick man carried to the hotel, but a few rods distant. At my appeal one of them carelessly approached the sufferer, and stood looking with perfect unconcern at the face already distinctly marked with that peculiar seal which is perhaps the most appalling of death's many signets.

"Cholera, eh? Nothing to notice here, stranger," said he; "Come, brace up, old Ben," he added turning, without the least notice of my continued and urgent appeal, to a stout-looking personage, who was nevertheless availing himself of a post for support; "no rest for the wicked, man—another grave's to be dug to-night! No baby's neither," he added, touching the struggling form with his foot; "some long inches to cover when they're once fairly straitened." Happily, I believe the brutal allusion did not reach its unconscious object; yet it was with some difficulty I kept myself calm.

"Suppose," said I, flinging him a small bill as the only argument that could at all avail, "suppose you are a little charier of your wit till the man is taken care of. Make some arrangements for taking him to the Eagle, and let a doctor be called without a moment's delay."

"Faith!" he replied, looking at the bill with a peculiar sort of meditative satisfaction, "doctors are getting scarce among us. Only one left, and he green as a frog-pond. But what do you want of one? You don't know much about the cholera, I reckon, stranger. Why, the fellow's caved in already."

"There's life yet," said I, "and therefore something to be done. Pray, don't waste any more words."

"Well, well," said the man, evidently one of those busy, bustling, officious spirits that are leaders in their class; "any thing in the way of trade. Dan Garnett is not one of them as turns his back to a job. Bear a hand, comrades," he called out to the others standing on the wharf; "best get a blanket—here's one the wharfman died on himself yesterday— good as any. Stir yourselves quickly! live men are lighter than dead ones, and he'll be heavier soon. We'll handle him kearfully enough," he added, in reply to my impulse; "but you see, stranger, we'd better by half let the council know there's another coffin wanted than to be troubling him now."

"Never mind—carry him steadily!" Alas! I too saw that a mightier hand than that of human strength was upon him; but I could not leave him thus.

"Bear ahead, then," said Dan Garnett; "hold up, old Ben—strike a bee-line, old rat! Aint got enough to steady you, eh? Well, the bar at the old Eagle aint drained out yet."

"You have the cholera badly in your village, I suppose," said I, remembering, as I hobbled on painfully beside the bearers, the dubious intimation of my new acquaintance.

Not at all, stranger—not a case among us—wound up here, sir—closed the concern teetotally. Them as is left here now is hard subjects. You'll find poor entertainment, I'm thinking, at the Eagle. You've staid there afore now, havent you? Well, there's some little difference in things now. Them as was flying about there two weeks ago, ladies and boarders and waiters, and what not, have all took private lodgings. Boss and the old cook have come through, and that's all. Wife and three young daughters all gone—pretty girls, gone too! proud as Lucifer—though but small room have they for airs now. Them's the last we buried this very morning. Plenty of quiet room for travellers, you see.—Let down your load, boys; let's see if boss is stirring. I rather think, though, he's hanging by the graves yet. What do you think now, stranger?

he asked, as the burden was lowered, and he turned a look of careless scrutiny to the livid face; "short work it makes, and sure—gone off, though, very quietly," he continued, still looking at the darkened face with perfect complacency; "they don't all go that way. Do you mind, Ben, the screech that old Hughes fetched as the last breath went out of him? I never stir if it didn't go through me like an ague-shake. The old fellow," he added, turning to me,

was the richest man in the place—griping old landholder—and you see he was bound not to die. But the grinning old skeleton held on to him jest as he would to a poor fellow that owed him; and now he's got but five feet of ground left.— One more hist, comrades! We must take the corpse round to old Judith; the Eagle, I 'low, will have to give it lodgings for to-night any how. It's going to be tremendous squally by appearance, and ther'll be poor chance likely to give it snugger quarters afore morning.

I had sunk, during these remarks, upon the steps of the portico, unable to stand from the fast increasing anguish of my limb; but connecting with the name of Judith (whom I remembered as the old black cook) the possibility of relief, I got up once more and hobbled eagerly after them. The old woman was sitting alone at the back of the silent and empty house, swaying herself to and fro with a leisure to which she was no doubt little accustomed. The approach of the ghastly burden borne towards her appeared to excite in her neither dismay, awe, revolt, nor surprise. Her mind was evidently already too full of the images of death to admit a single new impression.

"Come, Judith, bestir yourself," said Dan Garnett; "here's travellers ahead. One of 'em, though, don't want nothing but lodging. Where shall we stow him? in the porch here?"

"Well, I suppose," replied the old woman, her own stony aspect seeming more like the dead than the living, "you can lay him on that table thar; its whar they've all been laid out principally."

Well, there he is! Straiten him out, boys. Aunt Hetty ought to be here now to close his eyes—rather stary, I think!—but you can do that, Judith. Fix up his jaws, too, while your hand is in. Stow away his plunder, Ben—enough in that big trunk, I judge, for decent fixing without his being beholden. But go one of you and see if the councilmen have any thing to say about it,—and stay! take 'em the measure for the coffin—six feet good; and mind, Ben, you get the grave started before sun-up.

I had at once appealed to old Judith for some effort in my own behalf, and I was now waiting, not without some impatience, upon her tardy movements in fulfilling the melancholy office pointed out to her.

"Aunt Hetty, now, likes to fix up dead folks," said Dan Garnett, returning from the bar where, as he said with a significant nod at old Judith, he had gone to see if the brandy was likely to hold out provided it should be needed in some new case.

"If it was not such a night now," he continued (and in truth the storm-spirits were by this time fairly up), "I'd go and bring Duchy to smooth him up a little. I ought to do it any how," he added, his visit at the bar already calling the amenities of his nature into high exercise; "the good soul has along been sent for when a corpse was to be rigged out in their last gear, and she seems to sort o' look for it."

"And mighty well it was too, for them as had friends to bury," said Judith, seeming for the first time to reply in a tone of human interest;

she was not only willing, but she seemed to have a 'ticular strength like, when every body else was down, and them that wasn't weren't none too willing to lend a hand. But you'd be foolish enough to trouble her to-night, let the weather be fair or foul. I 'speck no body can hold out allays. She jist gone from dead to dead, and haint laid her head on a pillar a whole night since she first put her hand to it. Any how, what odds does it make to a stark body like that, whether you cover him up as he is, or in span clean rigging? He's got no friends, I 'low, to trouble themselves.

Judith's reasoning seemed for a time conclusive; and opening an inner door, she now pointed out to me a lounge, which she assured me was all fresh changed, and of which I was most thankful to avail myself. Dan Garnett meanwhile ensconced himself in an arm chair at my side, and whistled Dan Tucker with great self-complacency, and in strange dissonance to the dirge-like winds now shrieking without, which it required little effort of fancy to imagine were wailing for those they would wake no longer.

Meanwhile the preparations which the old woman had set herself earnestly about for my suffering limb proved of no avail. Specifics hitherto infallible in my case were vain. Even that of brandy—the one friend, Dan Garnett said, in all need, and which he insisted on pouring out more lavishly for my relief, failed. My distress was indeed extreme, and the inflammation was evidently assuming a rather serious character.

"Well, my good fellow," said I to Dan Garnett,—we got wonderfully meek when suffering forces home upon us our real dependence upon each other,—"it is storming fearfully, but if I wait on it long I shall be in a fair way to lose my leg. Bring your doctor to me if he is green; you are too old a stager to mind the weather."

"Of course," said my ready friend, his kindly mood having as yet had no chance to evaporate; "Dan Garnett aint sugar nor salt to mind a little thunder and lightning, and it aint a doctor's business to lie a-bed, no how. Get me a *numberil*, Judith; I don't want it for myself, but while I'm out I'll jist go round and fetch Aunt Hetty."

"I tell ye then again ye'd be mighty foolish, massa Garnett, that's sartain," she replied; "I s'pose though ye're not in earnest."

Dan, however, was not only in earnest, but with that maudlin pertinacity of purpose that was not to be overruled, terrible as the storm was,—bending the umbrella which he attempted to raise so roughly that he flung it back into the porch,—he started bravely ahead; and we had not long to wait the issue. A few minutes after the entrance of the physician, who came speedily at the summons, Dan returned himself, accompanied by Aunt Hetty. So at least she was addressed by Judith and the doctor—by the latter with great kindness and even respect; and despite my extremity of suffering, I could but look with something of curiosity at the person to whom such striking reference had been repeatedly made. All my preconceived ideas, however, of a weird old woman with an indurated and Meg Merrilies frame and spirit, was put aback by the quiet and quaint figure (for she was dressed in the peculiar garb of her countrywomen) that stood before me. She seemed scarcely forty, though the fair German complexion and the great length of soft brown hair, that could not have been so plainly arranged as to lose its grace, might make her seem much younger than she really was. Her features, too, small and perfectly regular, had a softness that it seemed no exposure could displace. But what riveted my attention was the intense sorrow that was the fixed expression of every lineament and motion. The expression was unobtrusive—silent, but not to be mistaken. It lay a strange depth of gloom in the light blue eye. The features, that but for it one would have instinctively associated with health, and hope, and all genial affections, were fairly steeped in it. It startled me in the soft German accent with which she replied in broken English to the doctor's kind inquiries for her welfare. Even in the ready movement with which she set about assisting him in some preparation for my suffering limb (ready, but most saddened), it was yet an accompaniment.

The especial task for which she had been brought was not now to be thought of. The storm was rushing violently through the porch where the body lay, repeatedly extinguishing the light with which Aunt Hetty strove more than once to shield it from the beating elements, notwithstanding Judith's assurance that "the dead man didn't mind it, any how," together with occasional asseverations of Dan Garnett's foolishness in troubling her at all about the matter—a reprehension in which even the doctor, a young but amiable man, who evidently gave a full heart's sympathy where skill proved unavailing, seemed disposed fully to join.

"Our friend Dan has certainly shown more thought for the dead than the living," said he, "a rather questionable duty, as I take it. But Aunt Hetty," he said, turning to her with a serious interest in his manner, "owes something to herself; and as soon as the storm lulls, I move she go home and waive the unpleasant office for which she has been summoned."

I looked at Aunt Hetty. The answer came slowly, after some minutes, during which she seemed hesitating whether to reply. She said in the lowest tones,—and oh! how mournful—"I has dressed great many as had moder and sister."

Judith's previous argument had already reversed the inference, but the doctor bowed to it without reply. The night wore on. By degrees there fell a hush, both on the elemental turmoil and the human sounds of the hour. Dan Garnett lay stretched on the floor in a profound slumber. Judith had swayed herself to sleep in her chair, and my own plaints, rather loud and deep for the credit of my manhood, were subsiding rapidly in a growing sense of ease. Only the tones of the doctor, still drawn out by my eager questioning, and dwelling with infinite feelings upon the details of the visitation that had depopulated the place, were now to be heard. How heart-rending were those details! What a power of human suffering did they attest! "Facts," said the narrator, "that make medical science a mere dream; that called out, too, in the most vivid opposition, the darkest and brightest traits of our nature. Friend fled friend. Others took post beside strangers and enemies. Throughout all I have described to you," he added, with a look of gratified recollection,

there was one humble and quiet spirit, that was never for a moment idle. From the hour the scourge was among us, she was always to be found amid the scenes of its most terrible triumph. A watcher by the dying, their tire-woman for the grave, Aunt Hetty was at all hours devoted to tasks from which the nerve of manhood might have well shrunk.

"Aunt Hetty!" I repeated, looking round for her, at the mention thus of her name. Where was she? She had passed from the room without a sound, or I should have noticed her. "She has probably," said the doctor, glancing at the partly open door, "settled herself out there with the dead body; such place seems always to suit her feelings in preference to any other."

He was not mistaken. Amid the dim light breaking through the still struggling clouds, I discerned her sitting on a low stool, in attitude now as motionless as the outstretched form whose ghastly length lay before her.

"Some morbid feelings," continued the doctor, "have doubtless had some bearing upon her singular devotedness, but even these have to me something in them almost sacred. Poor Aunt Hetty! Sorrow has in truth raised her above life's common instincts."

"And what have been her sorrows?" said I; "you seem to know them. I had already fancied there was a history in her face—pray, what is it?"

Well, it is a very brief one; a single fact, as it does that of many others, forming a sombre web to her whole life. She came a few years since with her husband and an only son, of some twenty years, from Germany. They settled here upon some rough grounds which they purchased upon the outskirts of the village, and which they soon converted into a pretty and pleasant home, alike marked by taste and toil. Industry and rural neatness with our German emigrants is rather a national than individual distinction; but Aunt Hetty's neighbors soon learned to distinguish her as a superior woman of her class—gentle, cheerful, active, self-sacrificing, true, and kind, with an ever-ready and open hand, and with her soft, broken English full of soul and sunshine.

But occasional clouds were flitting over this usually happy spirit—an evil daily deepening, that could but wake in a mother's prescient heart many a boding fear. The son, who was evidently the very daylight of her soul, a handsome and manly-looking fellow, with an open and generous nature, as I am told, was adventurous and dissipated—the fine elements of his mother's nature, which he perhaps inherited, being robbed of their beauty in his, by excess and perversion. No amount of indulgent tenderness,—for both father and mother were devoted to their boy,—could keep him under the paternal roof. Returning thither only occasionally, and with tokens of reckless habitudes that made these visits but seasons of troubled misgivings, he spent most of his time on the river, or at some of the various ports, but always it would seem in idle and profitless adventure. The father at last sickened. A painful disease fastened on him, with which his strong frame struggled for months; and all this time his son was wholly absent. Death finally released him; but ere he died, a rumor had come that the young man, having been engaged in an affray where one of the party fell a victim, was imprisoned in New Orleans. From what I know of Aunt Hetty's character, she would have gone to him at once; but she might not leave her dying husband to another's care. A few days after released her from this duty; but she returned from the grave to read a letter from one of her fellow-emigrants,—who could write a mother such things?—that her boy was to be hung—upon what day—and other horrible minutiae; though the terrible day was already past, for the letter had by some casualty been delayed. A young German girl at service in the place was with her when the dreadful missive was received. Long afterwards she was asked in my hearing, by some one more curious than feeling, how Aunt Hetty bore the news. She burst into tears, and wringing her hands bitterly, exclaimed, 'Mein Got! mein Got! may I never see such another agony!'

But from that hour nobody, I am told, has ever heard from Aunt Hetty herself the slightest allusion to her sorrows. Since that time, indeed, she has been rarely seen; going always when called for to the sick, but never otherwise leaving her own domicile voluntarily, till since our visitation from the cholera. Her little garden, however, was still worked and kept with its wonted neatness; being not only her means of livelihood, but, as my professional rounds among the destitute have led me to know, of many a little charity still extended to them through the medium of an orphan child in her service. But so carefully has she seemed to avoid all human eye, that even her out-door labors are done in the early morning ere her neighbors are astir, or when she can avail herself of moonlight hours, lengthened far into the night,—as are my yarns, I perceive,

added the doctor, looking at his watch with a sudden and good-natured change of voice and manner. "We are getting, I see, into the small hours, and you are easy—thanks to Aunt Hetty's suggestions, I suspect, more than to my own skill. You can sleep now," he said, taking his hat, with a bland smile, quite as soothing as the opiate he had administered; "I am not sure, indeed, but you've been dozing already, fancying, no doubt, you were some prince with a pensioned storyteller at your bedside. But settle yourself now to bright dreams—a privilege I shall hasten to take myself, if it may be permitted me."

And he left me—in a silence. And now I was at last permitted to think over all the gloomy images the last few hours had presented. What a night it had been! By what associations I was surrounded! and yet, thanks to our most concentrated human selfishness, I slept at once, profoundly forgetful of all the late anguish of the stricken household—of the many darkened habitations around me; awoke, too, after some hours of pleasant rest, to a sense of perfect satisfaction at finding myself still at ease. Some matin sounds indicated that the morning was breaking, but its cold gray obscurity afforded no incentive to shake off my slumber. A light, dim and feeble, I saw was burning in the porch, where Aunt Hetty had probably still kept her vigil, and I heard steps there; but my mind was as yet too inert to make any questioning in regard to them. I had again closed my eyes, and lay in the half dreamy state, when the outer sense receives what yet the thought takes no cognizance of. A low murmur of soft, sorrowful sounds had come fitfully upon my ear for some time, ere I rallied sufficiently to distinguish them from the seeming sighs and the various sounds that followed the storm. But my perceptions cleared. It must be Aunt Hetty! and raising myself at last, with a strong feeling of interest, I looked through the glass panel of my door, which she must have closed while I slept, to see if I were right. She was still as when I last observed her, alone with the dreamless sleeper, but not, as then, motionless. She was bending over the body with a near but dim lamp-light flickering on the fixed lineaments, and was adjusting the hair and the position of the head with great care. But while thus busied she was from time to time uttering in her own language, which it chanced that I familiarly understood, expressions of wailing tenderness and implied despondence, that I find it impossible to translate. At times she paused in her task, and stood for a moment contemplating the features, doubtless so changed that even love could not have recalled the lineaments—such is the effacing touch of the cholera; and then again turning from the earnest gaze, and renewing the endeavor to soften the dark traces of the spoiler, she would break into renewed utterances of the most heartbreaking pathos.

Ah! these thick black curls! so glossy yet. Some mother has been proud once,—smooth 'em out this way, and lay them round the great forehead. She will think this a sorrow—she will bow her head, when she should raise it and give thanks. Let the angels whisper it to her; let them bid her give praise by day and by night—her God has not hidden his face when her mother's heart cried to him.

So full of unimaginable sorrow were the tones, that in very pain of hearing, though I could but listen with my whole soul, I was glad when they were interrupted. The burly sleeper on the floor up roused himself, and the first sound of his voice drove back the broken wail to the sorrowing heart. She turned to him at once as he now stood beside her, with the same settledness of look she had previously worn.

"You said dere was tings to put on him?"

"Did I?" said Garnett, applying his hand to his head as if he would dig up the recollection; "well, I can't say exactly—sort o'foggy this morning. There's his trunk, though—remember bringing it along. Plenty in that, I reckon, by its heft," pushing it towards her, touching the lock too at the same time no ways gently with his foot; "open, too, I guess— the boat-hands flung it on the wharf as if it burnt their fingers. There!" he continued, wrenching open the lid as Hetty looked at it somewhat hesitatingly, and now flinging from it a quantity of decent and most neatly arranged clothing; "plenty for scores of dead men, you see, and nicer lots than they need be for such an outfit; money, too, if more's wanted," he added, as a kerchief with a corner tied up fell heavily on the floor.

Aunt Hetty was evidently disturbed by the unwarranted freedom. "Oh, I want nothing but dese," she said, laying by a few articles, and putting the rest back anxiously in their previous order. "Can you no fix de lock?" she said, examining it herself, and then assisting to tie a cord tightly around it. "Do you, Judy, put it away safe (for the old woman and myself were now part of the group) till de master may-be will be able to see no ting wrong is done."

She then turned back to the body. "Ah, yes! if you will be so good den," she continued, in reply to my proffer of the little assistance I was able to render, and putting in my hands the articles she had selected. Then raising the body herself—an effort of which, indeed, she looked incapable—she was reaching to me for some of the intended array, when a small volume fell from beneath the vest she had just loosened. Her eye fell on it with an intensity I can never forget. I stooped to pick it up. The binding had some marks of foreign style, and the leaves falling open as it fell, I saw it was a German Bible. The name "Henrique Van Ernstein" was written on a blank leaf, with the words in German, "Given me by my dear mother, April 27, 18—," and striking my eye as I raised it, I read them involuntarily aloud.

"Henrique Van Ernstein!" The sound was echoed back on my ear in a cry so startling, so strong, so thrilling, that months after I seemed occasionally to hear it. The body fell rather than was laid back from her hold, as she turned her head to clutch the book from my hand.

"My God! my God!"—again she spoke in her own language—"'tis his! 'tis my boy's! 'tis Henrique's!"—and then suddenly turning her gaze wildly, but with a fixed look, for a moment on the face of the dead, she uttered yet another cry, bearing in its prolonged tones the very extremity of human emotion, and then fell on the body, clasping it round in a hold in which all the vain yearnings of long years seemed concentrated. She was pouring out upon that dull, cold ear expressions and names of passionate fondness, with which a mother's heart only overflows. "Mine own! mine own! my boy! my Henrique! my beloved! my beautiful!"

Mightier indeed is Love than Death, said I mentally, as I would fain have drawn her from the ghastly embrace. The effort was all unheeded. Yet again and again, kissing the livid lips, she would raise herself to fix a lengthened gaze on the face, seeming with every moment, as she thus stood tracing the lineaments, to find some new line familiar to her heart,—all this while, too, continuing to pour out such a flood of the very agony of joy, of maternal passion in its utmost excess, as few of those whose lives reach the longest date can call to memory.

My boy! My Henrique! How was it I had forgot to know my own? A mother to look strangely on her boy! How should I think he had filled a grave of shame?—his mother?—but he comes himself—comes to tell her of the black falsehood. It is he—it is Henrique! Oh, thou great and merciful Lord God! thou art indeed a God of truth and justice and pity and forgiveness and loving-kindness!

But these bursts of the many mingling passions of the poor woman's soul at last subsided. They were finally merged in one absorbing strength of prayer, or rather of thanksgiving, poured out upon her knees beside her dead, in His ear who has all power to tranquillize the surging billows. And from the outpouring of thanks and praise, how calm she at last arose. Calm, did I say? There was a radiance in the serenity of that now still face, bespeaking a peace that the poor estimate of our more human feelings may not measure. With this look she now turned to the making arrangements for the burial of her boy. Again with kisses—oh! how fond, but now scarcely mournful—she arranged the curls of such unchanged beauty round the capacious brow, and once more, as she had been wont in other days, she folded the snowy shirt over the bosom, icy and unconscious now, but whose last pulse she knew had been true to her and to the teachings of those happier days. And there, too, she again placed the treasured volume that had been her last gift of love. That it had been the stay and solace of her wandering Henrique, there could be no doubt. It was much worn. Upon a second blank leaf, bearing a date of her most awful memory, he had written some brief expressions of intense thankfulness, seeming to imply an unexpected deliverance from some dark impending fate; and throughout the whole volume, many of whose pages were now scarcely legible, there were leaves turned down, marking those especial passages in which the soul of penitence finds utterance for its own emotions.

There are still tokens in our debased nature of better elements that were once a part of it. They who had, the preceding evening, looked with such reckless faces on the dying man, were again present. They had come with the hearse that had been sent round for the body. But their countenances now had taken a touch of feeling. Aunt Hetty's dissolute but open-handed boy had, it seemed, been well known to them, and of this her simple expression denoted her aware. Pointing to the body, she said quietly, "Look at him—it is Henrique!" Some others, too, were there. Despite the desolation of the place, a half dozen persons gathered around the mourner and her dead. They were perhaps of those who knew her only as a late tender of the bedside of her own dying. Among them, with his hat drawn over his brow, was the master of the house, whose steps, through my long waking hours the preceding night, I had heard traversing the empty chambers. All were at last ready and waiting to attend Aunt Hetty with the remains back to her cottage—for there where the father slept, the son was also to be laid. I had feared my kind doctor, who had also joined us (grasping my hand with a smile not at variance with the tears he struggled to suppress), might veto my attempt to accompany them; but he gave me his arm to help me to the little vehicle he had in waiting, without a syllable.

It was one of those mornings of soft brightness that so often follow a night of storms. The glad ministrants of nature, revivified by it, were pouring out balm, and beauty, and fragrance, and melody, on every hand. But these bright influences awake no thought of jarring dissonance with earth's tenderer sorrows. They have too much of holiness. The sound of bird and bee, and the stir of "young leaves," as we passed, seemed to melt into the deep funeral hush that was upon our sense. We reached the grave, as yet scarcely completed by those who had gone forward with the first dawn for that purpose. It was in a deeply shaded and grassy nook of a little enclosure pertaining to the cottage, and planted by him on whose grave their blossoms were yearly shed, with orchard trees. Even the face of Dan Garnett, now speedily completing the task in which he had voluntarily engaged, attested, as he at last stood leaning on his spade, the spell and power of some sanctifying presence. One of Aunt Hetty's German neighbors, who had been early an assist sharer in the scenes of the morning, read the burial service in their own language. The mother's hands were clasped, but seemingly in prayer—not in anguish. A few sobs and murmurs met my ear—not bitter, but low and tender—evidently Love's last farewell—and then her voice, singularly musical and deep, went up through the stillness of the secluded spot in an anthem of mingled faith and thanksgiving. Deeper and clearer the strain arose, as strengthening the soul that breathed it. The doctor whisperingly admonished me of the prudence of returning, but it was with reluctance that I turned from the spot. The triumphant tones were yet floating away to the still heavens, beyond which, no doubt, the angels were also hymning the safe housing of the erring Henrique.